The White Lady

HELEN FRY

THE WHITE LADY

The Story of Two Key British
Secret Service Networks
Behind German Lines

YALE UNIVERSITY PRESS
NEW HAVEN AND LONDON

For information about this and other Yale University Press publications, please contact:
U.S. Office: sales.press@yale.edu   yalebooks.com
Europe Office: sales@yaleup.co.uk   yalebooks.co.uk

Set in Adobe Garamond Pro by IDSUK (DataConnection) Ltd
Printed and bound in the UK using 100% renewable electricity at CPI Group (UK) Ltd

Library of Congress Control Number: 2025940614
A catalogue record for this book is available from the British Library.
Authorized Representative in the EU: Easy Access System Europe, Mustamäe tee 50, 10621 Tallinn, Estonia, gpsr.requests@easproject.com

ISBN 978-0-300-27511-7

10 9 8 7 6 5 4 3 2 1

In honour of
the men and women
of La Dame Blanche and
the Clarence Service
and
To the memory of my grandfather
John J.M. Jeffery, DSC, DFC
1922–2024

We must never forget their courage and sacrifice.

CONTENTS

CONTENTS

ACKNOWLEDGEMENTS

My first thanks are to Heather McCallum, the Managing Director at Yale University Press and my commissioning editor, for appreciating that this little-known history deserves wider readership outside Belgium. She has been a rock throughout this project. She and her incredible, dedicated team are hard-working and passionate, and a huge support at every stage of the writing and publication process. This praise extends to the marketing, media and sales teams, who are a delight to work with; and special thanks too to Rui Ricardo for designing another awe-inspiring jacket that captures the content of this book. I am ever grateful to my agent Andrew Lownie for his hard work and continued support of my career.

Enormous thanks and gratitude to François de Radiguès, grandson of Thérèse de Radiguès, and family – Rodolphe de Radiguès, Frances, Soline and Lala – for sharing the private family archive and making this part of the history available to me. It was a privilege to hear about the family's courageous roles in two world wars and to have been given a personal tour in Belgium of the key historic places in this book.

It has been a huge privilege to access the files of the Clarence Service ahead of their declassification. In this respect, my sincere thanks to Robin Libert (Chairman RUSRA-KUIAD, Royal Union of Intelligence and Action Services, and Board Member War Heritage Institute, Belgium) for his help with the official files and permitting their use. With thanks too for his expertise on the wider history of the Belgian resistance in World War Two, and especially the Clarence Service and Mill. Peter Verstraeten has been of immense practical support throughout the years of writing this book and has provided expert guidance on the Belgian archives of La Dame Blanche and Clarence Service. This book would not have been possible without Robin Libert or Peter Verstraeten.

I wish to extend thanks to the following for their support of the book: Colonel Bruno Plaetsier, Jeanine Tchaikowski-Reina, Baudouin Collett, Michael Bottenheim, John Scarman, Arthur Fleiss, John Howe, Lee Richards, Richard Bennett and Mark Scoble.

This book could not have been written without the help of the following archivists and curators: at the Imperial War Museum and the National Archives in London; Eva Muys, lead archivist at SGRS, Belgian Military Archives in Brussels; archivist Samuel Pauwels, National Museum of the Resistance in Brussels; at the Cegesoma Studies & Documentation Institute in Brussels; members of RUSRA (the Royal Union of Intelligence and Action Networks), Belgium; Bill Steadman of the Military Intelligence Museum (MIM), Chicksands (UK); and Fred Judge, former archivist of MIM.

A big thank you to my family for their loyal support and encouragement for over twenty-five years, and who continue to be inspired by these stories of heroism.

North Sea

Rotterdam

HOLLAND

Rhine

Ostend
Bruges
Ghent
Antwerp
(Anvers)

Maas

GERMANY

Scheldt
Malines
Hasselt

Ypres
Brussels

BELGIUM
Wandre

Lille
Tournai
Liège

Mons
Charleroi
Namur
Meuse
Malmédy

Douai
Valenciennes
Sambre
Ciney
St Vith

Dinant

Givet
GRAND DUCHY OF
LUXEMBOURG

Oise
Hirson
Gedinne

Nouzon

FRANCE
Charleville
Tintigny
Trier
Arlon

Aisne

0   50 miles
0   80 km

Thionville

PROLOGUE
CONNEUX CASTLE

4 August 1914, Conneux Castle, near Ciney, Belgium

The mood at Conneux Castle on the morning of 4 August 1914 was tempered by the mounting tension in Europe as Thérèse de Radiguès and her husband Henri sat with their eight children around the breakfast table.[1] Thirteen-year-old Gérard de Radiguès heard the postman pushing his bicycle over the stones of the driveway and leapt up from the table. He rushed into the hall and returned, clutching a newspaper and shouting with excitement, 'War is declared!'[2]

Henri's face became one of stern displeasure as he explained to his son that war would see intolerable suffering and high casualties.

Tensions in Western Europe had been rising since the assassination on 28 June 1914 of Archduke Franz Ferdinand, heir to the Austro-Hungarian empire. Some sixty-five miles away, the Grand Duchy of Luxembourg had been occupied by German troops on 2 August. The following day Germany declared war on France. On 4 August German forces invaded a large part of Belgium – an action that triggered Britain's declaration of war on Germany the same day.

The discussion around the breakfast table that morning of 4 August became solemn as twenty-seven-year-old Louis and his brother Xavier, just two weeks shy of his seventeenth birthday, declared that they would fight for Belgium. The next day the two brothers left to enlist in the army. Thérèse and her daughter Marie stood in tears on the steps of Conneux Castle; Henri was beside them, clearly moved. In this war, three sons – Louis, Jean and Xavier – would fight for Belgium, while the rest of the family would find other, clandestine means of resisting the German aggression.

The day after their two sons had departed for war, Thérèse and Henri gave over a section of the castle for use by the Red Cross. Their daughter Agnès commented that they 'tore the bed sheets to make bandages and lint' for the casualties that they were expecting from the fighting.[3] French soldiers began to move through the countryside around Ciney to protect Belgium from the advancing German forces. Agnès herself witnessed them passing through the area and wrote, 'They were magnificent with their helmets shining in the sun, in red breeches, blue jackets, mounted on beautiful horses which also drew small cannons . . . We made sandwiches as fast as we could . . . The army was full of enthusiasm and sang or shouted at us, "We will get them"!'[4]

The soldiers marched to face the enemy, full of expectation that they would halt and defeat the German forces. Their excitement was short-lived. Some 10km from Conneux Castle, there was fighting in the vicinity of Dinant. With the sound of intense gunfire in the background, the large shutters in the living rooms of the castle were lowered and Thérèse began to receive the first seriously wounded French soldiers.

Dinant saw the arrival of German forces on 15 August 1914. On the 23rd, 674 citizens of Dinant were shot and bayoneted, including men, women and children. Today, there is a memorial in the town to the massacre. The town fell on 24 August.

It would be a pattern repeated across Belgium. After the eleven-day siege of Liège ended with its fall on 16 August, followed by that of Namur, fighting around Halen held up the German advance on Brussels, but on 20 August 1914, the German army entered the Belgian capital. Antwerp fell on 10 October 1914 (apart from a small area around the river Yser). The fighting was accompanied by brutal massacres of Belgian civilians carried out by the German army as it swept across Belgium.[5] There was widespread looting and burning of buildings; civilians were murdered in the small town of Hervé; the city of Liège saw fifty people killed, and sixty people were put to death in the villages of Soumagne and Micheroux. In the tiny town of Andenne on the river Meuse, German soldiers butchered all civilians they could find; women were raped and children gunned down.

Within a week of the Dinant atrocities, Belgian refugees began to arrive at Conneux Castle with further accounts of German brutality, the burning down of houses and arrests of local Roman Catholic priests. Thérèse and Henri sheltered them, alongside fleeing French soldiers, who were hidden in the basement of the castle. Others were hidden in Ciney and nearby villages.

The Radiguèses were playing a very dangerous game in taking in these refugees, for the Germans had already come to Conneux. As Dinant was being captured, a German soldier, revolver in hand, had arrived at the castle and demanded the keys. Forty-nine-year-old Thérèse was not intimidated. She refused to hand over the keys and explained in perfect German that the castle was being used by the Red Cross and he was not allowed to enter their home. She displayed a total fearlessness: something that would mark out her strong character and defiance throughout this war. The soldier ignored her protestations and billeted his men in the outbuildings, in the castle's parkland and in nearby farms and houses around Ciney. Thérèse and Henri were allowed to remain in the castle, but under occupation by German officers for the next four years.

In October 1914, Thérèse received the first news of her sons who were fighting on the front line. Xavier was stationed near the river Yser; Jean, meanwhile, had been seriously wounded by shrapnel in his shoulder and transported to a hospital in France. Thérèse decided to visit him. The route would not be straightforward because fighting on the Western Front meant that she could not cross the border directly into France, so she travelled via Holland and England.[6] Her daughter twenty-three-year-old Marguerite accompanied her; she was looking for her fiancé, Edmond t'Kint, who was fighting with the Allies and was believed to be taken ill in England. This was indeed the case – he was recovering from an illness. Their wedding had been due to take place that autumn, but war had prevented it.[7]

Thérèse and Marguerite travelled via Rotterdam to the port of Folkestone on the south coast of England. Marguerite's travel permit, which survives among family papers, is stamped by the Belgian consulate in Folkestone for her entry into England on 30 November 1914 and subsequent exit on 14 December 1914.

Belgian visitors or refugees arriving on English soil were of great interest to British intelligence. Although the Belgian consulate in Folkestone had no direct concern in enrolling such assets in espionage activities, it did have a close association with Major Cecil Aylmer Cameron, who worked for British intelligence, and who was based in an office in the port town. Cameron was on the lookout for Belgians to recruit and send back to their homeland on intelligence operations for the British. It is possible that Thérèse and her daughter – by then already well versed in keeping secrets from the Germans – crossed paths with Cameron.

Thérèse and Marguerite returned to Castle Conneux on 22 December 1914. Thérèse discussed with her husband how to ensure the safety of their younger daughters, sixteen-year-old Marie-Antoinette and eleven-year-old Agnès, because of the fear of rape by German soldiers. They decided that Marie-Antoinette and Agnès should leave for England. On 18 January 1915, they stood on the steps of the castle and waved goodbye to their daughters. It was to be an all-too-familiar scene for this family. The girls travelled with another local Belgian family, taking the long slow journey, first to Holland by a horse-drawn carriage. Three days later, on 21 January 1915, they crossed the English Channel and arrived in Folkestone. They were seen at the refugee office and promised accommodation with other Belgian refugees in a house in Walton-on-Thames, Surrey.[8] By 15 February, Marie-Antoinette and Agnès were boarding at the Roman Catholic convent of St Maur in Weybridge.[9]

Back at Conneux Castle, Thérèse and Henri continued to make the German officers comfortable there, all the while sheltering French soldiers in their cellars, undiscovered by the occupying Germans.[10] But in the shadows another war was raging – a secret war – and one in which Thérèse (and later her daughters) would be involved for the remainder of the war and after.

In an astonishing act of courage, Thérèse quietly and covertly carried out intelligence-gathering for the British Secret Service, as part of a clandestine network that came to be known as La Dame Blanche (the White Lady). Its name was drawn from a German legend that, should a ghost of a white lady appear, she would herald the downfall of the Hohenzollern royal dynasty, the ruling family of Brandenburg-Prussia (and Imperial Germany). By choosing this name, it is clear that the network's leaders believed that, by its clandestine work collecting information behind the lines for the British Secret Service, it would bring about the downfall of the German invaders.

From within the walls of her home, and right under the noses of the German soldiers billeted there, Thérèse transformed Conneux Castle into an important centre in the Ardennes region for intelligence operations that she led. It marked the beginning of an extraordinary, heroic contribution by all members of this family, who joined the efforts of other patriotic Belgian families and individuals. The dangers of being part of a clandestine network for the Allies could not be more acute. The risks were known. The city of Liège became the headquarters for the leadership of the intelligence network.

Thérèse was recruited into the network by Walthère Dewé of Liège, an engineer whose cousin, Dieudonné Lambrecht, was the principal leader. Both men will appear prominently in this story. The families had been well known to each other since Thérèse's childhood, as she was born in Liège, the daughter of Charles Jean Minette, a lawyer and landowner in the region.[11] On 21 November 1888 she had married Henri de Radiguès (de Chennevière), a civil engineer and a widower of her own sister Marguerite.[12] By the end of World War One, Thérèse had created and headed an entirely new intelligence sector for the British in the Ardennes.

Like Thérèse, many patriotic and loyal Belgian women and men emerged in the war as strong leaders, agents and spies who were at the very heart of the White Lady network. Thousands of heroic Belgian women and men refused to be crushed under the German boot, spying on the enemy's troop trains and keeping the Allies supplied with a mass of general information about German morale and intentions. More than forty agents initially worked for the White Lady, with agent numbers estimated to have risen to 1,084 by the end of the war in 1918.[13] Women were prominent in the network, and not incidental to its success. For these women and men, it was a war without uniform, passing invisibly through enemy-occupied Belgium and northern France. Theirs was a great sacrifice, and if caught, they would pay a high price. Agents did suffer horrifying betrayal and capture by the Germans, and yet they continued their dedicated work, because they understood the importance of what they were doing for the Allies. And they did it all over again when the call came in 1939 and 1940, for the Clarence Service, the successor network in World War Two.

What emerges here is a story of defiance, heroism, ingenuity and leadership that saw Belgian women and men engaged in daring acts of espionage behind the German lines across two world wars. It is an inspirational history.

INTRODUCTION

In the history of the British Secret Intelligence Service (SIS/MI6), two of its intelligence networks have been given high acclaim. They were La Dame Blanche (the White Lady) in World War One, and the Clarence Service in World War Two. Both were in Belgium.

The slaughter in the muddy trenches on the Western Front and in Flanders fields have come to define the Great War.[1] One German soldier serving in Belgium wrote to his wife in December 1914 of 'mass and individual soldiers' graves in the midst of fields, some of which are still unharvested, trenches, gun emplacements, grenade craters'.[2] But as important as it is to remember Flanders fields, much more deserves to be known today by the general public on the key clandestine intelligence operations in Belgium by the British Secret Service.

For many members of the general public, the understanding of intelligence-gathering in Belgium during and between the world wars has been informed by television dramas. Maybe Agatha Christie's Belgian detective Hercule Poirot springs to mind – the inspiration for whom perhaps came from Christie's own nursing of Belgian refugees in Torquay, South Devon, during World War One – made famous on-screen by David Suchet. Or *Secret Army*, another well-known TV drama series, centring around a clandestine Belgian organisation that aids the escape of shot-down Allied airmen during World War Two – inspired by the true historical events of the Comet escape line in Brussels.

But Belgium's actual role in intelligence operations in both of the twentieth century's major wars has received comparably scant attention in the public eye, especially for an anglophone readership.[3] Material exists in intelligence histories,[4] but no significant fuller history has been published in English of the White Lady since Henry Landau's memoirs of the 1930s; and there is no published history in English for the Clarence Service of World War Two at all.

And this despite the high praise afforded both networks by official histories and principal actors. The White Lady is described in the official MI6 history as 'the most successful single British human intelligence operation of the First World War'.[5] Claude Dansey (who became vice chief of MI6) said of its successor the Clarence Service in the next war, 'By the quality and quantity of the messages and documents which it provided, Clarence was the highest among the networks of military information of all occupied Europe.'[6]

Such praise compelled me to research these networks, and they have now fascinated me for over twenty years. I explored the roles of the women in the White Lady and the Clarence Service in my previous book, *Women in Intelligence*. And in 2017 I was the historical consultant for a three-part Channel 4 TV documentary series on the origins of the British Secret Service.[7] It covered a number of British intelligence operations across the world wars, including the White Lady network, which featured in the first episode. That included a rare interview with the grandson of Walthère Dewé, who led the network from 1916.[8] I always hoped that one day enough files would be declassified to tell the story in more detail.

This book is a chronological history of the White Lady and its successors, the Clarence Service and the latter's sister network Mill, which was formed out of it, across two world wars. It explores their agents and how they operated and, where possible, details the intelligence gained from behind German lines. In the background are pertinent questions. What was the intelligence need? How was it gained? What was its impact? It will become clear that the intelligence networks in Belgium delivered critical eyewitness information that enabled the British Secret Service and Allied commanders in the field to build a picture of German fighting capability and German positions behind the lines, as well as helping them to predict the direction of the next German offensive against Allied positions. The importance of this clandestine work cannot be overstated.

The focus of this book is the White Lady, the Clarence Service and Mill, all networks of the British Secret Service (SIS/MI6). There was a similar network of train-watching and intelligence-gathering in the Grand Duchy of Luxembourg, which finally became operational from 1918 and was headed by a highly successful bourgeoise Luxembourg woman named Madame Lise Rischard.[9] Although it was a British intelligence network, it is not included here because it was distinct from the White Lady and run from a different location by a different chief.[10] Its official files have not been declassified or may have already been destroyed by SIS, although some relevant papers kept by its head, Captain Bruce, survive in a private archive in Scotland.[11]

Neither is there coverage in my book of the famous network of Gabrielle Petit.[12] Although a network of the British Secret Service, it was entirely separate from the network that came to be known as the White Lady. Petit had been recruited in the summer of 1915, while crossing the English Channel by boat from Belgium to England. She received training in England and returned to Tournai in Belgium, from where she ran her own intelligence network called 'Petit' in the Ypres region and around Maubeuge in France.[13] Her small network comprised three agents and herself.[14]

This book does not cover any of the other resistance groups or intelligence operations in Belgium run by the British, French or Belgians. It would be beyond its scope: this is a vast subject in both world wars, as attested by the thousands of files recently declassified in the State Archives in Brussels (Archives Générales du Royaume).[15]

That declassification means that there are now full files for the Clarence Service available to draw on. The history told here will be largely new to the public today also because of the secrecy that continues to exist around MI6, an organisation that does not release its files. In these pages is a story of strong leadership, particularly of men and women like Dieudonné Lambrecht, Walthère Dewé, Thérèse de Radiguès, the Tandel sisters and so many others. For a new generation of readers, *The White Lady* provides an understanding of the courage and sacrifice of the people of Belgium behind the German lines.

Sources

The primary sources for the White Lady are archives in London and Brussels. The Imperial War Museum, London (IWM) holds two red boxes of miscellaneous material, including some agent reports, tiny messages and codes in envelopes and a handful of photographs.[16] There are a few intelligence reports for 1918 which come from Thérèse de Radiguès's sector in the Ardennes. In the State Archives, Brussels, I was able to use the archives of La Dame Blanche, which contain agent files and reports, and the personal archive of Walthère Dewé.[17] I consulted the personal papers of the Tandel sisters in the Belgian Military Archives in Brussels.[18] I was able to use the unpublished papers in the de Radiguès private family archive.[19]

Files for the Clarence Service of World War Two are held in the IWM and the State Archives, Brussels.[20] The IWM archive consists of eight grey boxes that contain hundreds of intelligence reports, in French, sent to MI6 from February 1941 until August 1944. These contain a staggering volume of intelligence. The reports often run to over twenty-five pages each, and contain annexes of diagrams, maps and annotated photographs. Some unique Clarence Service material is held in the National Museum of the Resistance, Brussels.[21] The State Archives and Cegesoma in Brussels hold the files for agents, known as Intelligence and Action Agents (IAA), for all networks operating in Belgium in World War Two, including the files for 1,547 officially recognised agents of the Clarence Service. The archives include personal forms for the men and women who aided the Clarence Service, but who were not recognised officially as agents, usually because their activities were small.[22] This includes the names of couriers and those who ran safehouses and letter boxes. In addition to the above, there are 800 messages sent from the radio operators of the Clarence Service to MI6 in London.[23] To establish the criteria of who was to be officially recognised as an agent, there were three Decree Laws (of 20 January 1944, 1 September 1944 and 16 February 1946). These were refined by a Service Note, dated 23 November 1945, written by Paul Bihin (the then Administrator-Director-General of the Public Security). It was a very limitative procedure, overseen by Ludovicus Caeymaex (then Assistant-Administrator of the State Security and himself a former IAA). Over 10,000 people were given 'Certificates of Appreciation' after the war across IAA networks in Belgium. The recently declassified files show that so many more worked for the Clarence Service than the official agent number of 1,547.[24] Today, these files provide a fuller picture of operations and enable an important recognition of the role that thousands of men and women played for the Clarence Service. They are deserving of recognition in the history.

A number of excellent histories of the White Lady and the Clarence Service have been published in French by historians in Belgium.[25] Narratives of the White Lady appear in English in sections in intelligence histories, but not in huge detail or as a full history, and usually told from the perspective of British intelligence, rather than the Belgian agents. Two important sources are Alan Judd's biography of Mansfield Cumming, the first head of the British Secret Service (SIS/MI6), and Keith Jeffery's authorised history of MI6, both of which contain official material from the MI6 archives. The authors had private access to Cumming's diary which is not available in the public domain.

One of the key – and controversial – sources, which historians have frequently drawn upon, are the published memoirs of Captain Henry Landau, the British intelligence officer in Rotterdam who ran the White

Lady for Cumming from July 1916. Landau first published his memoirs in America in 1934 as *All's Fair: The Story of the British Secret Service Behind the German Lines*. This was followed by another book in 1935 entitled *Secrets of the White Lady*.[26] A variation of the latter was published in Britain in 1938 as *Spreading the Spy Net: The Story of a British Spy Director*.[27]

British intelligence had major issues with Landau publishing his memoirs when he did, given they named agents from the White Lady at a time when the Nazi regime was a reality, and the books remained in print throughout World War Two. These agents were carrying out the same work for the successor SIS network, the Clarence Service, and Landau's works exposed them, placing them at risk of arrest by German counter-espionage units.[28] It was an irresponsible act. Publishing memoirs at all was taboo for an intelligence officer: Landau had signed the Official Secrets Act and that vow of secrecy was to last beyond the grave. SIS and MI6 did not officially 'exist' until 1994, and so any attempt by former or serving officers to publish their autobiographies caused alarm in intelligence circles. On behalf of SIS, in 1934 Stewart Menzies (a future 'C') personally warned Landau, who was then residing in America, to not publish his memoirs in Britain.[29] Four years later, in 1938, Landau did publish in the UK – although SIS appears to have taken no action to prevent it.

During his lifetime and still today, Landau remains a deeply contentious figure. Very serious allegations of sexual abuse were made against him in Holland in 1917.[30] Landau's morally reprehensible private life aside, he had, in Keith Jeffery's words, 'a real gift for intelligence work'.[31] His heinous behaviour in private is separate from his value as a source for the history of the White Lady.

Landau's books were written twenty years after the fact, and contain numerous colourful descriptions of events and conversations, at some of which he was not present. There are places where his account differs from, or elaborates on, those given in the official MI6 history.[32] Caution therefore needs to be exercised when drawing on the memoirs. But it remains an important source. The descriptions he gives are remarkably close to the agents' written testimonies in the surviving reports in the IWM and declassified files in Brussels. The events he describes suggest that he may well have retained documents from his work for the British Secret Service, and drawn on them in his books. It is clear, for instance, that Landau had access to files pertaining to the White Lady and interviewed some of the agents himself.[33] And new sources are coming to light. For instance, while Keith Jeffery asserted that the closed SIS archives 'tell a slightly different story', a declassified War Office file now offers a picture of Landau's recruitment and a timeline of events that is fuller than that found in the official MI6 archive, and which buttresses Landau's account.[34]

The various networks' personnel and activities were recorded in detail by the post-war commission. The wider intelligence 'big picture' also survives in the archives, along with some agent reports scattered among other files in different locations. But telling the full story of the White Lady would not have been possible without Landau's account, as SIS destroyed many of their files relating specifically to La Dame Blanche. Mansfield Cumming's biographer Alan Judd says: 'If he [Landau] had not published as he did, one of the greatest espionage achievements of the twentieth century would have remained largely unknown even to SIS itself, as well as to history . . . The remains of SIS's early archive yields not a word about what must have been one of the brightest feathers in Cumming's cap.'[35]

Mansfield Cumming

Fifty-four-year-old Mansfield Smith Cumming of the Royal Navy was the first head of the British Secret Service, which had been founded in 1909 and was initially part of the Secret Service Bureau. From 1915 Cumming's organisation became known as MI1(c) and was the forerunner of the Secret Intelligence Service (SIS) or MI6. A bit of an extrovert, Cumming became famous for signing his name 'C' in green ink, a tradition that has been carried on by all heads of SIS ever since. He operated out of Flat 54, 2 Whitehall Court, just a stone's throw from the War Office in Whitehall.

In July 1914, Cumming recruited Major Cecil Cameron, known as agent AC, to his secret service, which was top secret, did not officially exist, and functioned under cover of the War Office.[36] Cameron's recruitment was in spite of the fact that he had a criminal record, having been convicted of helping his wife to swindle an insurance company by faking a robbery. Cameron may have been innocent of the crime and taken some of the blame in support of his wife, but he served a five-year jail sentence for it.[37] She got three years.

On 31 July 1914, Cumming met with Cameron and two others.[38] Cameron was given codes and instructed to travel to France to meet one of Cumming's contacts in Paris. This he did, then went immediately on to Dinant in Belgium to establish himself at Givet. On 2 August 1914 Cumming gave more codes to another of Cameron's colleagues and instructed him to leave for Brussels, which he did with a driver, travelling via Dover and Ostend. At this time Cumming had a handful of officers in Belgium, including Demetrius Boulger who was based in Dinant, along the line of the anticipated German offensive.[39] In Brussels he had Herbert Dale Long, George Marie de Goldschmidt, James Cuffe and, now, Cecil Cameron.[40]

Colonel (soon Brigadier-General) George Macdonogh left for France with the British Expeditionary Force (BEF) on 14 August 1914, to head the intelligence section at General Headquarters (GHQ), based initially in the Château Beaurepaire in Montreuil.[41] Just prior to leaving, Macdonogh had put in place a plan with Cumming on how the army in the field would receive intelligence on the enemy. It was agreed that a section would be established in France to run agents in enemy-occupied areas north of Luxembourg, and that this would be run from GHQ.[42] Cumming's organisation was to gather all information from inside Germany and be in direct contact with Macdonogh on what Cumming's agents had gathered.

The day after Macdonogh left for France, 15 August 1914, Cumming himself travelled to Brussels to brief his agents on requirements during the war and 'to regularise Cameron's position vis-à-vis the British embassy and smooth ruffled feathers over some indiscretion committed by Henry Dale Long'.[43] The advance of German forces disrupted Macdonogh's and Cumming's plans for intelligence-gathering in Belgium. Cumming's men in Brussels returned to England, with the exception of Herbert Long.[44] Roy Regnart and Cameron joined Macdonogh at GHQ, where Cameron was tasked with getting intelligence from behind the German lines.[45] No mention is made in the official MI6 history on whether Cameron might have initially become the eyes and ears of Cumming inside GHQ. Cumming began to focus intelligence-gathering on Belgium from a covert headquarters in Holland, with his networks under the control of his officer in Rotterdam, thirty-eight-year-old Captain Richard Tinsley.[46] Tinsley's operations soon became 'the most important intelligence collection point on the Western Front'.[47]

Tinsley was given £3,000 a month for his operations, which was approximately half the monthly budget of £6,313 for Cumming's whole organisation.[48] Known simply as 'T', Tinsley had joined the Royal Naval Volunteer Reserve (RNVR) in 1903, and served as a maritime agent of the Cunard Line prior to World War One. In 1914 he was working undercover for Cumming in an office along the Boompjes (waterfront boulevard) in Rotterdam as manager of the Uranium Steamship Company. It was an ideal cover and Rotterdam the perfect base from which to coordinate covert intelligence networks in and out of German-occupied Belgium because of the neutrality of Holland in this war.

The world of intelligence was a dark one. Like Cameron and Landau, Tinsley was no angel. He was a rough-looking character, a crook and a con-man, who spoke no French, Dutch or Flemish and had no experience in military intelligence. He was described as 'a liar and a first-class intriguer with few scruples' and 'an absolute scoundrel', who was purported to be blackmailing companies in Holland and conducting dodgy dealings with German businessmen who had been banned from

England.[49] Cumming tended to recruit men from the criminal world who could exploit human weaknesses in areas of sexuality, bribery and gambling, such that 'the line between criminal and secret agent was a thin one'.[50] Cumming thought Tinsley's tough stance would make him a perfect candidate for ensuring the networks ran efficiently from Rotterdam and that he would keep the Dutch authorities on side – which he did.

From 3 October 1914, Cumming was temporarily out of action after a serious car accident in France, in which his son, Lieutenant Alastair Smith Cumming, died and he himself had a leg amputated (said to have been a self-amputation).[51] Macdonogh took advantage of Cumming's absence and appointed Cameron to a post in Folkestone, where GHQ ran another office. Cameron set up a train-watching organisation in Belgium, running it from 8 The Parade.[52] Macdonogh had decided on a policy of recruiting agents from amongst the Belgian refugees who were coming to England, training them and returning them to Belgium as spies. Cuffe and Goldschmidt, two of Cumming's men who had withdrawn from Belgium with the advancing German forces, were politely commanded to hand their agents over to Cameron. Macdonogh set up a second intelligence-gathering organisation under Major Ernest Wallinger, who operated from 7 Lincoln House, Basil Street, London.

Folkestone had a branch office at 41 rue St Roch in Paris, run by Captain George Bruce. Bruce was responsible for recruiting Belgian and French agents already living in unoccupied France and sending them back behind the German lines to collect information.[53] He went on to recruit Madame Lise Rischard, mentioned above, to set up a train-watching network in the Grand Duchy of Luxembourg – a network that was distinct from the White Lady in Belgium, and therefore not included in this book.[54]

Intelligence Behind the Lines

The Belgian and French intelligence services were also gathering their own information from behind the German lines, with British intelligence concerned by an overlap of agents and operations in the same regions. To resolve this, a number of meetings were held between the different intelligence organisations and British intelligence. A conference took place at Furnes (Belgium) on 22 November 1914 to try to create a common intelligence agency between them.[55] Although this aim was not achieved, it was agreed that they would cooperate with each other on a daily basis and each open an office in Folkestone, under a new umbrella organisation called the Bureau Central Interallié (BCI). Folkestone was chosen because the English port was a focal point where thousands of Belgian and French refugees arrived by boat from the continent, with the occasional spy amongst them. Cameron was tasked with liaising with them.

In these early days of primitive networks, it was a matter of learning on the job. Sigismund Payne Best, an officer of the Intelligence Corps (later SIS), who was posted to Macdonogh's intelligence section at GHQ in 1914, commented that the whole intelligence organisation was 'based upon ideas which had been evolved during the South African War [Boer War]. No one had any idea what it was going to be like to fight a modern army.'[56]

By early 1915, there were three distinct organisations collecting intelligence from behind the German lines in Belgium. They were Cameron's and Wallinger's networks, headed by Macdonogh, and a third headed by Tinsley (T Service) that reported direct to Cumming in London. Inter-service rivalry developed between these three different intelligence organisations.[57] There was also intense friction between the different heads of British military intelligence, including between Cumming and GHQ.[58] They disagreed over who should run the intelligence-gathering networks behind the German lines in Belgium and there were repeated attempts by GHQ to cut Cumming out of operations altogether.

As the arguments in military intelligence raged in the background and Macdonogh made various attempts to take over Cumming's networks, German forces had created a hinterland across Belgium, Luxembourg and the occupied areas of northern France. Its military units criss-crossed the countryside as they headed from the east to the front line. With the advent of prolonged trench warfare, it became increasingly difficult to gain the relevant intelligence swiftly enough from the different areas behind the German lines. It resulted in Cameron and Wallinger starting to use Holland to smuggle out their intelligence reports. They maintained their own system of couriers, passeurs (smugglers) and agents. Information gathered by these agents was sent initially to Tinsley, who passed it to the British military attaché in Rotterdam. He was forty-year-old Major Laurie Oppenheim, who wrote up detailed intelligence reports that came from a number of different sources, and which were then sent to London. As well as information from the train-watching service, Tinsley's office produced some very valuable naval reports for Cumming.[59]

Holland was already the main channel for Cumming's networks, and it was feared that this could lead to a blurring of lines and an overlap of agents. Some agents began to sell their information to the highest bidder.[60] From November 1916, Tinsley headed all secret organisations in Holland, with Cumming in overall charge of intelligence operations on the Western Front. Operational zones were established to avoid crossover between GHQ operations and Cumming's. Cameron ran his own agents, reported the information to GHQ and was restricted to geographical operations from Lier in the north, the region east of Brussels and Charleroi to the French border in the south.[61] Cumming's organisation operated east of that line and inside Brussels.

With the occupation of Belgium, the inhabitants of villages and towns found themselves behind the German lines and witnesses to the daily movements of German soldiers and equipment, often across the countryside towards the front line. After various battles, they witnessed the German units withdrawing to their resting camps. They were perfectly placed as observers to watch the railway networks. A train-watching service would give the Allied forces advance warning of the areas where German troops were concentrated, and their movement of units and armaments. It meant that the next major German attack could be predicted even before it began, enabling Allied reinforcements to be moved to a particular area in time to repel those forces. An official War Office report stated that train-watching was of vital importance in drawing up the enemy's order of battle and would have 'a direct effect on the operations and movements of our own forces, and therefore became the first objective of the Secret Service networks'.[62]

It was a patriotic Belgian, Dieudonné Lambrecht, who would lead that army in the shadows. It was an army without uniform or guns, but one that would provide British intelligence with a substantial picture of the situation behind the German lines.

PART I
THE WHITE LADY

Chapter 1
A PIONEER OF THE RESISTANCE

Thirty-two-year-old Dieudonné Lambrecht was living in Liège and happily married, with a baby daughter of only a few months old and caring for his elderly parents, when he entered the clandestine world, believing that it would help his oppressed country.

In December 1914 he travelled from Liège to Holland to join the Belgian army and fight for his country.[1] While he was there he met Ferdinand Afchain, a Parisian and British Secret Service agent, a 'cut out' (a go-between) who was recruiting new agents for Cameron.[2] Afchain asked Lambrecht if he would be willing to return to Belgium to establish an espionage network for the British. Lambrecht agreed and said to Afchain that he could collect information around Liège and bring it into Holland himself. His work entailed travelling and permitted him to cross the Dutch frontier on legitimate business without suspicion from the German authorities – the perfect cover to smuggle intelligence. He first operated under George Marie de Goldschmidt of the War Office, with Afchain becoming his main contact in Rotterdam from May 1915, and then Tinsley.[3] Now Lambrecht's life in Belgium would be in constant danger from Germany's counter-espionage teams that sought to break up networks that helped the Allies.

Lambrecht was born on 4 May 1882 in Thier-à-Liège, a district in the north of Liège.[4] He was educated locally and raised as a Roman Catholic, of a cheerful, frank and open nature. After modest beginnings, working at the Demarteau printing press, then in an administrative post, he took over a small mechanical and armoury factory at rue Vivegnis in Liège, with his brother-in-law Oscar Donnay. The latter would also soon join the network. The local population around Liège consisted mainly of farmers, market gardeners, gunsmiths, engineers and industrialists. The telegraphic and communications engineers would prove to be ideal recruits for the technical radio communication side of Lambrecht's network.

It quickly became apparent to British intelligence in London that Lambrecht was a man with strong moral qualities and a leader who understood the importance of the methodical observation of enemy troops. On returning to Liège, he set up the Lambrecht Service and recruited Oscar Donnay, and two Jesuit priests in Liège called Father Arthur Dupont and Father Jean (Pére) Des Onays ('Belleflamme').[5] The three men helped to establish the first observation posts at Liège, Jemelle and Stavelot (the latter in the Ardennes region of Belgium, close to Luxembourg) by engaging the help of Belgian railway workers. Battalions were created initially at Liège, Namur and Brussels, with 200 agents enrolling immediately. The battalions increased across the war and were divided into companies, which were subdivided into platoons.[6] They began to note the transportation of large German military units coming from the Eastern Front towards the Western Front.

A key figure in the network from the beginning was Lambrecht's thirty-four-year-old cousin Walthère Dewé.[7] Tall and dark-haired, with a black scrubby beard and penetrating blue eyes, he would soon rise to become the chief engineer for the Telephone and Telegraph Company in Liège.[8] He was born on 26 April 1880 in an isolated house with several acres of land in the rue Coupée, high above the valley in Liège. In 1899, he studied at the University of Liège and became a highly skilled engineer. He married Dieudonnée Salmon and they went on to have four children.[9] Dewé recruited patriotic Belgians, such as his colleagues (local engineers) and civilians such as Thérèse de Radiguès (more about her shortly). Dewé had a wide circle of trusted friends whom he could recruit, and that included his university colleagues; and as a practising Roman Catholic, he was respected by parishioners at the church, as well as by local priests, monks and nuns. This made his job of recruiting from this section of society easier. Whatever the background of the new agents, they had common ground in their patriotism and faith, for many were observant Roman Catholics who attended mass daily. Their Christian beliefs and sense of service underpinned their drive for joining the clandestine network.

Train-Watching Posts

The network's agents worked at their observation posts along the railways, counting the number of trains and carriages and compiling intelligence reports on the transportation of enemy troops. They noted the number of trains and their wagons, empty wagons, types of soldiers and their units (identified by their insignia), machine guns, ammunition and heavy artillery. All this information had to be smuggled to Landau and British intelligence in Holland. A westward movement of German troops for several days from the Eastern Front through Jemelle alerted Lambrecht to an impending offensive. As one of the troop trains passed through Jemelle one night, he jumped onto the buffer and hid until it reached its final destination, where he alighted with the intelligence.[10]

Each night and day the observers at the train-watching posts, many of them women, watched the trains passing through the railway centres of Liège, Namur and Jemelle and noted all troop movements through Belgium.[11] Lambrecht acted as a courier, in what was considered to be one of the most hazardous jobs within a clandestine network, and often working at night. He succeeded in avoiding arrest by frontier guards and German patrols to smuggle his reports into Holland. Each time he travelled on 'industrial business' he was searched, but hid letters from soldiers and telegraphic messages, such that the Germans did not find them.

Lambrecht started to hire boatmen, professional smugglers and fraud-sters because the reports needed to be taken urgently into Holland. He was aware of the risk of engaging such shady characters who might betray him or an operation for money. The urgency of the situation perhaps clouded his judgement on the security risks of doing so. Smuggling the reports into Holland became increasingly difficult as the Germans stepped up their searches, but still the agents operated silently and invisibly across Belgium. Section leaders recruited people as 'walking agents' (*agents prome-neurs*), observers whose task was to wander a region and watch and cata-logue German troop movements occurring by road.[12]

The train-watching posts were essential to intelligence-gathering behind the German lines for four years. For the duration of the war, the Germans moved their troops and armaments from Germany through Belgium or Luxembourg to the front line in France; and later, when in retreat, they moved them in reverse. All this could be observed by rail and road and enabled British intelligence to analyse what military units were being moved and where. Ways to smuggle this crucial information out of the country had to be devised, and this saw the development of ingenious methods of spycraft.

Spycraft

Intelligence reports could be written in invisible ink on tissue paper and folded so small that they could be concealed in the buttons of a jacket.[13] The special buttons were made by Lambrecht's friend in Liège. The messages were revealed by Cumming's officers in Holland using an alcohol-iodine agent. Some of these tiny messages were handwritten in French or in code and survive today in the IWM archive. Messages were also written on rice paper that was sourced from Japan, and 3 × 2 inches in size.[14] These could be rolled up and hidden in a bicycle valve or a rubber tube. If inside a rubber tube, each end could be cut off and it could be carried in the mouth. If there was risk of arrest during a courier's journey, a message could be swallowed.

Other early spycraft techniques were adopted, including knitting codes into jumpers. Cottages located nearest to the railway lines became the new intelligence front line, as women, from the ages of eighteen to eighty, sat outside their cottages and by their windows inside and knitted. It was a seemingly innocent activity, but in fact they were watching the troop movements as the trains passed by their doors. Certain stitches indicated the number of German troops, the regiments and how many; as one British intelligence officer later wrote, 'They knitted their information in combinations of plain and purl to represent the composition of the wagons – plain for soldiers, purl for horses and guns. This had to be deciphered, written down and sent to the chief of service.'[15] The scarves and jumpers were thrown over the wire along the border between Belgium and Holland to a peasant waiting on the other side, who appeared to be working the land. Eventually they arrived at GHQ in France, where an intelligence officer decoded them.

British intelligence officer Sigismund Payne Best, who arrived in Tinsley's office in 1917, noted how he had to become even more inventive to secure a line for intelligence to be smuggled out of the country. He became a drug pusher, selling large quantities of morphine and cocaine to the border guards, which enabled him to regularly cross the frontier or pass through the electrified fence without being challenged by guards.[16] He later claimed in his unpublished memoirs that the British prime minister, David Lloyd George, sanctioned his unlawful actions, after which, 'If anyone wanted to come from Belgium into Holland, he came through our special door.'[17] It meant that intelligence reports could reach London in only two to three days.

On the German side, some ordinary soldiers were aware of the clandestine activities of spies and passeurs. Arthur Weiner, a German soldier stationed at the German passport office in Kemzeke on the Dutch border, mentioned the espionage activities in letters written home to his wife in Germany. He was billeted in a palace in Ghent that had been requisitioned from a French count. In December 1914 he wrote: 'Sadly, we'll be leaving here on Monday, the Dutch border to be precise, but I must ask you not to say a word about this to anyone, as there is a lot of espionage activity based there. The posting is hardly a dangerous one, and for that reason I'm letting you know despite the prohibition.'[18]

Weiner soon wrote more extensively of espionage activities by Belgians. 'We continue to mistrust the English in relation to Holland,' he wrote. 'Secret orders arrive frequently which point to a very strong espionage presence in our region of Holland. We know of some of the agents when they cross the border in disguise on their donkey carts.'[19]

Weiner and his comrades were occasionally called by the Etappen command (the German communications command behind the lines) to aid them after the arrest of Belgian civilians suspected of espionage. The Etappen consisted also of military courts and field police. It tracked down spies and agents, including those of Lambrecht's network, as Weiner wrote to his wife:

> Where assistance is required, e.g. for the investigation of suspicious wagons, automobiles, people, for requisitions, punitive sorties against villages, the Etappen Command requests our help as necessary . . . The Etappen itself is not an easy posting because of the proximity of the Dutch border and the extensive spying activity conducted via Holland. Not a day passes without our arresting a suspect. Our guardroom here in the village serves as the custody point, sometimes 8 or more people are there, including soldiers under arrest. During the night women are held in the lock-up, but there is a double guard at the door and the window. Occasionally very elegant ladies appear. The duty officer is often able to secure their release without further ado where there has been an error. Otherwise, the case is heard by a 'Kriegsgerichtsrat', a senior official in the Courts Martial and, where appropriate, passed on to the Inspectorate. Minor charges, e.g. smuggling of intrinsically harmless letters or newspapers, result in an immediate fine or custody . . . Of course, you mustn't say too much about what you've read, but sometimes you learn something which was clearly deliberately hushed up.[20]

The reference to elegant ladies could be Lambrecht's aristocratic agents, who were arrested for espionage. Weiner wrote a total of 700 letters to his wife from the front line in Belgium. Written in old German Gothic script, they provide a rare perspective of the war in Belgium from the German angle.[21]

Escape Lines and Espionage

As so often happened in World War One, the intelligence networks became mixed up with escape lines. British, French and Belgian soldiers were smuggled across the frontier into Holland. Some of Lambrecht's leaders and agents conducted both escape and intelligence-gathering activities, but this was risky: it blurred the lines of operations, and if members of one network were arrested by the German Field Police, it could compromise the others. A fine line existed between Lambrecht's intelligence work and his agents aiding British and French soldiers. It would be an argument in the next war, 1939–45, that the escape lines should be run entirely separately from SIS's intelligence networks to avoid either being compromised if one went down.

Countess Gabrielle de Monge is a prime example of intelligence work for the British Secret Service overlapping with an escape line.[22] In November 1914 she founded the Service de Monge, which she ran from her home at Château de Wallay-Reppe in Ohey, east of Namur.[23] With the support of Thérèse and Henri de Radiguès, Gabrielle arranged for soldiers to be hidden in nearby Conneux Castle as well as the estates of other aristocrats and in religious abbeys. Her close circle of aristocratic friends provided shelter before the soldiers could be safely smuggled into Holland.[24] Service de Monge was well organised for an early escape line and had a section for forgery, printing photographs and the production of fake identity cards for the escaping soldiers. A team of Belgian women was tasked specifically with recruiting others into the escape line. There was another dimension to their work: collecting information for the British Secret Service and sending it out via Holland. They worked closely with Lambrecht's intelligence network.

On a grey and foggy morning, 24 November 1914, Gabrielle came downstairs into the smoking room at Château de Wallay-Reppe to meet with a group of patriotic Belgians, one of whom was her own brother-in-law, whose name is not given in her memoir.[25] They were planning the first escape for six French soldiers and it was decided that she would act as a scout to go ahead and check that the route was clear of German patrols. Her brother-in-law suggested that she break up the journey with a stop in Liège, where his brother Jean could help. There were considerable physical distances to be covered – a total of approximately 150km to the Dutch frontier. The first stage comprised a 15km journey to Huy from Gabrielle's castle. This was followed by a 25km journey along the river Meuse to Liège. She decided that the best way to travel these distances was by bicycle.

The first stage took Gabrielle to Huy; the soldiers followed on foot with a guide, not too far behind. She agreed to meet them at certain points along the route. In the inns or at trusted meeting locations she obtained up-to-date information from local Belgians on the state of German occupation of the area. She assessed any potential security risks for the escapers coming along behind her, and established what German guards were on duty on the bridges across the Meuse. German guards strictly controlled the movement of civilians in occupied Belgium.

During the first journey she undertook with escapers, there was a sentry posted on a bridge they had to cross. Not able to produce the required identity pass, she quickly came up with a scheme.[26] She let down one of the tyres on her bicycle and wheeled it towards the guard.

'Pass,' he said.

'I don't have one,' she replied in German, which immediately softened his approach to her, 'but I am just going to get my bicycle repaired on the other side of the bridge. There is no need to ask for a pass for that.' She started to back away, saying, 'I don't have time for this [delay] today.'[27] The guard relented and allowed her across the bridge.

Out of sight on the other side, she pumped up her tyre and continued to the next location, where she was rendezvousing with the escapers.

The ruse of the flat tyre worked on a number of occasions for the rest of the journey. The dangers of crossing occupied Belgium could not be underestimated, but Gabrielle and her network of guides and couriers succeeded in smuggling men over the frontier into Holland. 'I owe you my life,' said one of the French men.

Gabrielle wrote of these men, 'They dare not believe their eyes, these poor soldiers who, for months, had been holed up in the woods like game and hunted [by German patrols].'[28] Once in Holland, she accompanied them a further 30km to the French consulate in Maastricht. The consul-general was not in, and they were received by the first secretary, who listened to the soldiers' escape story. 'How did you manage to cross occupied Belgium and reach neutral Holland, whose frontier is guarded?' he asked.

'That's how,' said one of the men, pointing at Gabrielle.

Gabrielle then completed the journey in reverse back to Ohey, all the while observing her surroundings and gathering intelligence. The risks in operating this escape line were great. The Germans issued a notice across the Ardennes region warning that anyone found sheltering or providing food to Allied soldiers would be shot, and German patrols were increased in the villages in the Ardennes.

Léon Parent

One of the key early helpers in the Service de Monge was nineteen-year-old Léon Parent.[29] He was patriotic and wanted to serve his country. He began working for Gabrielle's escape line and soon entered Lambrecht's network as well.[30] He lived in the small village of Vonèche, located in the province of Namur on the French frontier in the Ardennes. The woods around there provided ideal cover for evading French soldiers.[31] Parent had already proved his mettle. When the first patrol of ten Germans had arrived in the neighbourhood, Parent had warned a Belgian post at Beauraing and this led to the capture of the German soldiers. A few days later, as French soldiers advanced from Gedinne towards Beauraing, Parent had slipped through the German lines to give the French commander a report on the strength of the German forces opposing them.

Having grown up in the village and knowing every part of the dense woods, he helped French soldiers to find suitable hiding places. But he knew that he could not smuggle them out of Belgium on his own; he would need support. Around late November–early December 1914, he decided to visit Gabrielle de Monge in Ohey. She had just returned from smuggling her first group of French soldiers into Holland. She agreed to work with him and use her contacts in Liège, so that he could escort small groups to the town. She procured the necessary frontier guides for the final stages of the journey to Liège; usually no more than ten men were escorted at any one time.

On his first mission Parent was accompanied by Gabrielle as far as Liège and she introduced him to local people who were prepared to help with food, resources and shelter.[32] The escapers left at dawn, dressed as villagers and workmen, and made their way in pairs to each meeting point, so as not to draw attention to a larger group of men walking through the countryside. Like Gabrielle, Parent used a bicycle to go ahead of them as a scout. He met the men at each agreed rendez-vous and rested until the entire group had caught up. It was a tough journey as so many of the men were recovering from wounds, often having only just escaped from a hospital.

The first stage of the journey ended at Conneux Castle, where Thérèse de Radiguès ensured there was always food prepared for them. The men were sheltered in an empty house in nearby Ciney, where the cupboards were always well stocked with food and blankets by local helpers. The next stage of the journey was to Huy, then Liège, where Gabrielle found lodgings for them in private houses or small inns. During the first month of the escape line, Parent successfully escorted sixty-two men out. He returned to Vonèche to find more soldiers waiting for him.

While Parent was travelling back and forth to Liège he came into contact with Lambrecht's network. He was approached to join.

Towards the end of March 1915, Parent returned from a mission to Liège and brought with him a piece of white paper for Gabrielle de Monge. It was from her cousin, Baroness van der Straten, and contained a message in invisible ink, asking her to go to Honnay as soon as possible, which she did.[33] It is the first hint of Service de Monge using traditional spycraft such as invisible ink. In her memoirs, Gabrielle does not reveal the nature of the visit to Honnay, but the following evening she called at Conneux Castle. It was the first time she had seen Thérèse and Henri de Radiguès in person since the foundation of the escape line in November 1914. She wrote, 'Like my cousins at Honnay, they were part of my organisation.'[34]

After supper, and seated around a wood fire, Gabrielle shared with them the secret message that she had received from Baroness van der Straten. The latter had Belgian and French soldiers who needed to be smuggled into Holland, but would only entrust them to Gabrielle. Henri assured her that the group could receive hospitality at Conneux Castle.

The following morning Gabrielle returned to Honnay, where she saw Parent and one of her servants informed her that there were fifteen men hiding in the potato cellar. At 4 a.m. the men were split into two groups and led out of the cellar by separate paths to the woods around Conneux Castle. Gabrielle went ahead to warn Henri de Radiguès that the men were hiding in the woods. She crawled through the barbed-wire fence surrounding the estate, and walked along an avenue of fir trees, to find Henri waiting for her. The men were brought into the castle and given food. At dawn, they moved off in the direction of Ciney and onwards to places where Gabrielle had arranged cars to pick them up. They were smuggled out of the country into Holland. This work would be made almost impossible by a new high-voltage electrified wire which the Germans began to construct along the Belgian–Dutch border in spring 1915.

The Wire of Death

Construction of the electrified fence reached its peak in May and June 1915 and totalled around 350km along the border from Knokke on the

Belgian coast to Aachen in Germany. Its aim was to prevent Belgians from leaving the country and to stop British and French spies from entering and exiting Belgium. Dubbed 'the wire of death' by Belgians and the German army alike, it was guarded by a combination of sentries, who were posted every few hundred metres along its entire length, and mounted patrols, police dogs and plainclothes secret police. Remnants of this fence still survive on the Dutch border.[35]

Throughout the war, at least 850 people lost their lives trying to cross through the wire. Its construction caused enormous challenges for Cumming and his officers in trying to obtain intelligence from inside occupied Belgium; there was a risk that the flow of information to Tinsley in Rotterdam would dry up. But Belgian and French agents nevertheless found creative ways to enter and exit surreptitiously.

Passeurs and spies were undeterred by the electrified fence and found ingenious ways to cross it.[36] One method was to use a collapsible wooden frame inserted between the wires and opened out into a square, so that those passing through were isolated from the electric current. Some simply wore long rubber boots, sleeves and gloves to prevent themselves from being electrocuted.[37] They passed through the wire into Holland with the help of two teenagers, Leonie Rameloo and Emilie Schattemann, who lived in a border village.[38]

The situation became trickier after the Germans became wise to these activities, but members of Lambrecht's network found new ways to smuggle intelligence out. For instance, messages were hidden inside a slit cut into potatoes, which were thrown over the wire to be collected on the other side. Intelligence continued to flow to the British.

War was raging in May 1915. At the end of the month, the first German Zeppelin airship raids began on London; in Turkey the Gallipoli campaign was well underway. On the Western Front, a large Anglo-French offensive was mounted in Artois, northern France. Behind the German lines, Lambrecht's observation posts operated for twenty-four hours a day, every day. They observed the German divisions that were being transported via the Luxembourg railway network from the Serbian front to fight in Flanders.[39] There were frequent movements of German divisions across Belgium, with observers seeing dozens of trains crowded with troops, and trains being loaded with equipment and passing across the railways. As agents and their families divided up day and night into manageable shifts, Cumming in London waited for vital intelligence.

Occasionally there is a fleeting mention of a clandestine mission in a memoir, as when Marie-Antoinette de Radiguès wrote in her unpublished diary entry for Wednesday, 21 July 1915, 'National Day – Harold left this morning for Holland – special mission.'[40] The nature of that mission is unknown, but other activities by Lambrecht's network are coming to light in declassified files. For instance, it is clear now that missions were planned and undertaken for airmen to be landed by plane into Belgium.[41]

Landings by Plane

In May 1915, a French spy was landed by plane in the Ardennes region of Belgium with two baskets of carrier pigeons. He linked up with his contact on the ground, agent Paul (Paulin) Jacquemin.[42] Jacquemin lived in Monthermé in the Ardennes and was already hiding French soldiers around there for Gabrielle de Monge. The pigeons were sent back with messages about enemy troop movements behind the German lines. French intelligence had realised that the Ardennes was a suitable region to land agents on the ground by plane and had already started to liaise with Jacquemin for such operations. The unnamed French spy who landed in May 1915 made two trips to Charleville, bringing back information for Jacquemin to report to French intelligence on the exact location of the headquarters of Crown Prince Wilhelm, Prince of Prussia and heir to the Kaiser.[43] Jacquemin set up a small platoon, working with the French too, and in liaison with Léon Parent.

By the middle of June 1915, Jacquemin and Parent were compromised after the Germans discovered that a number of spies were being landed in the Ardennes.[44] One of those spies, known only as 'Robert', was tracked by the Germans to a small farm belonging to M. Tutiaux, a farmer in Vieux-Moulins de Thilay. The farmhouse was surrounded by German patrols, and although Robert managed to escape into the woods, his intelligence reports were found. Tutiaux was questioned, and it is not known if he gave any information away, but other arrests swiftly followed. Jacquemin was shot while running away from the police in Monthermé. He was posthumously awarded the King's Commendation for Brave Conduct (military).

The principal agents of Jacquemin's platoon were also either shot by the Germans or died in prison. Mme Hélène Levy of Charleville, one of the key women in his platoon, was arrested, tried and condemned to death, with her sentence later reduced to life imprisonment.[45] She had organised the intelligence reports, aided escape and evasion, and run the pigeon service.[46] Sister Marie Angèle, the mother superior of the convent at Les Hauts Buttes in the Ardennes, sheltered some of the airmen in the convent. She was recommended for an honour for her 'patriotic collaboration . . . and precious services rendered' in the war, which was personally signed by Henri Philippe Pétain, Marshal of France.[47]

Parent avoided arrest, and tried to cross the Dutch border in order to join the Belgian army-in-exile. At Liège he learned that the frontier guide who was to take him to the border had been arrested. He returned to his parents' home in Vonèche, but the German secret police had already discovered his involvement with Jacquemin and were looking for him.

At 7 a.m. on 18 August 1915, Parent was arrested, along with his father and mother, and taken by car to Givet and imprisoned in Anvers. From there, in early October, Parent was transferred to a prison in Antwerp and held in solitary confinement. On 8 October, he was tried in the fortress of Antwerp, without the presence of a Belgian lawyer, and refused to give up the names of his colleagues. Aged twenty, he was condemned to death and awaited his fate.[48]

News of his sentence caused outrage in Belgium and thousands of Belgians signed a petition to the German Kaiser for his release, but without success. His parents, who were given fifteen years' hard labour, were permitted to say goodbye to him. They were then transferred to a prison in Germany. The German secret police was determined to find evidence of Parent's espionage and placed a stool pigeon in his cell. This was a fake prisoner who pretended to also be condemned to death for espionage, so he could gain the trust of Parent. Weeks of solitary confinement wore down Parent and he became too trusting of his cellmate. Gradually the cellmate drew a confession from Parent, who admitted to having been involved in espionage.

Parent was shot at dawn on 8 December 1915.[49] He had sacrificed his life for his country, but not before saving around 350 soldiers who were back on the front line fighting for the freedom of Belgium and France: a heroic personal contribution to the cause for freedom.

The deaths of Jacquemin and Parent were not the end. Across Belgium, the male and female agents carried on their quiet and methodical intelligence-gathering, alongside aiding and sheltering airmen who continued to be infiltrated into the country. By now, Tinsley had twenty-seven members of staff in his office in Rotterdam, consisting of British, French and Dutch personnel.[50] Behind the scenes, the higher echelons of military intelligence were still arguing over who controlled the network in Belgium.

Control of Belgian Networks

Brigadier Macdonogh continued to manoeuvre his position to gain complete control over the networks in Belgium, believing that secret service work there should come under his authority, and not that of Mansfield Cumming ('C'). On 13 May 1915, Macdonogh asked that all original intelligence reports from British, French and Belgian sources that were being sent to the War Office by military attaché Major Laurie Oppenheim in Rotterdam be forwarded to him without delay.

He took the view that not only did such work belong to the intelligence section of the army in the field, but he wished to be the first to assess their contents.[51] By implication this meant Cumming's networks, too.[52] No agreement was reached and the arguments rumbled on in the background.

In September 1915, Cumming and Major Walter Kirke of the Intelligence Corps attended a conference in Paris to try to thrash out a solution on Allied agents operating via Holland. The aim of the conference was to put an end to rivalry, indiscretion and double-dealing by some spies.[53] In spite of having collected excellent intelligence behind the lines, one official report noted, 'There is little doubt that denunciations, buying up of other services and agents, duplication of reports, collaboration between agents of the various Allied systems were not uncommon; so that the information arrived at the various headquarters in a manner which was not only confusing, but sometimes unreliable and apt to be dangerous.'[54] No agreement was reached at this conference either.

The first breakthrough came on 29 November 1915 at the War Office in London, where it was decided that intelligence-gathering should be divided into different regions of Belgium. Cumming's organisation would cover the easterly section of Belgium and GHQ would have control of the westerly areas, to enable the latter to largely gain tactical information.[55] In spite of the best intentions to operate in separate regions, it was not possible to avoid a duplication of work, and coordination over border crossings and routes could have helped each service.[56] In the background to all this, the intelligence section of the War Office was itself undergoing reorganisation. A new Directorate of Military Intelligence and a Directorate of Military Operations were formed, which were distinct from each other.

Although the 29 November conference appeared to provide a solution by carving up Belgium into regions for the sole jurisdiction of particular sectors of British intelligence, it was impractical in the end. The artificial limiting of territory to certain networks prevented the natural flow of information, especially if that information crossed a line into the zone of another organisation. This potentially deprived them of useful information from reliable sources in an area where they did not have jurisdiction.[57] Rotterdam was the only realistic route whereby any of this intelligence could be brought out. By early 1917, the British Secret Service was given exclusive control of the agents working for the network that came to be known as La Dame Blanche (the White Lady). Cumming finally had a free hand for his operations, managed by Tinsley in Holland, and without official interference from elsewhere.

In reality, many of the operational issues were ironed out by the Belgian leadership and agents on the ground, who were unaware of the organisational problems within British intelligence. Through instinct, common sense and ingenuity they organised their sectors right across the regions behind the German lines, and thus became one of Cumming's greatest successes.

Chapter 2
BETRAYAL

The high-voltage fence was not the only challenge for British intelligence in 1915. The networks in Belgium and France had begun to be decimated by an effective German counter-intelligence service and betrayals, which led to the arrests and deaths of leaders and agents.[1]

It was devastating for British intelligence, but Lambrecht's network was still operating. That summer, it proved its value by the quality of information it was sending to British and French intelligence. During August 1915, Lambrecht was able to inform the French authorities of the movement of a large convoy of German troops in the direction of the front lines, which led to French forces intercepting it. German prisoners of war were captured, but on this occasion they did not yield any intelligence during interrogation. Observing the movement of German troops was a significant result in itself: it showed that the Germans were planning a new offensive. Lambrecht expanded his network of observers to cover the provinces around Liège and Namur, and closer to the Luxembourg border. He found ways to send agents into France, specifically to Charleville. He recruited women and men whom he could trust to run observation posts from Belgium and across the border into France. These new agents were trained for regular missions and in spycraft to enable a rapid transmission of intelligence reports to Tinsley in Rotterdam.

Expanding the observation posts produced results, as one of those new recruits was one Captain Ernest Evrard, who was about to deliver vital information on a new German offensive.[2] He was entrusted with a perilous mission in occupied France to blow up the Saint-Joseph Bridge between Revin and Fumay and gather military intelligence from these areas. He took with him an Alsatian, eighteen-year-old Alfred Schwenck ('Aubry'). At 5 a.m. on 23 September 1915, the two men were landed by plane on a hill near Dauphiné, along with supplies of explosives and devices. Schwenck was soon captured in military uniform and transported to Germany.[3]

In the meantime, Evrard had tracked the positions of German soldiers in the region, evaded them and reached the banks of the Meuse. He was then escorted by a guide and helper, Jules Yon, to Fumay. In Fumay an agent, known simply as Martin, hid him in a slate quarry.[4] With the help of Martin and his wife, Evrard set up headquarters in that unlikely location, with supplies and pigeons. Evrard conducted espionage, noting the movement of trains and troops in the region and transmitting the information by pigeon to the British Secret Service. He sabotaged local telegraph wires to disrupt the German communications. Alongside his work, the covert train watchers across Belgium observed a large, slow movement of German troops from the Russian front.[5] It was clear that these troops were moving to reinforce German positions in the Champagne area of France for an attack against the British and French.[6] The cumulative intelligence was sent to the British and French intelligence services in enough time for French forces to bring forward their Champagne offensive by at least two days.

On 25 September 1915, British and French forces launched a new combined offensive on the Western Front, with the French soldiers fighting in the Champagne and Artois region and the British at Loos, in the famous Battle of Loos.[7] Marie-Antoinette de Radiguès, who had by then returned to Conneux Castle from England, noted in her diary, 'The Allies advance. It is said that the great offensive has begun.'[8]

By the end of the first day and in spite of sustaining huge casualties, British troops had broken through German positions near Loos, but

were only partially successful at Hulluch. However, the lack of immediate reinforcements for them meant that any further advance faltered.
Within three days, German troops had pushed British forces back, but
not to their original lines – the British kept some forward positions. It
is fair to say that without the original intelligence on the large movement of German units from Lambrecht's agents, the casualties, fatalities
and loss of ground could have been far worse. For both the Allied and
German sides, this war showed very early on how difficult it was for
either side to break through the Western Front.

After the failed Allied offensive, German troops began to move in
huge numbers across Belgium. From late September and into October
1915, Lambrecht's network observed it all, and sent every detail in its
reports to the British Secret Service. Lambrecht received a message back
from British military headquarters that his report on the movement of
troops around Liège and the east of Belgium was very good and more
such reports were to be sent.

Evrard was still operating from his headquarters in the slate quarry.
He and his men attempted to blow up the Saint-Joseph Bridge, but they
were spotted by German soldiers. Evrard managed to evade capture, but
the others were caught. He sent a message by pigeon to be picked up by
plane immediately, but no plane came. Loyal patriots aided his escape
back to the Ardennes in Belgium, where he was hidden in a house.

By the end of November 1915, many of Evrard's agents had been
arrested by the Germans and condemned to death or given sentences of
hard labour.[9] Evrard himself was arrested and sent to a fortress in
Germany, then to a POW camp, from which he managed to escape and
returned to France.[10] Désiré Lambert, one of his fellow agents, said,
'Evrard was the most wonderful figure I have encountered, with a patriotism that is unfailing, an indomitable courage, a tireless zeal.'[11]

The end of 1915 saw a slew of bad news reach the British Secret
Service in London. On 19 December, Countess Gabrielle de Monge
was arrested with two young Belgians as they tried to cross into Holland.
Suspected of espionage, they were taken to Gemmenich prison, east

Belgium, for interrogation. Gabrielle pretended she had been entering Holland to find work, but she was found to be carrying a false identity pass in the name of Julia Massage, aged twenty-seven, and 235 francs in her handbag.

On 5 January 1916, Gabrielle and the two young Belgian men were transferred to Liège.[12] She wrote: 'We were paraded through the streets of the city. I looked pitiful among my guards: with my big shoes covered in mud, without a hat and my hair in disarray due to lack of a comb as I had not been able to comb my hair for five days.' They were taken to St Léonard prison in the suburbs of Liège. Her arrest was a substantial loss to British intelligence as her escape line had already saved over 400 Allied soldiers. At her trial, Gabrielle's lawyer pleaded insanity and produced a medical certificate to say as much. In doing this, he hoped she would avoid the death penalty, but she had to spend several difficult months in a psychiatric asylum where she underwent various torturous treatments. Eventually, there was a hearing in Namur and she was sentenced to three years in prison and hard labour.

New Year's Day 1916 saw the arrest of Henri and Thérèse de Radiguès, the principal leaders of the network in the Ardennes. They were imprisoned in Givet prison for fifteen days, after which they were released on parole and returned to Conneux Castle. The following day, 16 January, the authorities returned to the castle and Henri was re-arrested. He was taken to Namur prison, where he faced charges of aiding French soldiers and young Belgians by hiding them in the Ardennes and arranging their safe passage out of the country. Four of the soldiers had been too sick to be moved and were arrested too. They confessed to everything during intense German interrogation and were sentenced to prison. Baron van der Straten was also arrested at this time, and together with Henri de Radiguès he was sentenced to eight years' hard labour. Henri was transferred first to Siegburg prison, then Rheinbach in Germany. The nuncio of the Roman Catholic Church intervened on his behalf and his sentence was commuted to eighteen months. He remained in prison until January 1918.

The entire sector of the network had gone down in the Ardennes, but it was not the end. Thérèse de Radiguès revived the network in the region. She was a tough, determined and courageous woman, and despite her husband and close friend being in prison, was resolute in continuing her clandestine work.

The Work Must Go On

Lambrecht remained focused on keeping the Lambrecht Service network going. The intelligence on German military build-up and operations had to be monitored and the information had to continue to flow to London, including movement of trains across the Belgian railways during the night. On 28 January 1916, an unnamed Belgian agent returned from a mission in England and wrote to Lambrecht, 'I confirm to you the great congratulations which I received on my last trip to the English General Headquarters. All the information from the different posts is much appreciated by the great chiefs and, in particular, that of Jemelle, of December 15 last, giving the numbers of the regiments which have been recognized as exact and of capital importance. Would you like to convey these congratulations to all the agents and tell them that they will not be forgotten.'[13]

In addition to watching the train lines, some agents were given special tasks of reporting on enemy defences, artillery, weapons, aerodromes and the movement of shipping from the ports of Ostend and Zeebrugge. Superb intelligence was being received throughout 1915, so much so that the British Secret Service asked Lambrecht to expand his network further into the south of Belgium and near the front line. He was asked urgently to form new observation posts at Bertrix, Autelbas and Virton in Belgium, and Mohon, Mézières and Montmédy in France.[14] Lambrecht began the immediate expansion, and in so doing, exposed himself to a greater risk of being caught by the Germans.

The expansion of agents and sectors paid off, because in the late winter of 1915 and into early 1916, information came about the forthcoming Battle of Verdun via the indiscretions of a German major who was billeted at the home of Lambrecht's sister.[15] To corroborate it, Lambrecht sent agents into the occupied regions of France to establish the final destination of the troops; they were indeed heading for Verdun. In addition, the agents observed and reported on the mass movement of German troops across the Belgian train network, and they too were heading for the same place. The Allies also received information from German deserters and this corroborated the picture coming from the Lambrecht Service.[16]

The Battle of Verdun lasted nine months from 21 February to 18 December 1916 and marked one of the longest and bloodiest of the war. French and German forces all sustained huge losses. With the build-up of German troops and artillery around Verdun, Lambrecht maintained contact with the French Secret Service in Holland. He had two particularly active agents there. They were Emile Fauquenot and Franz Creusen, who were screening French refugees and interviewing them as potential spies to be sent into Belgium for Lambrecht.[17] Fauquenot and Creusen were already on the German secret police's wanted list for having led a group of saboteurs in disrupting German military operations and communications in Belgium. Their efforts at recruiting new agents increased at the time of the attack on Verdun because General Joffre, the commander-in-chief of French forces on the Western Front, was preparing his own offensive on the Somme and needed intelligence on German troops and positions.[18]

Fauquenot interviewed a newly arrived female refugee in Holland called Marie Birckel, a young French schoolteacher. There was an instant connection between them, as she found her interrogator to have an intense patriotic streak. They later married after the war. Marie volunteered to spy for Fauquenot and joined Lambrecht's organisation. She agreed to mount a train-watching post on the Hirson–Mézières line, which had thus far been largely unsuccessful for the Allied intelligence agencies. She was to be sent over the frontier with a Dutch guide, Bertram, because the other trusted guides were engaged on missions.

He was working for the French Secret Service in Maastricht, but unbeknown to Fauquenot and Creusen, Bertram was a German double agent.[19]

Having crossed the border, Marie continued to Liège, where she became aware that she was being followed. She did not go to the letter box to pick up reports, but instead waited in her overnight lodgings, knowing arrest was imminent. She was apprehended and taken to St Léonard prison in Liège.

Back at the British Secret Service headquarters in London, Cumming waited for reports, but no information was coming from behind the wire. It was clear that new methods had to be devised to bring intelligence over the frontier. Lambrecht found himself increasingly cut off from all communication with his contacts in Holland, and became concerned that the new, valuable information that was being collected by his network was piling up in dead letter boxes in Liège. This intelligence would quickly become outdated. Everything seemed to be breaking down.[20] Rumours began to circulate that some Belgian refugees in Holland had sold their information to the highest bidder among the various Allied secret services, sometimes to several buyers at the same time. This potentially compromised the security of Lambrecht's agents. A number of black marketeers sold information to the Germans, and this led to the death of male and female agents in occupied Belgium. Further, the personal safety of Lambrecht was about to be compromised, in a security lapse caused by his own misjudgement of events and desire to get intelligence reports swiftly to Holland and onwards to London.

Betrayal of Lambrecht

In Holland, Ferdinand Afchain was working hard to find ways of reaching Liège and engaging suitable trusted people to undertake a dangerous mission to pick up Lambrecht's pile of reports. Afchain received an urgent telegram from an intelligence officer at British GHQ and he decided to risk a mission. The exact chain of events that followed is unclear, but it is known that a letter intended for Lambrecht ended up in the hands of a Dutchman by the name of Keurvers, who was working for German counter-espionage.[21]

Keurvers arrived at the dead letter box in Liège, which was located in a modest cigar store owned by one of Lambrecht's cousins, M. Leclercq. Leclercq was out at the time, so Keurvers spoke to his wife and introduced himself as a Dutchman who had just arrived from Holland with an urgent letter for her husband. She was aware of her husband's clandestine activities, but became suspicious of Keurvers' accent, which appeared to be more German than Dutch, and she refused to accept the letter. Keurvers persisted and gave her a coded password: 'The seven boxes of tricolor cigars have arrived safely.'[22]

She still did not trust him, even though she recognised the code. 'My husband told me nothing of cigars,' she said. 'Besides, we are not expecting any letters from Holland.'[23] As soon as Keurvers left, she sought out Lambrecht and informed him of what had happened. Instead of praising her discretion and security consciousness, he rebuked her for being overcautious. The Dutchman had given her the right code.

When Mme Leclercq hurried back to the cigar store, she found that Keurvers had returned during her absence and given the letter to her servant. Before he left, he told the servant that he would come back the following day at ten o'clock. The letter was swiftly taken to Lambrecht. He opened the small rolled-up paper and read the message in Afchain's handwriting:

> I confirm the long list of merchandise orders delivered to you, January 28th, care of our friend Dupont [Leclercq's codename], but regret having received no reply. Our delivery man, who brought you the above orders, being unable to continue with his duties, I am using the present carrier, who will contact you once a week. I believe he is the only one who can do this at the present moment. I hope

you will be able to pull us out of our present critical situation by giving him a report, as complete as possible, of all the merchandise in your store. It is absolutely necessary to make use of the present opportunity, as none of our competitors are in a position to deliver.[24]

Lambrecht was primed to accept Keurvers as genuine, as he thought only of the priority of the six weeks' worth of reports that had accumulated for British intelligence. The bundle was too bulky to smuggle out of Belgium, so he stayed up all night and made a summary of their contents.

The following morning, he arrived at the Leclercq cigar store in the rue de Campine. As he entered, he saw Keurvers in conversation with M. Leclercq. Leclercq led Lambrecht into a small parlour at the back of the store, where he expressed suspicions about Keurvers. But Lambrecht could not be persuaded.[25] He had Afchain's letter and that was sufficient for him. After all, Keurvers had given him the correct coded password. Lambrecht believed Keurvers to be genuine and handed over the intelligence reports.

As Lambrecht was returning home, he noticed that he was being followed. Instead of believing that he was at risk, he thought only of the safety of Keurvers as the courier of the reports. He jumped on a tram and managed to shake off his tail. He knew he had a chance of finding Keurvers in one of the cafés on the Grand Place. He peered through the window of the Café du Marronnier and saw Keurvers sitting with two well-known German secret police officers (Landwerlen and Douhard), who had been involved in the arrest of nearly every spy so far in the area.

Lambrecht made what turned out to be a fatal decision. Instead of hiding with friends in a safehouse until he could be smuggled into Holland, he returned home to warn his wife and ask her to go off to alert Leclercq. Lambrecht walked through the front door of his house to find the secret police waiting for him. They had been watching the cigar store for several days. They had photographed Afchain's letter and had the intelligence reports given to Keurvers as evidence for a trial.

Lambrecht was held in the infamous Fort de la Chartreuse, Liège. Although he knew his own life could not be saved, he could save the network of over thirty agents, because Leclercq had never known their names and therefore could not give them up if he was ever arrested. Lambrecht's primary focus now was not to betray any of the agents under interrogation. The Germans employed third-degree measures during interrogations to try to break Lambrecht, but he did not give away a single name.[26] He even managed to convince them that neither his own wife nor the Leclercqs knew anything of his activities. His influential friends, the Marquis de Villalobar (the Spanish ambassador) and van Vollenhoven (the Dutch ambassador), tried to intercede on his behalf with Herr von Bissing, the German governor general of Belgium. Petitions by the Roman Catholic Church also failed. Lambrecht was condemned to death.

On the eve of his execution, 17 April 1916, he wrote a moving letter to his wife:

> Oh! My well beloved, what a terrible blow to you, who had such high hopes! Poor wife! Poor parents! My soul is filled with intense sadness thinking of you all . . . May God give you the courage, which He has never ceased to grant me, so your suffering may be less. In heaven, I will watch over you . . . Think of my life as having been given up for my country – it will make my death seem less painful to you. After my faith, my country is what I hold most dear; in sacrificing life for it, I am only doing what so many have done before me, and will do again . . . I will leave you, as a last souvenir of me, the cross you sent me, and I will place on it kisses for you, Riette, and my parents. I will join to it my wedding ring . . . For our darling little daughter, for my parents and for you, receive on this letter, the last affectionate kisses of he, who was. Your Donné.[27]

Lambrecht was shot on 18 April 1916 at the Fort de la Chartreuse in Liège.[28]

The Germans failed to discover that the headquarters of the clandestine network was in Liège, but they lost no time in placing posters about Lambrecht's execution on the walls of public buildings across the town to discourage others. Instead of deterring Lambrecht's agents who were lying low across Belgium, it served as a catalyst for defiance. They would continue because they knew the value of their information being smuggled out to the British Secret Service: intelligence that had the potential to change the outcome on the battlefields.

In death, Lambrecht became a powerful figure who inspired others to continue his work. Like a phoenix rising from the ashes, from the remnants of his espionage service emerged one of the greatest spy organisations of World War One.

Chapter 3
THE MICHELIN SERVICE

When Walthère Dewé read the execution notice announcing the fate of his cousin Dieudonné Lambrecht, there was no question in his mind that the network had to continue. The British Secret Service and Allied military commanders needed the intelligence that Belgian agents could provide from behind the German lines. Dewé immediately became the network's principal leader, placing himself and his family at even greater risk than at the beginning of the war.[1] In this he was supported wholeheartedly by his wife Dieudonnée, who was fully aware of the dangers for her husband as leader of an extensive clandestine espionage network across Belgium. This network would change its name to the Michelin Service, which appears to have been inspired by numerous advertisements for Michelin tyres around Belgium.[2]

One of Dewé's first actions as the new leader was to recruit forty-year-old Herman (Henri) Chauvin, a professor of physics at the Institut Montefiore, a well-known engineering college in Liège.[3] He became Dewé's co-chief. In contrast to Dewé, Chauvin was small in stature, with light hair, a long beard, blue eyes and a soft voice. The challenges facing the two men were immense. In the two years since the outbreak of war, German counter-espionage had hunted down members of the resistance and broken up networks. In Liège alone, around fifty spies had been shot and several hundred were sentenced to various terms of imprisonment. To protect the network after Lambrecht's death, Dewé knew that they must adopt new ways to evade German counter-espionage and avoid arrest.

On 22 June 1916, Dewé met with Father Des Onays and Oscar Donnay, two of the original leaders alongside Lambrecht.[4] He went over the history of Lambrecht's network with them to establish how it had failed. Two factors became apparent: first, that Lambrecht had undertaken the most dangerous work himself, particularly when operating as a courier; and second, all his agents knew his identity, and this could have compromised his personal security at any point. At the meeting, it was decided that all agents and couriers should be isolated from the main organisation by dividing Belgium into four operational regions, each with its own head. If a security breach occurred, each sector could be isolated from the others and survive. It was believed that this would protect the whole organisation. Dewé established a counter-espionage section for the Michelin Service to spy on the German secret police and its activities. It was headed by Alexandre Neujean, who was Chauvin's father-in-law and Belgian chief of police in Liège – a position that had come under the control of the German secret police.[5] This family connection meant that Neujean was able to warn of impending raids and police searches, and provide photographs of secret police officers, so Dewé's agents could avoid crossing paths with them. The secret police proved to be an ongoing menace and threat, as it recruited local Belgians as informers to determine who was working for the Allies. Most of the arrests made by the secret police were due to these traitors. Neujean was able to identify the traitors, too, and warn members of the Michelin Service.

Another matter that had to be addressed by Dewé was lack of funds to restart the organisation after Lambrecht's death. Help came from two Belgian bankers, Marcel Nagelmackers and Paul Philippart, who advanced money on condition that they were given full reimbursement after the war. British intelligence honoured that commitment at the end of the war, and the men were repaid. In lending the money, Nagelmackers and Philippart risked their lives, because if caught they would have been found guilty of espionage for bankrolling a clandestine network. Their willingness to help Dewé meant that the old train-watching posts at Liège and Jemelle became operational again.

The network initially had forty-one agents who worked from six observation posts around Liège, Jemelle and Stavelot. The most difficult task that still remained for Dewé was to try to establish contact with British intelligence.

'The Office', London

In late spring 1916, another man was doing just that. Captain Henry Landau arrived at 2 Whitehall Court, just a stone's throw from the War Office in Whitehall, for a meeting.[6]

Born in South Africa on 7 March 1892, Landau was the son of a merchant and had received a diverse education, including at Dulwich College (London), followed by a period of study in Germany, at Gonville & Caius College, Cambridge, and then at the London School of Mines.[7] Up to April 1916 he had served as an officer in the Royal Field Artillery, but was currently back in England on medical leave.[8]

Unbeknown to Landau, the woman he was courting – the sister of his adjutant, who had introduced them[9] – happened to be Mansfield Cumming's personal secretary. She had noted Landau's facility with languages (he spoke French, German, Dutch and Flemish fluently) and told him that his country needed personnel with language skills. She was the person who, in effect, recruited him. It was not long before Landau received a letter asking him to attend an interview at the War Office. The day after that interview a telephone call invited him to attend a meeting at 2 Whitehall Court. In his memoirs, Landau said that he reported to Colonel B (this was Colonel Freddie Browning), who informed Landau that he had been transferred to the Intelligence Corps and attached for special duties to the British Secret Service.[10]

Landau was sent to the top floor to meet the chief. That man would turn out to be Mansfield Cumming, the head of the British Secret Service.

The magnificent Victorian building with its white stone façade had been built around 1884. Adjoined by the National Liberal Club, it had several occupants in 1916 – a hotel, the Authors' Club and prestigious apartments with views overlooking the river Thames. Only two years earlier, permission had been granted by the managers of Whitehall Court for an extra room to be built on the top floor. That was where Landau was now headed. He took several flights of stairs to the top floor and walked along the corridor to Flat 54. He noticed an eerie silence that disconnected him from the outside world. He did not yet realise that he was about to enter the inner sanctum – the 'Holy of Holies' – of one of the most secretive organisations in British history, one that officially did not exist. This was the headquarters of MI1(c), then part of the Secret Service Bureau, later renamed the Secret Intelligence Service (SIS/MI6).[11]

According to Landau's own colourful account, he knocked and entered an office that resembled the state room of a ship's commander. A high-backed chair suddenly swivelled around from the dark polished desk to reveal a rotund man in naval uniform, in his late fifties, staring directly at him. Cumming wasted no time with pleasantries. His intelligence networks behind enemy lines had been destroyed by a series of betrayals of their agents.[12]

'You are just the man we want to join Tinsley in Rotterdam,' he said. 'Our train-watching service has broken down completely in Belgium and in north-eastern France. We are getting absolutely nothing through.'[13] Cumming told him, 'It is up to you to re-organise the service. I can't tell you how it is to be done – that is your job. You have carte blanche. You have been transferred to the Intelligence Corps and are attached for special duties to the British Secret Service.'[14]

Landau was left in no doubt as to the importance of the task given to him by Cumming: he was to revive the British Secret Service network that the Germans had closed down after Lambrecht's execution. He exited the building and made his way to Harrods to acquire some extra clothes, as he was due to travel from Victoria Station to Harwich at 8.30 p.m. that evening for a boat crossing to the Hook of Holland.[15] In truth, the timeline was not quite so swift. There was a delay between Landau's meeting with Cumming and his leaving for Rotterdam, due to the Directorate of Military Intelligence not responding swiftly enough to Cumming's correspondence. Cumming had written to the Directorate requesting that Landau be attached to MI1(c) for what was described as light office work abroad.[16] That is not exactly how Landau understood the outcome of the meeting and the responsibility being placed on his shoulders.

Rotterdam

By the end of June 1916, Landau had not yet left for Rotterdam. Memos were still being sent to army administration asking for orders to be issued to transfer Landau as soon as possible from the Royal Field Artillery to Military Intelligence.[17] The MI6 archive shows that Landau himself wrote to Colonel Freddie Browning, Cumming's deputy, to see if MI1(c) still wished to engage him, as he was about to be posted back to France.[18] Instructions were finally issued for Landau to report to Room 254 at the War Office for duty on 7 July.[19]

The following day, Landau arrived in Rotterdam to work with Tinsley.[20] Landau did not realise that he had been placed there on a temporary trial basis, and that Cumming had written to the Directorate of Military Intelligence at the War Office that if he proved satisfactory, he would remain in Rotterdam for the duration of the war.[21] Tinsley explained to him how the whole network of forty observation posts had been compromised and nearly all his agents arrested.[22] An agent in Maastricht had tried to restart the network, but was unsuccessful. Tinsley would provide Landau with the money for him to revive the network in Belgium and to meet its operational costs.

Tinsley had created four sections in the Rotterdam office: military, naval, counter-espionage and press, the latter to monitor foreign newspapers for information. He appointed Landau as head of the military section to oversee all military espionage in Germany and France, and behind the German lines in occupied Belgium. Landau was to consult with Major Laurie Oppenheim, the British military attaché at The Hague, about what information was needed by British intelligence. Urgent military intelligence received from Landau would be telegraphed in code by Oppenheim; otherwise it was sent to London via the diplomatic bag.

The highest priority was to ensure that the intelligence reports left Belgium and were taken as swiftly as possible into Holland. This could only be achieved with a loyal workforce along the border, and so Landau created six different sections along the frontier, such that if one was compromised the others could continue. He knew that he must keep a close watch on the couriers because so many had already been arrested by the German secret police.

Before successfully making contact with Dewé, Landau started to build his contacts by interviewing refugees to recruit spies and initially working with individual agents. One of the early agents was an unnamed German deserter who gave Landau 'the biggest Secret Service scoop of the war'.[23] It was a copy of the German Field Post Directory, which listed the locations of all German units and their designation numbers. It proved to be one of the most valuable sources of information for British intelligence.

Working with individual agents was fine, but Landau needed to make contact with the train-watching network in Belgium. The delay in doing so was partly due to Dewé's own security consciousness and also Landau's inexperience in running a network, which meant that it was a while before the two men connected. In the meantime, Dewé was exploring his own way to reach Allied intelligence agencies as well as his own country's secret-service-in-exile.

French Agents, Belgian Secret Service

Dewé knew that the only way to get intelligence to the Allies was via Allied agents in Holland, but identifying and making contact with them was not easy. In the early days of his leadership, Dewé's network was also beset by mistakes made by those agents, which saw some of the operatives arrested by the German secret police. The first channel of communication was to reach out to the French Secret Service, which Dewé did.[24] Emile Fauquenot and Franz Creusen, French agents already working for the network, liaised with Dewé. One of their French recruits, Marie Birckel, had already been arrested.

On the night of 30 June 1916, Fauquenot and Creusen started their own journey to the frontier for a secret meeting in some woods near the village of Eijsden, on the Dutch–Belgian border. They entered the woods, close to the electrified wire. Just as they thought about turning back, they were hit over the head with a blunt instrument. A dozen German secret policemen were hidden in the bushes on the Dutch side of the border and dragged them into Belgium. It was a breach of Dutch neutrality, but who would know? They were taken to St Léonard prison in Liège, where Marie Birckel was incarcerated. These two men were about to do more damage than the secret police could imagine – because now, Dewé had two agents inside the prison who were prepared to smuggle out coded messages on who was imprisoned there and what they had been asked in interrogation. This information gave Dewé an important picture of what the Germans knew about his organisation.

The arrests of Birckel, Fauquenot and Creusen in such a short space of time meant that Dewé could ill afford any further security risks. Around this time, one of his co-leaders, Father Jean Des Onays, received a bundle of letters and a message from a French Secret Service agent named Féchy (who was operating in Maastricht), asking him whether Féchy could start an espionage service. It offered the first concrete opportunity to get intelligence to the Allies from a different sector. Des Onays told Dewé and Chauvin about the offer, but they declined. They had just learned from

Neujean, the head of the counter-espionage security section, of the arrests of Birckel, Fauquenot and Creusen. Dewé and Chauvin were right to be cautious. A few days later, the man who had brought the original letter from Féchy to Des Onays was arrested. Féchy was later discovered not to have been the betrayer, but nevertheless, the chain of the network had to be protected if past mistakes were not to be repeated.

After the betrayal by Bertram, Dewé and Chauvin interviewed a Belgian engineer by the name of Bihet, who was to be their delegate to Belgian General Headquarters in France to make contact with the Belgian Secret Service and find a trusted courier to take the intelligence reports into Holland. For security protocol, it was agreed that at 11.30 a.m. every day (except on a Sunday), a woman wearing a green felt hat would be waiting inside St Denis church in Liège, for the courier from Holland. She would not know his identity until he gave a password, 'Yser', and she was to reply, 'Lion d'Or'. He would then hand over a message and arrange a time and place for their next meeting. Bihet was to insert an advertisement in the personal column of a Dutch newspaper to indicate that he had arrived in Holland. On a moonless night, a frontier guide took Bihet safely through the high-voltage electric wire, using India rubber socks and gloves to avoid electrocution, and he made it safely into Holland.

Two weeks later, on 23 July 1916, an announcement appeared in a Dutch newspaper.[25] This was the agreed message from Bihet. The woman in the green hat duly arrived at the rendezvous at the St Denis church to wait for the unknown courier, but no courier came. Dewé and Chauvin began to believe that all communications with Holland had failed and they would have to begin again. Then on the last Sunday in August, while Dewé was out, a peasant arrived at his house with a letter from Holland. The peasant left his name and address with Dewé's wife, but refused to wait. When Dewé returned home, he was alarmed by the breach of protocol by Bihet, who had received explicit instructions that no agents' names were to be given, not even to personnel at the Belgian General Headquarters. Yet the courier sent by Bihet knew

Dewé's name and address, and these details were clearly written on the envelope. This could have fallen into the hands of the German secret police or a German agent. Alarmingly, too, there were explicit instructions inside the envelope which outlined the kind of reports needed and the fact that there was collaboration with the Belgian Secret Service. The letter went on to say that Dewé was to dispatch his reports swiftly, send new passwords in case a different courier was used in subsequent missions, provide details of how the courier should contact Dewé and send a list of some of his agents. The reasoning for the latter was that the courier could contact another member of the network if Dewé was ever arrested. This all amounted to a serious breach of security that could have led to the network being compromised.

Dewé became suspicious. His own cousin, Lambrecht, had been lost through a lack of security. He wondered why the courier hadn't gone to St Denis church as agreed. He and Chauvin decided that if a police raid occurred in the coming days or weeks, they would deny all knowledge. The courier returned a week later, on a Sunday, and Dewé refused to speak with him. In the end, time proved the honesty of the courier because Dewé was not arrested. This was one incident that showed the careless and dangerous ways some members of the network operated early on in Dewé's leadership. Dewé never discovered why Bihet had disregarded security procedures or why the courier had travelled on a Sunday – the only day when the woman in the green felt hat would not have been in the church. The Germans had successfully infiltrated the courier lines so many times that Dewé knew lessons had to be learned. And twice he had failed to contact the Allies via the French Intelligence Services in Maastricht.[26] He did not give up hope of finding a direct contact to the British Secret Service. This came a few weeks after Landau had arrived in Rotterdam.

Meeting Landau

Precisely how Dewé first connected with Landau and the exact date of that visit is unclear from surviving records. On Dewé's first visit to

Landau, which he made under an assumed name, St Lambert, he explained that he had a number of patriotic Belgian men and women who were prepared to work for an espionage network.[27] The Michelin Service located its headquarters in Liège and originally operated three battalions in the regions of Tournai, Arlon and Conneux.[28] The battalion at Tournai covered the region of Lille, Douai and into northern German-occupied France. The Arlon sector operated into the Grand Duchy of Luxembourg and observed enemy troop movements along the Trier–Luxembourg railway line, and had a post on the Aachen–Herbesthal–Liège line. These posts could observe German troops moving westwards from Germany to the Western Front, along the stretch from Verdun to the coast. The sector of Conneux, run by Thérèse de Radiguès, covered the region in the Ardennes and southern Belgium. The castles around Conneux and Ciney, south of Namur, became key centres of the network in the south.

One of the early contacts with the British Secret Service was secured via one of Dewé's agents, M. Boseret. Boseret's father-in-law, Gustave Snoeck, was president of the Crédit Anversois, one of the largest Belgian banks. He had several foreign banking contacts in Holland and England, to whom he sent financial reports. Fifty-year-old Snoeck had considerable wealth and so much to lose by engaging in espionage, yet when Boseret contacted him, Snoeck agreed to use his own premises as a letter box and courier for the network. Towards the end of August 1916, the courier took the first Michelin Service reports out of Belgium and passed them to Mr Van Geysel, agent of the Crédit Anversois at The Hague. He took them straight to Abbé de Moor ('Marcel'), one of Major Cameron's agents in Holland.[29]

Between August and the end of November 1916, intelligence reports from the observation posts in Namur, Charleroi and Brussels were dropped at Snoeck's letter box twice a week for dispatch to Holland. Dewé and Chauvin waited for feedback from Holland as to whether their information was of value, but there was no response. Dewé became concerned. Were the reports reaching the British? He sent numerous messages in which he asked for an answer, but again there was only silence for three months.

Dewé and Chauvin decided that an emissary had to be sent to Belgian General Headquarters in Holland. Boseret volunteered for the mission, and on 2 December 1916 he was sent through the high-voltage electric wire, with the same frontier guide who had taken Bihet across earlier in the year.[30]

While Boseret crossed the frontier, in Antwerp, Snoeck continued his intelligence work, giving reports to his courier who took them to a dead letter box being run by one of the female agents, Delphine Alenus, at Baelen-sur-Nethe, a small village near the Dutch border. Alenus then took the reports on to a peasant who worked the fields adjoining the electrified wire. The reports were written on fine tissue paper, rolled into small cigarette-shaped tubes and hidden inside farming tools. When it was deemed safe, out of view of German border patrols, the messages were pushed into a clod of earth and thrown over the wire. This was not easy. To keep animals away from the electrified fence, a 15ft barbed-wire fence had been constructed on each side of it. The clumps of earth containing the messages had to be thrown at least 30ft in distance and a height of 10ft to clear the fences. The Dutchman picking up the earth on the other side could not throw anything back because the patrols would immediately become suspicious and investigate. Consequently, the messages hidden in clods of earth could not receive responses, including from Tinsley's office, and this was the reason for the silence.

Meanwhile, an Antwerp courier had been followed by the Germans and this led to Snoeck being arrested. Snoeck knew that none of the intelligence reports had been seized by the secret police, and argued that the reports were solely of a financial nature. The German police believed his defence and he was released. The Michelin Service remained intact and survived.

M. Liévin had replaced Abbé de Moor as the intermediary in the courier service. It was through Liévin that contact was made again with

British intelligence in Holland, after his courier met with an agent at a specified inn in Antwerp. As a security measure Boseret had not given any of the addresses of the Michelin chiefs to Liévin; but Liévin was pressing him for an address. Finally, Boseret handed over the name and address of Father Des Onays, before travelling via England to France to join the Belgian army-in-exile. While in England he met several times with Major Cameron, who emphasised the significance and importance of the work of the Michelin Service.

With Liévin's success in re-establishing contact between the Michelin Service and British intelligence, the Michelin chiefs expanded the network to include new observation posts at Arlon, Dinant and Tongres. Itinerant agents travelled Belgium to observe the movement of German divisions in and out of the rest areas in Flanders and Luxembourg and along the Belgian borders.

Landau recruited Victor Moreau ('Oram'), the son of a former high-ranking official of the Belgian State Railways.[31] Oram became instrumental in recruiting Belgian railwaymen and refugees as frontier agents. In the field of operations, he became chief of the agents in Holland. He gave each of his frontier agents a number and arranged for the couriers to pick up the reports. The fundamental value of these couriers lay in the fact that they could pass unnoticed among the peasants, smugglers and other frontier types who lived in the border villages. A key factor in the success of British Secret Service operations at the frontiers was the discipline and loyalty of Oram's frontier agents, in contrast to frontier agents employed by the other Allied secret services, who often worked for the highest bidder.

Oram had six separate means of communication inside Belgium, so that if one went down, he had five others. The chief of each sector gathered the intelligence reports from their network and these were deposited at letter boxes in Liège, Antwerp and Brussels. Couriers carried the reports to the frontier, where they were passed into Holland. On the Dutch side, the intelligence was overseen by Landau and Oram, with Landau responsible for sending the intelligence reports to British GHQ.

Challenges remained for the network when, in November 1916, the German navy captured a number of mail boats running between Holland and Britain. This severely disrupted the supply of reports to London, and the British Secret Service was deprived of news at a time when it most needed it.

Arrest of Father Des Onays

By June 1917 the Michelin Service was facing severe financial concerns. Fresh funds were needed from the British, but there was no news forthcoming from the couriers in Holland on advancing funds for the operations. Alexandre Neujean reported that M. Lechat, who had replaced Des Onays as one of the 'letter boxes' in Liège (for reasons not given), was under suspicion by the German secret police. Neujean warned Lechat and nothing compromising was found on him when his property was raided, but he was still arrested. Acting on the knowledge of Lechat's arrest, Dewé and Chauvin sent an emissary, Gustave Lemaire, a Belgian engineer, across the border into Holland to warn Liévin that his courier system was compromised and he should petition the British for urgent funds.[32]

Lemaire crossed the frontier on 5 June 1917. He met with Landau, during which time Landau offered for the Michelin Service to come formally under the auspices of the British Secret Service.[33] Lemaire agreed, but on two conditions: the network's expenditure must be fully covered by the British and its members must be enrolled as soldiers.[34] Landau promised him military status for them (still without Cumming's knowledge).[35] He guaranteed that weekly sums from the Secret Service would cover the entire expenditure of the Michelin Service. Lemaire remained in Holland long enough to satisfy himself that the liaison between the Michelin Service and the War Office was working smoothly. His secret mission successfully accomplished, he did not return to Belgium, instead travelling on to Le Havre to offer his engineering expertise to the Belgian government-in-exile.

On 13 June 1917, at the same time as Lechat's arrest, Father Des Onays received a visit from the secret police while taking a Latin class at the Collège St Servais. He had compromising material hidden on him, and delayed his arrest by insisting that the police first speak to the head of the college. This gave him enough time to place the compromising documents inside a prayer book and pass the book to a student. Des Onays and Lechat were taken to Brussels and interrogated along with other members of the network, M. Montfort (a courier) and Baron Fayen (operating as a letter box for reports from Brussels, Mons, Charleroi and Namur).[36] Montfort was found to have intelligence reports hidden in his sock, which he had collected from a Michelin Service agent. During the subsequent interrogations, the men were shown photographic copies of all correspondence that had passed between Liévin and the Michelin Service.

At the time, the arrests were suspected to be due to betrayal, but the exact circumstances did not emerge until after the war, when Liévin made a statement about the betrayer.[37] He was one of Liévin's own agents, Georges Gylinck (known as Saint-George), who had given exceptional service to the network in 1916 by penetrating some of the most difficult regions of Lille, Courtrai and Tournai to collect reports.[38] Nevertheless, tempted by money, he had sold his services to the German secret police in 1917. Because of his treachery, eight of Liévin's agents were shot.

Father Des Onays denied the charges of espionage at his trial and was spared the death sentence because the German police failed to produce their double agent to testify against him. He was taken to a prison in Germany and survived the war. The Germans never discovered that he was one of the leaders of the Michelin Service. Liévin believed that the betrayals demonstrated a failure of leadership, ultimately by Landau in Holland, and he drove his own agenda to control the Michelin Service himself.[39]

Liévin is a typical example of the competition and rivalry that occasionally arose among the Allied secret services in Holland. Such tensions meant that they unintentionally lost sight of their main objective (and one in which they were all united): the defeat of the occupying German forces and the liberation of Belgium and Luxembourg. From the perspective of the British Secret Service, significant changes among the Allied secret services in Holland in June 1917 would be advantageous. The French intelligence service decided to use Switzerland as its main base for operations and drastically reduced its presence in Holland. Then, handicapped by a lack of funds, the Belgian Secret Service was not able to operate effectively in Belgium. It left the way open for the British Secret Service to fill the void.

Chapter 4
THE WHITE LADY

Dewé had no intention of giving up, despite the betrayals in the early summer of 1917 which had marked another sombre catastrophe for the British network in Belgium. He revived the network with Herman Chauvin and Joseph Falloise. Aware that the German secret police knew the name of the Michelin Service from captured photographic copies of correspondence, the network's name was changed to La Dame Blanche (the White Lady), with all its connotations of bringing about the downfall of the Germans. Later the White Lady network was also known as the Corps d'Observation Anglais au Front (English Observation Corps of the Western Front).[1]

In July 1917, Dewé formally joined the British Secret Service and explained to Landau that from now on his men and women would work for the network only if they were given military status and a rank. He was clear to Landau that they were to be considered not as spies, but as soldiers of a separate unit of the British army. Dewé's insistence on this point meant that Landau faced a dilemma, because he had no authority to grant military status to the Belgian agents, nor to set up a new unit within the British army. Furthermore, there were Belgian women in the network. How could they be included as soldiers of the British army alongside the men, equally with military ranks and roles like the men, when the British army did not have British men and women in the same military unit?

Landau told Dewé that he would have to defer to the War Office, though he knew that neither Cumming nor the War Office would make a swift reply. It could take weeks or months to get a response, which might even be a refusal. Landau could not take that risk: the train-watching observation work was of paramount importance and must continue without delay. Even if consent came, the War Office needed agreement from the Belgian government-in-exile and vital time would be lost in trying to gain this. Landau waited just one day before telling Dewé that he had received approval from London, even though he had not.[2]

Landau knew that to honour this agreement, he would have to obtain approval from the War Office at the end of the war. What if it was refused then? For now, he took the risk because the work behind enemy lines was too important. He promised Dewé the sum of £10,000 a month (just short of £800,000 in today's value) to run the network – monies he secured from Tinsley. In return, Landau asked him to commit to expanding the network around Chimay and Hirson.[3] From archives in Brussels, it is now possible to identify early July 1917 as the official moment when the White Lady was given military status.[4] This marked an important point in the history of espionage in Belgium and in British military history.[5] Members of the network swore an oath of loyalty on enlistment, as did new agents joining them subsequently:

> I declare and enlist in the capacity of soldier in the Allied military observation service until the end of the war. I swear before God to respect this engagement, to accomplish conscientiously the offices entrusted to me . . . not to reveal (without formal authorisation) anything concerning the organisation of the service, even if this stance should entail for me the penalty of death.[6]

The network increased its surveillance of German troop movements by creating a further fifty-one railway observation posts across Belgium and the Grand Duchy of Luxembourg. As before, the posts operated every day and night of the year. The network continued to gather intelligence by watching the trains moving across Belgium and north-eastern France, and cataloguing the movement of enemy troops from Germany to France and the Western Front. The transfer of a division via a particular train junction could still take two days or more – sufficient time for intelligence reports to reach the British. Information continued to be collected on enemy plans, the formation of new troop divisions, new types of guns, innovative methods of attack by the enemy, the arrival of reinforcements in a region and the number of German soldiers being moved.

The leaders reviewed ways to tighten the network against the German secret police and counter-espionage sections. All agents were given false names to use in their reports and when contacting each other. Dewé used a number of codenames for himself: 'Van den Bosch', 'Gauthier' and 'Muraille'. Neujean was known as 'Petit', and Chauvin used the names 'Dumont', 'Beaumont', 'Valdor', 'Granito' and 'Bouchon'.[7] Women took on leadership roles, as in the case of the four specialist extension squads who were responsible for expanding the White Lady across Belgium. These four squads consisted entirely of women.[8] In addition to the recruitment squads, women directed battalions and established new observation posts.

The total number of agents in both Belgium and France connected to the White Lady was, according to Landau, over 2,000.[9] It has been estimated that around a third of these agents were women.[10] We do know that by the end of the war the membership of the White Lady in Belgium totalled 1,084, comprising 904 soldiers (278 women and 626 men) and 180 auxiliaries.[11] The majority were Roman Catholic and the leadership consisted almost entirely of professionals, academics and members of religious orders, including eighty priests and nuns. It was one of the largest intelligence services in Western Europe in World War One.[12]

The Headquarters

The White Lady operated its headquarters from two locations in Liège. Its main HQ was located in a house with five exits: one door to the front street; another into the back garden, which gave access to a side street via a small alleyway; one through a skylight onto the roof; and on each of the two floors, ordinary wall cupboards in a closet leading into the adjoining house, where an elderly couple lived. The second HQ house also had several exits. It benefited from a windowless room where the council met late at night during the curfew. In addition, the network had three houses used to hide agents who had been compromised. The arrest of Des Onays, a Michelin Service leader, had taught Dewé and Chauvin a lesson. They systematically removed all direct connections between themselves and their frontier posts. Those couriers and frontier 'letter boxes' who knew their identity were retired and new ones were recruited via trusted intermediaries.

The headquarters operated with a council of eight members, a Roman Catholic chaplain, and separate sections for counter-espionage, finance, the hiding of compromised agents, overseeing couriers and extending the network.[13] A separate committee prepared the intelligence reports that came from the various letter boxes. The fourth platoon of each company was engaged solely on collecting the intelligence reports from the three other platoons. It deposited the reports at the designated 'letter box' for that company; each company had a separate one. A different agent took the reports to the relevant battalion letter box. A secretariat (committee) for each battalion typed up the intelligence reports, after which they were scrutinised by the battalion commander. Couriers took these reports to one of three letter boxes for the headquarters in Liège. The couriers and letter boxes were isolated from each other to protect them if one was compromised.

The reports were analysed by Dewé and Chauvin at headquarters in Liège, then passed to the headquarters' secretariat, from where a special courier took the reports to a letter box on the frontier. The frontier letter box was run solely by the British Secret Service, which used its own couriers to cross the frontier into Holland. The role of this letter box was the most dangerous, as here was the highest risk of being captured by the German patrols. As a contingency, the names and addresses of the letter boxes of the three battalions were sent to Landau in code, in case the headquarters was raided and seized. Landau would then be able to contact the battalions directly.

In spite of these enhanced security measures, the White Lady was engaged in a life-and-death struggle with the German secret police for the whole of the war.

Soldiers Without Uniform

Women were an integral part of Lambrecht and Dewé's network from the start of the war. From 1917, when it changed its name to the White Lady, it recruited more women, most of whom were employed as educators or domestics, though a good number of them had no occupation prior to the war.

These women were usefully 'invisible' because the Germans did not expect women to be involved in intelligence. They tended to hold a stereotypical view that women would be at home raising their family and looking after the household, and if they were spotted outside, it was to do with their domestic roles (such as buying bread and provisions, or visiting elderly relatives). This preconception meant that women were ideal agents for moving around enemy territory, gathering intelligence and couriering messages. They hid messages in their corsets, bread baskets, hems of garments and broom handles.[14]

The women played a central and often sophisticated role in the White Lady – so much so that the network could not have succeeded without them.[15] As with the men, the women disapproved of being designated as spies. They swore an oath of allegiance, and Dewé petitioned Landau to accept them in a military capacity, with military ranks, like their male counterparts.[16] The militarisation of women took time because the British army had no formal structure for them to be enlisted in military or combat roles. But it was a ground-breaking move that permitted women to 'function in so-called masculine roles, such as spy, courier and saboteur'.[17] For the first time in British military history, women could serve in roles traditionally fulfilled by men and be placed on an equal footing with men. In some cases, they outranked their male colleagues.

Women undertook positions of responsibility in the daily running of the network and offered distinguished service. In one secret service section, Lieutenant Julienne Demarteau and her sister Lieutenant Anne Demarteau worked as secretaries. Julienne undertook liaison duties in equal status to two male liaison officers. The position was extremely important and dangerous, because she oversaw the centralised intelligence documents coming in from the various units and then organised their delivery to Holland. She founded several observation posts in Luxembourg and recruited for the platoons.

Families set up safehouses, ran letter boxes and established courier networks. The Weimerskirch sisters, Emma, Alice and Jeanne, joined the White Lady and ran a letter box from the family's Catholic bookshop in Liège. One of the sisters had spent six months in the prison of St Léonard for disseminating anti-German propaganda. The sisters successfully ran the letter box until the end of the war without being betrayed. They were all in the Service of the Guard and responsible for the White Lady's security.[18] Sergeant Emma Weimerskirch was personal assistant to the commander of an observation post and keeper of the intelligence reports for the post.[19] An elite security section was headed by François Rodelet, and in his section were Juliette de Brualle, Julie Brever and Germaine van den Berg. The women carried out liaison duties with prisons. An auxiliary section was responsible for counter-espionage; eight of its members were men, with one woman, Sergeant Isabelle Wauthier.

After Anna Kesseler lost her only son fighting on the front line in 1914, she was determined to play her part for her country. She and her four daughters all enlisted in the White Lady.[20] Two of the daughters, Germaine (aged twenty-three) and Maria (aged twenty-one), worked as couriers between Brussels and Liège.

Jeanne Delwaide

One of the earliest figures to enlist in the White Lady was Jeanne Delwaide, who was designated agent number 20.[21] Since 1915, she and her younger sister from a Belgian bourgeois family had been aiding young Belgian men to escape over the Dutch border to join the Belgian army-in-exile. Hiding places were found close to the border, before a guide smuggled the men through the electric wire. Occasionally the men were hidden under the floorboards of a barge heading to a Dutch port. Until 1917 the sisters had not been part of the British intelligence network in Belgium. As soon as Jeanne joined the White Lady, she ceased all work for the escape line. Operating from her home at Pepinster, near Verviers, she set up a new train-watching post on the Aachen–Herbesthal–Liège line, a strategic rail line between Germany and Belgium. Such was the importance of this rail line that, via an influential Belgian contact in Holland, the British Secret Service asked M. Siquet (the proprietor of a small inn in Verviers) to establish a duplicate observation post in the event that the one being run by the White Lady was compromised. Somehow Jeanne found out about Siquet's activities.

'For what happened next, Jeanne Delwaide was not to blame,' Landau wrote later.[22] La Dame Blanche agents knew to keep clear of other espionage organisations, as such entanglement increased the chance of them being discovered by German surveillance. But through one of its Namur agents, the network received a request to smuggle the intelligence reports into Holland of an espionage organisation run by British GHQ, called the Biscops Service, whose own frontier network had broken down. For the first time since being leader, Dewé with Neujean, using their assumed names of 'Gauthier' and 'Petit' respectively, met a delegate of the Biscops Service. Although they refused to transmit the reports for the Biscops Service, they did agree to help it find a new clandestine frontier passage. Dewé and Neujean turned to Jeanne Delwaide, who had established and was running their train-watching post in the region. She gave them the password 'Balafré', which was the codeword for them when making contact with M. Siquet. Dewé and Neujean put him in touch with the Biscops Service, and soon Siquet was receiving the reports to run into Holland.

At this time, former colleagues of the escape line and Jeanne's sister had been arrested and it was believed she herself had been compromised. Dewé knew that Jeanne had to be isolated and sent immediately over the border into Holland. With no time to hide, she decided to arrange her own exfiltration from Belgium and asked Siquet for help. Siquet informed her that a group of refugees was to be taken to Holland, via the Belgian–German border, the following night by one of his guides.[23] Even though Jeanne was uneasy about this route from her own knowledge, it was her only swift way out. She arrived at Siquet's inn the following evening. Escorted across the countryside, during which time they picked up three other Belgian civilians and four escapers (French and Russian), they crept carefully to within less than fifty metres of the border. A group of German secret police jumped out from behind a hedge, their guns pointing at the party. They were arrested and taken first to Herbesthal, then to prison in Namur.

Because the Germans initially believed that Jeanne was a refugee, she was held for three weeks in solitary confinement before she was interrogated. Those who had been arrested with her were already receiving intense interrogation, during which the Germans used a stool pigeon, posing as a priest, to gain their trust. One of the refugees was taken in and betrayed details about Siquet. Siquet's arrest followed.

At Siquet's inn the secret police found intelligence reports and other compromising correspondence. They lay in wait there for other members of the network and the next day arrested a female courier of the Biscops Service. She had no defence, as reports were found sewn into the hem of her skirt. She refused to give up the network and said that the reports had been given to her by an unknown man whom she believed because he had showed her an official letter, stamped with an official seal, from the Belgian government at Le Havre.

In prison in Namur, Siquet was taken in too by the fake priest, whom he had thought trustworthy because he had seen him being beaten up. It was a ruse by the Germans that worked, as Siquet confided all he knew to the phoney priest. The secret police turned their attention to Jeanne, because the stool pigeon had been working on the others in the prison.

The White Lady's counter-espionage section learned of her arrest and informed Dewé immediately. One morning a priest slipped a note to Jeanne with details in it of a code that would permit the leaders to secretly communicate with her. The note ended with the words of encouragement, 'In our hearts we are with you.'[24] She replied in code and the following day received this from Dewé, using the pseudonym 'Theo':

> Remember you are a soldier. Remember your oath. Deny everything. Refuse to use the German language; you can defend yourself better in French. I congratulate you on your heroic attitude. Be calm. No bravado. We have taken our precautions here; none of us has been arrested. I am with you with all my heart. I will pray for you. I have advised your parents. Theo.[25]

This coded message urging her to keep her oath was intended to keep her strong, as Dewé did not know how she would fare under interrogation.

During her interrogation Jeanne denied belonging to any espionage organisation and, to protect the frontier guides, even denied trying to escape. She concocted a story that she had gone to buy butter from a farm near Welkenraedt, and on her way back that evening, had encountered a group of young men. Being afraid of the dark, she had decided to walk close behind them. She was therefore surprised to find herself arrested.

Her interrogator whispered a few words to an orderly, who left the room. The door opened again, and there stood the guide she had been trying to protect. She did not realise that he was Rosenberg, a member of the secret police at Namur. Rosenberg's mistress, a woman named Mariette, was a traitor to her country, as an active member of the German counter-espionage service who was operating as one of the stool pigeons in Namur prison.[26]

The secret police pressed Jeanne for the identity of the man whom she had originally sent to Siquet and who had used the password 'Balafré' – details confided to the priest by Siquet. They were convinced that Jeanne knew the identity of the man as well as 'Gauthier' (Dewé) and 'Petit' (Neujean), who were mentioned in the Biscops reports. She did indeed know their real identities, but for the following seven months, as the secret police tried to gain the information from her, she did not give them away. Her determined spirit remained strong, and it meant that the secret police could obtain no evidence from her. If she had given away under interrogation the names of the leadership of the White Lady, it would have been a severe blow for Cumming's organisation and consequently the network's ability to keep the British Secret Service abreast of military information from behind the German lines.

Delwaide never gave the network away.[27] At her trial the military prosecutor pressed for the death sentence. With only the word of Siquet's stool pigeon, there was no other evidence against her and she was sentenced to life imprisonment and a fine of 1,000 marks. She was taken to prison in Bonn and then transferred to the infamous women's prison at Siegburg, near Cologne in Germany. She remained at Siegburg until the Armistice in November 1918.

Siquet was shot at Namur on 25 April 1918. If he had not become involved with an external espionage organisation, the Biscops Service, he might not have been compromised. He had done it from a sense of patriotic duty which had overridden any security considerations. It was a hard lesson learned by the White Lady. Most members of the Biscops Service were eventually arrested by the Germans. The men and women who were not went on to enlist as agents in the White Lady in the last year of the war. They established valuable train-watching posts for Dewé and Chauvin in the Valenciennes area of occupied France, which became supremely valuable as the only intelligence reports for the British Secret Service from that region.

The Ardennes

The Ardennes region in the south of Belgium continued to be significant for the White Lady, in terms of intelligence-gathering along the French–Belgian border and in support of evaders. The two kinds of clandestine operations went hand in hand. The thick forests offered perfect shelter and proved ideal for hiding Allied soldiers. Since the early days of the war, the local population had supported escapers with shelter, clothing and food from their own limited rations. It was within the same region that Thérèse de Radiguès and her aristocratic friends were operating. Two particularly active agents in this area were members of the Grandprez and Grégoire families, both of whom ran observation posts from the spa town of Stavelot where they were living.[28] Every day and night André Grégoire and his wife, whose three sons were already fighting on the front line, took turns to watch the trains passing on the Trois-Ponts–Stavelot–Malmédy railway line. They monitored the main rail route by which German troops and armaments were moved across Belgium from the German border, which was less than 30km away.

Likewise, members of the Grandprez family undertook train-watching duties and gathered a significant amount of information for British intelligence on the movement of German troops. Elise Grandprez was unmarried and in her late forties, and she operated in the region with her sister Marie and two brothers François and Constant. Elise and Marie ran a letter box and worked as couriers. Using invisible ink, the sisters wrote secret reports onto ordinary objects, such as packing paper, box covers and bookplates. They had originally worked for Dieudonné Lambrecht.

After Lambrecht's execution, they decided to abandon their espionage activities. At the end of January 1917, a man who gave his name as Delacour called at their home in Stavelot. He claimed to be a Frenchman, formerly of Roubaix, who had managed to cross the electrified fence and was on a mission from the French Secret Service. Constant Grandprez let him into the house. Delacour explained the importance of setting up the train-watching network again. Constant was cautious and gave nothing away. After a couple more visits, though, he gained Constant's trust, and Constant agreed to meet Delacour at 160 rue Fétine in Liège to pass him the first reports. It was a ruse.

As Constant was leaving the rendezvous, Delacour suggested he order a taxi, which he did. When Constant got into the car, two German secret police were waiting for him. He was taken off for questioning. The following day, all the other members of the Grandprez family, along with André Grégoire and his wife, were arrested on suspicion of espionage.

At the trial, Marie Grandprez was acquitted because of lack of evidence; François Grandprez and Mme Grégoire, however, were sentenced to fifteen years' hard labour. André Grégoire and Constant and Elise Grandprez were sentenced to death. They were shot at the Fort de la Chartreuse, Liège, on 8 May 1917. As she faced the firing squad, Elise pressed a small Belgian flag to her chest.[29]

Their executions did not deter patriotic Belgians from working for the network, nor from being recruited as the war progressed. Four specialist extension squads that consisted entirely of women continued to recruit agents for the White Lady across Belgium.[30]

Laure and Louise Tandel

New agents and couriers were enlisted into the White Lady throughout the war by members of the White Lady recruitment squads; and many of the recruiters were women.[31] One of them was Marie Delcourt, who was twenty-seven years old when she joined as an agent in 1914, unmarried and living in Liège, without a known profession. She recruited operatives and carried out secretarial duties until January 1918, when she established a major new observation post in Luxembourg. She operated the post until it was dissolved in September 1918. Delcourt had already worked for the network for three years when, on 10 November 1917, she recruited two sisters, Laure and Louise Tandel.[32] They became prominent members in the network and soon took up leadership roles. Laure Tandel had just been released from prison in Germany, for her part in an underground organisation called Le Mot du Soldat, which sent parcels of clothing, money and letters to Belgian soldiers at the front line.

At the outbreak of war, Laure was thirty-nine and her sister was thirty-seven. Both were unmarried and teaching at a girls' school for prominent Catholic families from Luxembourg and Switzerland. Laure was the headmistress. Throughout 1914 and 1915 the sisters helped wounded French and British soldiers through the Red Cross. In July 1915 they joined Le Mot du Soldat. They were both arrested on 31 March 1916 for these activities and imprisoned in Brussels.[33] They were transferred to Mechelen prison in northern Belgium, where Laure was interrogated across several days. She admitted to working for Le Mot du Soldat, but insisted that her sister was entirely innocent. The Germans believed her and, on 7 April 1916, Louise was released.

Laure was accused of espionage and sentenced to a year's imprisonment. On 30 June 1916, she was transferred to Siegburg. Her diaries and drawings from the prison survive today in the Military Archives in Brussels and make for moving reading.[34] Nine months later, Laure was released from prison and returned to Brussels, living with her sister. In spite of all that she had endured, she was determined to continue her patriotic duty.

On 23 December 1917, Laure and Louise took the oath of allegiance to the White Lady in front of Marie Delcourt and Leopold Blanjean as their two witnesses.[35] Laure immediately set up one of the twelve secretariats in Brussels that were responsible for typing the collected documents and information. In November 1917, Louise Tandel accepted the role of manager at the head office of the White Lady in Brussels, from where she set up new observation posts west of the city.[36] The sisters soon became two of the network's most prominent members.

In September 1918, Laure was appointed commander of Battalion III in Brussels and promoted to the rank of captain. She directed the battalion's companies of Mons, Tournai, Ghent and Brussels. Louise was appointed deputy commander. They established new observation posts at Malines, Mons and Gard, which observed the trains passing through Malines, Mons, Louvain and Charleroi as well as German military equipment and troops in these regions.[37] The battalion had 190 agents, almost a third of whom were women.[38] The women acted as couriers for passing documents and reports between agents and locations, as well as maintaining correspondence with the main leaders in Liège. In terms of the status of the women, 60 per cent were married, 7 per cent widowed and 34 per cent unmarried.[39]

In January 1918, Marie Delcourt, who had successfully recruited the Tandel sisters, established a major observation post in Luxembourg. She continued to recruit, as well as carry out secretarial duties, until the post was dissolved in September 1918.[40]

Spy Techniques

From summer of 1917, the White Lady network had dozens of couriers crossing occupied Belgium and France with their secret contraband of intelligence to move between the letter boxes. The majority of the network's couriers were women; theirs constituted the most dangerous work undertaken by anyone in it.[41] They understood that their intelligence-gathering was linked to the survival of their country in the long term, because the defeat of the occupying German forces could be achieved by their aiding British intelligence.

But the story of the White Lady isn't just about the men and women who operated in it. It is also one of ingenuity and creativity in spycraft: the agents were developing early methods of intelligence-gathering, without training, and in emergency conditions of wartime. This they did alongside the use of all kinds of traditional methods of spycraft.

The couriers continued to find clever ways to conceal documents and deliver them to Rotterdam. Miniscule messages and information were handwritten or typed on sheets of fine tissue paper and collected into small cigarette-shaped rolls, which could be hidden inside broom handles and other similar objects and smuggled into Holland. Dewé and Chauvin knew a man in Liège who could hollow out special walking sticks so that the handle unscrewed to expose a cavity in which it was possible to hold up to six rolls, each roll consisting of twenty-five sheets.[42]

Another way of transporting a rolled-up message was in a small brown metal tube that could hold just one roll. It was used mainly by local couriers who were not travelling far and had only a small number of reports to deliver. The advantage of this device was that it could be hidden in a courier's sleeve. Although the Germans never discovered these methods, there was a near-discovery for one courier, known only as Juliette.[43] She operated a courier route from Namur to Liège, in which she travelled by train to Liège to deliver documents and then smuggled funds back to Namur. On one occasion she arrived at the ticket barrier of the station to find a random inspection of identity cards. She was instructed by the secret police to go into a side room. She knew she was about to be searched and questioned about her long journey to Liège. Her small compromising roll had been sewn into a piece of black cloth and hidden up her sleeve. In the room, she noticed a radiator and with one swift move she dropped the roll behind it. The secret police entered the room and questioned her.

Juliette was quick-thinking and explained that she had been visiting a sick relative in Liège. She was taken to another room, where a female

German officer searched her clothes and handbag for hidden items and slit open the hem of her dress. Nothing was found and Juliette was free to go. She deliberately took her time to dress, and by the time she had finished, the officer had left. She entered the other room, retrieved the secret roll of intelligence and carried on her journey.

The network used codes to transfer information and intelligence. A simple code was devised that was based on either the Lord's Prayer or a universally known verse or poem.[44] A more complicated code was used between the White Lady and the office in Rotterdam that worked from a pocket dictionary plus a key – a column of arbitrary numbers that were marked on a small cardboard strip. The numbers on the slip were changed continually, and different editions of a dictionary were used (known to each side), such that this code was undecipherable without the key. If a military word did not appear in the dictionary, a grid code was used for those terms, which was also changed regularly.[45]

And so it was that, without any formal espionage training, ordinary women and men used their initiative and adapted to operational needs behind the German lines, to ensure the information they had gathered could make it out to British intelligence in Holland. Their methods of spycraft were often simple, sometimes complex, and were incredibly effective.

Chapter 5
THE HIRSON PLATOON

Towards the end of August 1917 Landau received news that the White Lady was hiding a French refugee in the home of Julienne Demarteau, one of its agents in Liège. The refugee was Edmond Amiable, a young man in his twenties, who had begun training for the priesthood but had decided to cross the frontier into Holland to join the Belgian army instead.[1] He made contact with the White Lady via a Jesuit priest. 'Gauthier' (Dewé) and 'Dumont' (Chauvin) gave Amiable an important verbal message for SIS and Landau. They also requested that one of Landau's own frontier guides smuggle Amiable into Holland, but SIS was not keen to do this because the mixing of frontier guides from the White Lady and SIS laid both organisations open to compromise and security risks. The headquarters in Liège was insistent, and on this one occasion SIS relented and sent Charles Willekens, one of its most trusted frontier guides, to collect Amiable.

Once in Holland, Amiable explained to Landau the difficulties in leaving the Hirson region of France and crossing into Belgium. Hirson was in the region that Landau had been trying to infiltrate for the last two years, but without success. Other Allied secret services had failed, too. The Hirson–Mézières railway line was an important main line that ran parallel to the German battle front, and this region assumed a far greater strategic importance as rumours grew of a large new German offensive.[2] It was at Trélon that the Kaiser had the Château de Merode, where he frequently took up residence. The town was the location for the headquarters of one of the German armies. Hirson was only 15km from this pivotal railway network and the general railway headquarters. Landau knew it was essential to establish new observation posts there. He persuaded Amiable not to join the army, but to return to Hirson instead to set up a train-watching line for him. He gave Amiable the codename 'A.91' and dispatched him back to Liège with Charles Willekens as his guide again.

The White Lady briefed Amiable on how to create a new post and explained that it needed him to watch the rest areas being used by German troops, in addition to other areas where German troops were amassing. Watching the Hirson–Mézières line gave the White Lady precise details of the transfer of German divisions from one sector to another, with itinerant agents reporting on the concentration of troops in areas away from the railway line. This information enabled British intelligence to locate the next area for a German attack on Allied positions and to pass on the information to French General Headquarters.

The Mission

On 29 August 1917, Chauvin accompanied Amiable on his mission and they left for Namur. Amiable still only knew his colleague's name as Dumont.[3] They arrived at a battalion headquarters of the White Lady in Namur where Abbé Philippot, the commander of the Second Battalion, gave them a letter of introduction to a trusted friend, Ghislain Hanotier, in Chimay. Hanotier had served in the Biscops Service for two years before that network was compromised, and as he had not been discovered by the Germans, he was able to enlist in the White Lady. On 31 August 1917, Amiable and Chauvin arrived in Chimay. Chauvin immediately went off to find Hanotier, and briefed him on establishing a letter box in Chimay. They recruited two couriers: one between Chimay and the French border, and another between Chimay and Namur.

With the letter box established, Amiable and Chauvin headed for the Franco-Belgian border. Moreau ('Oram') agreed to act as their frontier guide – a perfect choice because Oram lived at Baives, a small village in France near the border, and occasionally crossed into Belgium legitimately to buy supplies for his family. He would not arouse suspicion. During the night of 7 September, Oram crossed into Belgium, met Amiable and Chauvin and secretly escorted them back into France via the small French village of Macon, where Oram said goodbye to them.

Disguised as local workmen, they had crossed the border without difficulty. Amiable was dressed in a dirty pair of blue jeans and a cap, and Chauvin in an old raincoat and scruffy hat. A local glass factory employed Belgian workers who daily crossed into France on special work permits, and Landau secured two such travel permits for Amiable and Chauvin. At one point they stumbled on a group of German soldiers, with no chance of escaping. They confidently walked on, believing their disguise as local workmen would work. It did, until they walked towards a road that led into the village and a German soldier hesitated and called out, 'Halt!'

The two men pretended not to hear and walked faster. A bullet whizzed past them and they threw themselves into a hedge. Chauvin dashed out the other side and ran off, then in the darkness fell into a ditch. He waited there for over an hour and when heavy rain began, he thought it safe to carry on. He decided to head back to Macon, where Landau was staying, and arrived at the house at dawn. Landau drove him by cart to Chimay, where they discussed with Hanotier the events of the previous night. Chauvin believed Amiable might have been captured.

But in fact, Amiable had not been found. He ran alongside a fence for a while, found an opening and hid in the centre of a thick bush. A group of German soldiers passed close to him and he heard them discussing the two runaways. He waited in the bush for three hours, then with the heavy rain felt it was safe to head off to his father's home on the outskirts of the French town of Trélon. He explained to his father the urgency of setting up a train-watching network around Hirson. His father agreed to set up the Hirson Platoon for the White Lady. He advised his son to return to Belgium because Amiable was of fighting age and would attract attention if he stayed in Trélon to run the organisation. Oram smuggled him back across the Franco-Belgian border.

When Amiable reached Chimay, he was surprised to be greeted by Chauvin, whom he thought had been captured. The two men returned to Liège and for six weeks they worked through and assessed the intelligence reports with Dewé.

Agent Pierre

Amiable's father immediately set up the Hirson Platoon and took the codename 'Pierre'. He visited Félix Latouche ('Dominique'), a former railway employee, in the village of Fourmies. Latouche wanted to avenge his being forced to remain in post at the railway to work for the occupying German forces, who had threatened him and his family with deportation if he refused. His cottage was situated right on the Hirson–Mézières railway line: a perfect location for clandestine train-watching during night and day.

Latouche's wife and two daughters, aged fourteen and thirteen, were active in the observation post. During the day, through a narrow slit in curtains, the two young sisters observed all trains passing by, and at night it was 'Dominique' and his wife. They wrote down what they saw in code, using foodstuffs to represent military subjects: beans meant soldiers, chicory meant horses, and coffee meant cannons.[4] They hid their coded reports inside the hollow handle of a broom, which they left in a corner outside to be collected by the courier. It was an incredible tribute to this family that the Fourmies Post ran from 23 September 1917 until the Armistice, and, as Landau later wrote, 'not a single German troop train was missed on this, the most important railway artery behind the German front'.[5]

'Pierre' continued to recruit agents. At Glageon, halfway between Trélon and Fourmies, he enrolled Crésillon, an employee at a local sawmill that was being forced to manufacture essential items for the German war effort. Next to the mill was a German site that manufactured anti-tank mines, barbed wire and an array of hardware for trench warfare. In an area of such high military activity by the enemy, Crésillon noted regimental numbers and numbers of troops. He set up a letter box in his own house and received the reports from Fourmies, Avesnes and other local areas. Twice a week he personally couriered them to 'Pierre' in Trélon. 'Pierre' feared that his regular meetings with Crésillon in a local café might attract attention, so he handed over the courier duties to his wife, who was 'invisible' to the Germans. She was a midwife and able to travel freely without suspicion. She hid the reports around the whale bones of her corset.[6]

Pierre passed the reports to Oram, who took them over the frontier to another courier in Macon.[7] During the course of his clandestine operations for the White Lady, Oram was often arrested, but the secret police failed to find any reports on him because he found clever ways to hide them, often concealed in clumps of earth. If he was working in a potato field, he buried the reports the day before, close to the electrified fence. In a swift move, he could retrieve the rolled-up reports hidden in a potato and throw it over the wire to a Dutch peasant on the other side. It was a simple method – perhaps crude, but it worked. Or he could carry some potatoes across the frontier himself and not arouse suspicion.

Women of the Hirson Platoon

Women were extremely active in the Hirson Platoon. Roman Catholic nuns acted as informants for the platoon and passed information that they gleaned from the conversations between German soldiers in hospitals where they were giving pastoral care. Reports from the network's observation posts were brought by courier to a convent of French nuns in Chimay. A German military hospital for wounded soldiers was set up in the convent. Sister Marie-Mélanie and Sister Marie-Caroline worked for the White Lady from within the convent. They ran a small shop which was also patronised by the German soldiers from the front line, affording an ideal opportunity to gain information from them.[8] The soldiers chatted among themselves and gave away snippets of information – all of which found its way into the intelligence reports that were compiled by the nuns for the White Lady.

The new German 'big gun' was one of the vital pieces of intelligence provided by the nuns. Sister Marie-Mélanie encouraged one particular German gunner who was convalescing in the convent to talk to her. Before returning to front-line fighting, he spoke about a new big gun, known as the 'Kaiser-Wilhelm-Geschütz'. This, he said, would turn the war in Germany's favour because it could fire a distance of 120km and reach as far as Paris. She told him that she doubted it, encouraging him to boast to her that he had seen the installation in Laon himself, not suspecting her of subtle espionage. The mention of Laon recalled to her how the nuns had given shelter to a French refugee a few weeks earlier, who had spoken about Crépy-en-Laon having been evacuated of its civilians for the Germans to place artillery there. It was there that the German military had constructed concrete gun platforms and located ammunition pits at a site called Dandry's Farm.

An agent was secretly sent to the farm to spy out the place to confirm the soldier's casual conversation with the nuns. Within three days he was back and able to report to the Hirson Platoon of a monster gun. This intelligence was passed straight to Landau and on to London, which corroborated other intelligence coming from Allied agents in Germany about a high-trajectory gun with a barrel thirty metres long. From a spy in Germany, British intelligence had already received full details of the trials of a high-angle gun on the coast of Heligoland, but with no further information on it.

One of the most courageous couriers for the Hirson Platoon was Eglantine Lefèvre, an employee of the *Poste Française* newspaper, who operated as a courier from April to October 1918.[9] She moved around areas that even Crésillon's wife could not, without arousing suspicion. Lefèvre reported on when the Kaiser was in residence at Château de Merode, near Trélon, and all roads were heavily guarded. Crésillon's wife had no excuse to go near the castle, but Lefèvre was able to navigate the fields and woods to get close to observe German activities.[10] She alerted the Allies to a secret visit by the Kaiser to the front line and the route of his train. The Allies tried to bomb the train, but missed their target. In October 1918, Lefèvre contracted Spanish influenza but vowed to continue to carry the reports to Trélon – which she did. On the 23rd she returned to Pierre's house (Amiable's father) with the reports, collapsed on the floor and died the following day.[11] She was only twenty-eight years old. She had sacrificed her health and life for the network.

The work of these women was vital in building a military picture of German forces and supply lines in Belgium, and it also saved the lives of British agents who could be killed going too near the front line to gather intelligence. The Hirson Platoon swiftly grew to over fifty members. It meant that the Trélon–Glageon–Fourmies–Avesnes sector was covered by an invisible network that noted down every German military movement for SIS.

The Chimay Company

The Chimay Company was the last of the White Lady companies to be formed and came under the umbrella of the Hirson Platoon.[12] A plan was drawn up to land a spy, a soldier by the name of Valtier, near his home village at Signy-l'Abbaye, near Rethel, in the Ardennes region of north-eastern France.[13] He was to recruit friends to a new observation post. Pierre Aubijoux volunteered to pilot the aircraft. They took off before dawn from a field near Jonchery. After flying for several hours, Aubijoux had lost his bearings and the plane was almost out of fuel. With no chance of returning to Allied lines in France, they made an emergency landing in a field, crashed into a barbed-wire fence and survived unharmed.[14] Two German soldiers rushed towards the plane. Aubijoux turned his machine gun on them, then set fire to the plane. He and Valtier dashed towards a wooded region where they hid from further German patrols. They received help from the nuns at the French convent in Chimay, who understood the importance of the mission.

Sister Marie-Mélanie sent a messenger to consult with Hanotier about Valtier and Aubijoux. It was decided that the two men should be smuggled into Holland, because they were still being hunted down by German patrols and would therefore be of little use to the network locally. Hanotier started them on their journey towards the Dutch frontier and left them to continue on their own. But Valtier disagreed with the decision to send them into Holland. He was on a mission and determined to see it through, even if it cost him his life. He and Aubijoux retraced their steps, and five days later they were back in Chimay. They persuaded the local leaders to take them on to Hirson, from where they set up their network of observation posts. Their courier began to bring the first intelligence reports to Sister Marie-Mélanie in Chimay. Having set up the posts, the two men decided to return to France and rejoin the army. They were arrested at the Dutch border. The Germans believed that they were French pilots whose plane had been forced down by recent heavy fog. They were taken to a prisoner-of-war camp in Germany, but not before they had succeeded in establishing the Chimay Company. The latter, which came under the Hirson Platoon, had itself formed four platoons: three operating in the regions of Hirson, Chimay, Charleroi, and one that consisted solely of couriers.[15]

Another agent penetrated the defences around the airfield at Bourlers, near Chimay, and reported back on the fake wooden tanks that the Germans had assembled there to deceive the Allies about their fighting capability. This agent also stole the briefcase of a German aviator, which yielded several priceless maps that marked all the military airfields behind a large section of the German Western Front. In February 1918, one of the Hirson Platoon's agents sent British intelligence the definitive evidence that from this sector the Germans were about to launch their great offensive of March 1918.[16] This corroborated information that had already been sent back from the Chimay Company about an imminent German offensive.

The Hirson Platoon and Chimay Company functioned until the end of the war without a single arrest. It was a remarkable achievement given the threat of German counter-espionage.

Chapter 6
VILLA DES HIRONDELLES

One of the key centres at the heart of operations was Villa des Hirondelles at Wandre, situated on the banks of the fast-flowing river Meuse. It served as the regional secretariat for the White Lady and the final place for typing the regional intelligence reports before dispatch to Holland.[1]

The villa had prepared for a raid by the German secret police, with twenty-eight guns and ten thousand rounds of ammunition stored inside. The front windows were heavily shuttered and a strong oak door secured the front entrance. In the event of a raid, one of the operatives inside could distract the secret police by talking and buying time, until all compromising documents had been destroyed and the other agents fled. A boat was moored on the banks of the river, ready for a swift escape. The villa still stands on the banks of the Meuse today, slightly set back from the river. The front entrance directly faces the water, and a back entrance is accessed through a long rear garden, leading to a quiet residential street.

In March 1918, the villa became the subject of a serious compromise, focused around agents Louis and Antony Collard, brothers in their twenties who were working for the White Lady.[2] In October 1917 they had left Tintigny, the small village of their birth in the valley of the Semois, and travelled to Liège.[3] Their aim was to cross into Holland

and join the Belgian army. While in Liège they were contacted by recruiters for the White Lady and persuaded to return to Tintigny to organise an intelligence network. They arrived back in Tintigny on 7 December 1917 and set up a regional network for Dewé that not only covered the whole of the Virton section via its observation posts, but also successfully established a train-watching post at Longuyon, on the strategic Longuyon–Sedan railway line. Their network set up observation posts in France and also began to penetrate the German-occupied Grand Duchy of Luxembourg. Louis and Antony became the couriers between Virton and Liège.[4] They occasionally stayed at Villa des Hirondelles.

On 8 March 1918, they and other operatives working at the villa were inadvertently compromised by a young woman called Marcelle. She was working in domestic service in Liège, employed by Ernest Reymen, the owner of Villa des Hirondelles.[5] Although she knew nothing of the spying activities at the villa, a relative who was envious that she was courting a rich Belgian man wrote an anonymous letter to the German secret police alleging that Marcelle had entered the country from France without a passport. Lieutenant Landwerlen, chief of the secret police at Liège, dispatched two plainclothes officers to bring her in for questioning. They also decided to question her employer, knowing that he resided somewhere in Wandre. Making enquiries with the local people, they established that Reymen might be at the Villa des Hirondelles, which he rented to tenants.

The plainclothes officers arrived at the villa and waited for a few minutes behind bushes in the garden. They saw two men, couriers Paul Franchimont and Henri van den Berg, leaving the house as they had just deposited their reports there. The two undercover officers appeared from the bushes.[6]

One of them, Müller, asked, 'Who lives here?'

The couriers did not reply. Müller pulled out his gun and ordered them to follow him towards the villa.

Jeanne Goeseels

At the time, there were four agents of the White Lady working down-stairs in the villa. They were thirty-five-year-old Jeanne Goeseels, who was in charge of the secretariat and using the pseudonym 'Madame Lebrun'; Rosa, a servant who worked for the network and also cleaned the villa; and Louis and Antony Collard, who were working in a back room. The latter had just arrived from Luxembourg and had decided to stay overnight in the villa. The stenographers, who transcribed the reports, were not in the villa at the time.

Müller knocked on the door, his gun pointed in Franchimont's side.[7] From behind the door, Jeanne Goeseels called out, 'Who's there?'

Under his breath, Müller told Franchimont to reply. When Goeseels heard the familiar voice, she opened the door and was confronted with reality. She instantly thought about how to alert the Collard brothers. She had been involved in intelligence operations since the beginning of the war, and even after several arrests previously, she had outwitted the Germans.

The reports which Franchimont and van den Berg had just dropped off were hidden down the side of a sofa, and might not be found, but Louis and Antony were in their room, copying out information that they had just brought back from the Luxembourg region. Goeseels had seen the reports spread out on a table. How could she warn them? To buy time, she talked in a loud voice to Müller, who asked whether Reymen lived there.

'No,' she replied. 'You are in my home.'

'Have you ever been arrested?' he asked.

'No. Neither by you nor the Belgians,' she lied.

'You are Mademoiselle Marcelle?' he replied.

'No, I am Madame Goeseels.'

'You are French?'

'No, I am a Belgian,' she answered. Müller remained suspicious and thought she could be hiding refugees, and decided to search the villa.

Louis and Antony heard nothing of the conversation. They were so engrossed in their work they did not realise the dangers until they heard footsteps outside their door. By then it was too late to escape, and the notebooks in their pockets had evidence of their activities. Antony threw his notebook out of the window, but reports were scattered across the table, and these were seized with Louis's notebook.

In the meantime, Goeseels slipped upstairs with a gun hidden in her blouse, and waited on the landing for one of the officers to leave the room.

Müller appeared. 'Trying to hide something?' he said as he moved into one of the bedrooms to search it.

Goeseels closed the door and tried to lock him in, but he was too quick, shoved open the door and pointed his gun at her.

Meanwhile, Franchimont and van den Berg were downstairs in the kitchen with the maid Rosa. Franchimont made a sign to van den Berg and the two men jumped out of the window and into the garden. They headed for the boat moored on the Meuse. The boat's chain was stuck. As they tried to free it, they looked up to see one of the secret police officers standing near them, pointing his gun. He had seen them pass under the window of the villa.

Franchimont recalled, 'While running to the boat I made a big mistake. I should have directed our attempt, not towards the Meuse, which obliged us to pass in front of a window from which the Boches [Germans] could see us . . . and I believe that our escape would have succeeded.'

They were taken back to the villa and questioned in the dining room. The officer with his gun in hand warned them, 'The first one who moves, I'll shoot.'

The villa was searched and a stash of guns and ammunition found. Franchimont and Creusen were arrested, along with Goeseels and the Collard brothers, and all were taken to Wandre police station. From there they were transferred to Liège for questioning. While each one was taken away for individual interrogation, Goeseels spoke to her fellow agents in the room.

She turned to Franchimont and said quietly, 'Tell them I am your mistress and you often visit me at the villa. You know nothing about my activities.'

She said to van den Berg, 'You are Franchimont's friend. You dropped in on a casual visit.'

To Louis and Antony she said, 'You are two of my lodgers. I don't know who you are, or anything about your activities. Remember your oath as a soldier. Reveal nothing . . .'

In her own defence, Goeseels invented the story that she had been helping refugees and had stored a few guns and some ammunition for them. She believed this would be seen as a less serious offence in the eyes of her captors than espionage.

Louis and Antony found it difficult to explain away the reports that had been seized, and so they told the interrogator that they were about to cross into Holland and had compiled the reports with the intention of selling them to an espionage organisation there. They did so to divert attention away from the White Lady, and believed that German law at that time would protect them. The law stated that a spy could not be executed unless it had been proved that he or she had directly or indirectly communicated with the enemy. An intention to spy was not punishable. However, the interrogators did not believe their story, as many of the reports were in code and undeniably espionage.

Lieutenant Landwerlen, Liège's chief of the secret police, was convinced that Goeseels was guilty of espionage, but had no direct proof. She held firm during intense interrogation and gave nothing away.[8]

Security Concerns

Two days after the arrests, on 10 March 1918, the White Lady's counter-espionage section discovered that the Collard brothers had been arrested at the villa. They were being held in solitary confinement and could not request visitors. However, two other agents, Fauquenot and Creusen, who were already imprisoned in Liège, continued to operate for the White Lady from inside the prison and managed to speak with Louis and Antony Collard. They smuggled out coded messages to the White Lady with insider help from Maryan, a Polish guard, and they asked the brothers about the arrests.

Fauquenot and Creusen sent a coded message to the White Lady headquarters in Liège warning that intelligence reports were still hidden in the sofa at the villa. Dewé sent Reymen, the villa's landlord – who must therefore have also been involved in the network – to retrieve the intelligence reports. While at the villa, Reymen discovered Antony Collard's notebook lying on the ground where he had thrown it from a window, and picked this up too.

Afterwards, Reymen received a letter from the White Lady, almost certainly sent by Dewé, thanking him for the items:

> We have the honor to acknowledge receipt of your reports. We find them very well done but very incomplete . . . We inform you of our desire to have a detailed plan of Villa des Hirondelles. At this point we will shortly send one of our agents to draw a sketch. Regarding your arrest, your report ends at the most interesting point, namely, your interrogations, which we ask you to give in detail . . . LDB.[9]

It seems that Reymen was not an innocent, unsuspecting landlord, but was working for La Dame Blanche too.

During his first interrogation, Franchimont was asked, 'Did you spy? Did you cross the border? Did you want to cross it?'[10] He replied 'no' to all, signed a declaration to that effect and was sent back to his cell. In other interrogations he was shown Goeseels's false identity papers in the name of Madame Lebrun. He kept his word to her, and denied knowing her except as his mistress. He was then shown a report on the region of Louvain and asked if it was her handwriting. It was not, and he denied knowing anything about reports. The interrogators believed the testimony of Franchimont and van den Berg and released them.

Fauquenot and Creusen continued to send more than fifty coded messages from the prison, providing verbatim details of the interrogations of other members of the network.[11] It enabled Dewé and Chauvin to learn how much the secret police knew, and so the leaders could immediately isolate and warn imperilled sectors of the network. One coded message confirmed that the Collard brothers had been beaten by the guards in an attempt to break them. Landau later wrote, 'Every third-degree method was tried; and not even Vérin, the most successful stool-pigeon in St Léonard [prison], was able to move the two martyred brothers to betrayal.'[12]

What Dewé and Chauvin could not ascertain was how the villa had been betrayed. Was there a traitor? Security concerns lingered over the coming months. Only later did the truth come out about Marcelle's jealous relative who had inadvertently compromised the operation. There were other dangerous moments, like the occasion when the secret police became suspicious of the Weimerskirch sisters (Emma, Alice and Jeanne), who ran a letter box in Liège. Their house was searched, and nothing compromising was found, but Dewé and Chauvin were working in a back room at the time and could so easily have been arrested. They had heard unusual male voices at the front door and escaped through the rear of the property.

The arrest of the Collards broke the chain with other members of the network, because the brothers had acted as both couriers and heads of the regional sector. The secret police found a few names in Louis's pocketbook and subsequently arrested the brothers' widowed father, as well as Abbé Arnould, and Monsieur and Madame Joseph Bastin. Joseph later gave an account of his arrest at their home in Tintigny:

On 21 March 1918, three German police officers came to my house around 5 o'clock in the evening and after searches, they arrested my wife and me to the prison of Neufchateau. The next day we left at

2 o'clock in the afternoon for Liège, where we arrived around 8 o'clock in the evening. We were put in the cell around midnight. On 24 March, we were questioned twice by the police, and a third time on 2 April. My wife was interrogated again on 17 April. On 1 May, we were photographed and on 3 May had our fingerprints taken.[13]

They first appeared in court on 27 June. Their German lawyer pleaded to reduce their proposed sentence of fifteen years to five years for Joseph Bastin and acquittal for his wife. It failed. The couple remained in prison until their release at the end of the war, on 11 November 1918.[14] The White Lady financially supported the young children whose parents were in prison.

Double Prison Breakout

The leadership of Dewé, Chauvin and Joseph Falloise planned to rescue Fauquenot and Creusen from prison. It was arranged and agreed in advance with the prisoners to take place on Maundy Thursday, 28 March 1918, when the German security and prison guards were reduced in capacity due to the Easter holidays.[15] Early that evening, Dewé met Chauvin in his study at the Institut Montefiore in Liège to finalise the escape. A model of the prison lay in front of them on the desk and they went over the exact route.

Dewé pulled out his watch. 'It's eight o'clock. We have no time to lose.'

They hid the model in a secret cupboard and went out, passing a woman in the entrance hall who had been on the lookout during the whole time they had been in the building. She had a concealed electric alarm which could be triggered if they were in danger, and this would have alerted Chauvin in his study.

At rue Pont d'Avroy, they stopped at a cigar store and Dewé went inside to buy cigarettes to use to signal to the two watchers in the prison that the coast was clear. They took a taxi from place de la Cathédrale to the vicinity of the prison. They walked into a small alleyway that ran from rue Regnier to rue Jonruelle and took up their position at the corner of the street to watch for German patrols. The area where Dewé and Chauvin had stationed themselves was badly lit and most shutters on the houses were closed. All was clear, so they each lit a cigarette to signal to the two watchers.

Fauquenot later recalled, 'With my pillow I fixed up a dummy to make the bed appear occupied. I placed some of my clothes on the chair, as if I had just taken them off. At eight o'clock, Maryan, the insider who agreed to help us, opened the cell.'[16] Maryan would have been shot if caught. Creusen was waiting for Fauquenot and hiding in a store cupboard, having already been smuggled out of his cell by Maryan.

Maryan gave them a small hammer and an iron spike, then wished them luck and disappeared. Fauquenot and Creusen made their way to the chapel, climbed a spiral staircase into a loft, and then made their way onto the roof of the prison.

At 9 p.m., Chauvin asked Dewé if he had heard a whistle, which was the prearranged sign from the prison that all was ready to break out Fauquenot. Then a silhouette of a figure appeared on the prison roof and promptly disappeared. 'Did you see him?' Chauvin asked Dewé, but Dewé had not.

A different shadowy figure suddenly emerged from the darkness of the street. It was one of their own agents, Juliette Durieu. She informed them that Maryan had reached the safehouse.

Meanwhile Fauquenot fastened a sheet to the skylight and began to slide down to the gutter. As he recalled: 'The roof was slippery and much steeper than I had imagined. From the gutter, I let out the sheet. To my horror, it was too short to reach anywhere near the prison wall. I pulled myself back to the skylight, and whispered the tragic news to Creusen, who was still in the loft . . . Then I heard a hiss from Creusen: "The pile of sheets, I'll go back and get some." '[17]

Creusen soon reappeared with a bundle of sheets and tied them into a long rope. Fauquenot slid swiftly down the drainpipe to the ground and ran towards Dewé and Chauvin. He gave the password, 'Joan of Arc'. Just as they enquired about the whereabouts of Creusen, his head appeared over the wall.

'The two Collards?' Dewé and Chauvin asked simultaneously.

'They are in a different wing in solitary confinement.'

After a short distance on foot, the men got into a taxi for place de la Cathédrale. They separated into two groups to avoid suspicion and met again at the safehouse, where Maryan was waiting.

An hour or so later, the breakout was discovered when German guards noticed the rope of sheets hanging down the prison wall. It took no time to discover that it was Fauquenot and Creusen who were missing. A full-scale search was mounted of the prison and environs.

It was decided that getting Fauquenot and Creusen over the frontier into Holland was no riskier than hiding them in Belgium, so Dewé and Chauvin decided on the former. Two guides of the White Lady network were procured for the mission. It was planned that Fauquenot, disguised as a Lutheran minister, would cross the frontier north of Antwerp. Creusen took another route through the Campine.

Spies in Disguise

The White Lady acquired the necessary vestments for Fauquenot's disguise, and set the crossing for 5 July 1918. That night, as he travelled by car to meet a guide who would take him over the frontier, Fauquenot happened upon a member of the secret police who had spent the evening with a girl from a brothel and was waiting to flag down a car for a lift back to Antwerp. The secret police officer got into the car, turned to Fauquenot and declared that there were too many spies disguising themselves as priests. He took Fauquenot back to Antwerp for investigation.

This was a disaster. Fauquenot would not be able to hold his cover, especially if interrogated by a real priest. As soon as the car was going faster, he opened the door and rolled out into a ditch. He escaped into the darkness and made his way back to Liège, where the network hid him until the Armistice.

Creusen's journey was not straightforward. His guide brought him within 100 metres of the frontier and left him hidden in the grass, while the guide staked out the frontier guards. Creusen was weak and exhausted from two years in prison and the trek on foot across the Campine. He fell asleep, and the guide failed to find him again. When Creusen woke at dawn, a frontier guard was standing over him and arrested him. During interrogation, he gave them a false name, Desmet, and said he lived in Flanders, close to the electrified fence. He was believed, but it was nevertheless clear that he was trying to smuggle himself across the frontier, and he was sent to Hasselt prison. The secret police never discovered that Desmet in Hasselt was actually the escapee Creusen from St Léonard, the very man they were hunting for. His identity was obscured, too, because of a beard and moustache, which he had grown since his escape. Landau commented, 'This failure to identify Creusen, in spite of his fingerprints which had been taken in St Léonard, is proof of the lack of cooperation which existed between the various Secret Police posts.'[18]

In the early hours of the morning after Fauquenot and Creusen's escape, Marie Birckel was brought out of her St Léonard cell for interrogation by three secret police officers. She was one of Fauquenot and Creusen's recruits, arrested in 1916.

Her interrogators watched closely for a reaction as she was asked, 'Do you know that Fauquenot and Creusen tried to escape last night? Fauquenot was shot dead and Creusen was badly wounded.' It was, in fact, not true. They wanted to see if she knew about it.

Through Maryan, Marie had known about the plan because it was suggested they break her out, too: she refused because she believed it would lessen the men's chances of escape. She gave nothing away to her interrogators.[19]

A second interrogator added, 'Creusen confessed before he died that it was planned that you were to escape with them.' This contradicted what the first interrogator had said, and in that moment Marie knew her friends had survived. She was soon returned to her cell. A few weeks later, she was transferred to a prison camp in Germany. After the war and her release from prison, she and Fauquenot married.

Restarting the Network

Eighteen-year-old Marie-Thérèse Collard was a courier for the White Lady and was out when her father was arrested at their home. She did not know where he had been taken, nor her two brothers who had been arrested at Villa des Hirondelles.[20] She tried to establish their location, but the local police refused to tell her anything. Irene Bastin was another network member who had escaped arrest. On 11 April, Marie-Thérèse and Irene sought out Marie-Thérèse's cousin in Namur for advice. He sent them on to Liège, where the two young women lodged for approximately six weeks in the house of Monsieur and Madame Duchêne. One morning they walked with M. Duchêne to St Léonard prison, where Irene's parents and Marie-Thérèse's brothers and father were being held. As they walked around the exterior of the dark prison walls, not seeing a single prisoner, they felt a sense of gloom and pain. Irene later wrote, 'And that fierce-looking sentry with his spiked helmet, who stood watch at the door!'[21]

While in Liège they were approached by members of the White Lady. A time was arranged for them to meet important members of network on Wednesday, 29 May 1918, at the Duchênes' home. They did not know at that point who they would meet. It was Dewé who arrived at the house at around 6 a.m. He asked them what they knew about the arrests at Villa des Hirondelles, and enquired for their welfare and whether they had any material needs. They were asked if they would consider enrolling as soldiers in the White Lady. Irene wrote after the war, 'It was with a glad heart that we accepted the mission that these gentlemen wanted to entrust to us.'[22]

Chauvin arrived at 7.30 a.m. One at a time, Marie-Thérèse and Irene each placed their hand on the cross of Dewé's rosary and, with the two men as witnesses, took the oath. 'It was a solemn moment,' wrote Irene. After swearing the oath, they were given false names as 'sisters' called Marthe and Madeleine Vailly.

Chauvin left at 8 a.m., but not before he reassured the women that he was doing everything possible for their families in the prison. Dewé began instructing Marie-Thérèse and Irene in espionage techniques and how to operate the network securely. Nothing could be written down; everything had to be committed to memory, and Dewé repeated instructions to ensure they remembered the key methods. The women were then instructed to travel to Jamoigne, near Chiny, in the province of Luxembourg within Belgium, close to the French border, and seek out Father Raulet. They were to mention a certain interview that Raulet had had with Dewé the previous year. With this message, Raulet would know that Dewé had sent them.

Dewé gave them money to pay the first agents in their new sector and cover their own travelling expenses. He departed around 10 a.m. The two women spent the rest of the day going over what they had been taught, then resting ahead of their journey.

At around 7 a.m. the following morning, Marie-Thérèse and Irene left by tram, accompanied by Monsieur Duchêne, to Liège, from where the two women would take a boat. Irene commented in her report how they felt a sense of sadness at leaving the place that held their loved ones, but they knew their mission was important. During the course of their journey, there was a random check by a German soldier on their identity cards. It was a tense moment, as it could have led to questions about why they were moving around the country, but all was fine. After the boat, they travelled by train to Namur, arriving later that same day.

These two eighteen-year-olds demonstrated much courage in restarting the network in the Virton region. They re-established contact with those agents who had not been arrested, and soon the network was up and running again. They headed the whole sector and ran contacts between couriers and agents. On one occasion they travelled to

Jamoigne with parcels containing bundles of intelligence reports, and deposited them in one of the first houses in the village. The secret police discovered that they were travelling regularly to Namur and Liège, and they were soon arrested, imprisoned for several weeks, and underwent three intense interrogations. No information was obtained from them and they were released.

The Trial and Farewell

While the two women revived the network, back at the fortress in Liège the interrogations were concluding. The prisoners were put on trial. The final judgement of the tribunal came on 2 July 1918, when Louis and Antony Collard, Abbé Arnould and Jeanne Goeseels were sentenced to death.[23] Léon Collard, father of the brothers, was sentenced to twelve years' hard labour; Irene Bastin's father Joseph received ten years' hard labour and her mother two years' hard labour. The sentences for Goeseels and Arnould were eventually commuted to hard labour for life.

The prison governor permitted a final farewell to take place between Léon Collard and his sons in the office. Louis and Antony fell to their knees and asked for their father's blessing. He returned the gesture. Without shedding a tear, the sons were led away by the guards. Their father rushed to the door and caught sight of his sons turning the corner of the corridor. They called back to him, 'We'll meet in heaven.'[24] That was the last time he saw his sons.

Dewé and Chauvin hatched a plan to rescue the Collards during their transfer from St Léonard prison to the Fort de la Chartreuse where their execution was due to take place. All transfers took place at night, accompanied by six prison guards. The road leading up to the fortress was narrow and steep, and the prison van had to ascend in low gear. There was an opportunity to intercept the van and get the men out, and a dozen armed men were on standby to rescue the brothers; but all attempts to find out the exact night of the transfer failed.

On 18 July 1918, Louis and Antony Collard were shot at the Fort de la Chartreuse. They were buried on the spot where they were shot. After the war, the British and Belgian governments posthumously bestowed on them the same high decorations as Dieudonné Lambrecht.[25]

The Collard brothers sacrificed their own lives, and their silence saved the lives of so many of the White Lady's agents and couriers. The silence and strength of Jeanne Goeseels in the face of German brutality also prevented the capture and killing of many agents. She later wrote, 'There are even things on which I am obliged to remain silent, things experienced and suffered that the world will never know.'[26]

Only she, Dewé and Chauvin knew the full operational details of the Villa des Hirondelles. If Jeanne had cracked under interrogation, more lives would have been lost. In pretending to be Franchimont's mistress, she had saved him from a similar fate to the Collard brothers.

The day after the Collard brothers were shot, Marie-Thérèse Collard and Irene Bastin wrote to Dewé and Chauvin in Liège to confirm that they had re-established the network. Their letter survives in archives and reads, in translation from French:

Dear Gentlemen,
    The mission with which you have honoured us has been easy for us to accomplish. A faithful and dedicated agent has already, on our return, reorganised [the network] in a part of the country . . . If you have orders to give us, send them to us, as we are at your disposal. More and more happy to be chosen by you to continue the work of our parents, please receive, with our sincere thanks, our respectful friendships.[27]

They signed off using their codenames, Marthe and Madeleine Vailly.

The daring rescue of Fauquenot and Creusen from St Léonard prison was a magnificent achievement, but it was not possible for Dewé and Chauvin to repeat it.

At the time of the Villa des Hirondelles affair, the Germans were planning a new spring offensive which they believed would bring the decisive victory for Germany. At this precarious moment for the Allies, the silence of the agents in the prison during their multiple interrogations saved the White Lady at one of its most crucial operational periods. SIS in London needed intelligence on the enemy spring offensive. The White Lady was quite literally the eyes and ears of the British Secret Service on the ground in Belgium.

Chapter 7
POST 49

In January 1918, the White Lady was given a directive by the British Secret Service for agents to gather intelligence on the training of troops behind the German lines. This was important because the General Staff of the British army could thus be informed in good time of new methods of attack, new defence systems and other enemy tactics.[1] The Allies anticipated a last big offensive by the Germans.

Thérèse de Radiguès received news that Conneux Castle should expect further German soldiers and artillery troops, which duly arrived. As had happened at the start of the war, Thérèse was asked by a German officer to hand over the keys to the castle. On this occasion it was one Lieutenant Barth, but again Thérèse refused. The Radiguès family remained on polite terms with their occupying guests, and even nicknamed Lieutenant Laeisz 'the Ambassador' because he behaved like a diplomat. He knocked on the drawing-room door, entered and bowed as he asked Thérèse in an English accent, 'Madam, will you allow me to play a bit of piano?' (He had spent time in England before the war.) The family listened as the German officer played for them. One of the soldiers performed duties as cook and was nicknamed 'Sausage' by the family. 'He's the kind of nice guy with a round face, always laughing, saying hello to us every time we pass,' wrote Agnès de Radiguès, Thérèse's daughter.[2]

It was a surreal situation – the family fraternised with the German officers and made them feel at home in the castle, but all the while Thérèse was secretly leading an entire intelligence sector for the White Lady. This was a new observation platoon in the Ardennes region called Post 49, created in January 1918, the very month the British Secret Service had issued their directive. Post 49 consisted of Thérèse's three daughters, her wider family and aristocrats from her circle of friends. They included Count François and Countess Caroline d'Aspremont-Lynden, Baron Albert de Garcia de la Vega, Countesses Henriette and Anne de Villermont, Baron Gui de Villenfragne and Baron van der Straten Waillet.[3] Balancing the imperatives of intelligence-gathering under the noses of the Germans took a steely nerve.

Thérèse was also worried about her fifth son, Gérard. He and his friend Baron Jean d'Huart had been arrested in Moresnet-La Calamine and had been held in the Chartreuse fortress, Liège from 31 October 1917 before being transferred to Paderborn in Germany. Both would be released on 25 November 1918, but nineteen-year-old Jean d'Huart died on 27 February 1919 from his mistreatment while in captivity.

The arrest of her son did not deter Thérèse from playing a leading role in the White Lady. Using the cover name 'Lieutenant Dubois-Lefevre', Lieutenant Thérèse de Radiguès was the battalion's commander and recruited agents, organised the missions and analysed the intelligence reports. Her three daughters, Marguerite (twenty-six), Marie-Antoinette (twenty) and Agnès (fifteen), also worked for Post 49, as did many of the members of the old Service de Monge. Thérèse recruited from her own close aristocratic circle, as her grandson, François de Radiguès, recalls:

In this charming region south of Namur, in the provinces of Namur and Luxembourg, there are lots of castles of the Belgian aristocracy, whose owners were of patriotic mindedness. My grandmother recruited them, and it included Baron and Baroness Adolphe de

Moffarts, Count André Eggermont, Count and Countess Françoise de Villermont, Baroness Clémie de l'Epine, Baron and Baroness de Bonhomme and Count de Béthune. It was often the case that several members within a family worked for my grandmother. They in turn recruited priests, teachers, members of their own staff and other trusted people in the area.[4] Conneux became the centre of a sector having surveillance of German troop movements crossing south of the provinces of Luxembourg and Namur. What particularly interested Dewé and Chauvin was the Trier–Luxembourg–Longuyon–Mézières–Charleville–Hirson–Fourmies–Valenciennes–Lille railway line, which was of fundamental strategic importance since it allowed the movement of German forces to and from the Western Front.[5]

Every week, the aristocratic women of Post 49 carried a considerable number of reports to meetings attended by the chiefs.[6] Baron Adolphe de Moffarts provided the general management for Limbourg. A post-war report on Post 49 noted how the work became 'more intense and more interesting. We were provided with a typewriter and long evenings were spent typing our reports with eight to ten German officers as roommate. Every week one of us continued to carry our ever-increasing reports and we attended meetings with our heroic leaders [in Liège].'[7]

Dewé and Chauvin looked to expand the network further to establish a flying squad (a sub-post) of Post 49 in Charleville in occupied France, to cover the Trier–Luxembourg–Sedan–Charleville–Mézières–Hirson line. It would enhance the work of the Hirson Platoon that now had observation posts along the Hirson–Trélon line.

Two other flying squads already existed at Tournai and Arlon. From Tournai, it was possible to bring back intelligence from Lille and Douai in the northern part of occupied France; and from Arlon, agents infiltrated the German-occupied Grand Duchy of Luxembourg. The Arlon post watched the vitally important Trier–Luxembourg line, which, together with the observation post on the Aachen–Herbesthal–Liège line, enabled British intelligence to note all train traffic going westwards out of Germany to points on the Western Front between Verdun and the sea.

The new annexe of Post 49 was to be called the Conneux Flying Squad, and was also known as Post 249.[8] Crossing the Franco-Belgian border was perilous and so to ensure a greater degree of success, it was decided that two young women should be found to undertake the mission. They would draw the least attention to themselves from German patrols. Marie-Antoinette de Radiguès and her twenty-three-year-old friend Baroness Clémie de L'Epine volunteered for it.[9]

Conneux Flying Squad

Marie-Antoinette ('Esther') and Clémie ('Alsace') already knew people in Charleville whom they hoped to recruit, but they had been out of touch with them since the beginning of the war. It was best to go personally to recruit them, and avoid the need to carry or send incriminating written messages. Clémie's family had an estate at Gedinne on the French border, approximately 60km from Charleville, an ideal base from which to coordinate a crossing. In the Gedinne area, a 10ft-high barbed-wire fence (a relic of pre-war days) separated Belgium from France; along it German sentries and the secret police kept a strict surveillance to prevent the passage of spies and their reports.

Charleville, situated on the banks of the Meuse, was occupied by Germany in both world wars. From 1916, the headquarters of Kaiser Wilhelm II and the Crown Prince was established in Château Renaudin, high above the town, and the town itself became the German military headquarters.[10] Importantly, from here ran the branch train lines to Rethel and Givet. Countess Françoise de Villermont (twenty-two) and her cousin, Countess Anne de Villermont (twenty-four), who originally worked for Post 49, set up a new train-watching post at Givet and on the Fumay line.[11]

In September 1918, Marie-Antoinette and Clémie set off from Conneux Castle by bicycle and headed for Clémie's family estate at

Gedinne. They found an experienced guide to smuggle them across the frontier. He was a twenty-year-old potato smuggler, known to them only as Georges, and carried half a sack of potatoes on his back. They arrived at a small farm, and to his horror, Georges noticed that half the potatoes had fallen through a hole in the sack, leaving a trail behind them.

Suddenly there was a sharp 'Halt!'

Two members of the secret police emerged from hiding in nearby bushes and demanded to see their identity cards. Fortunately, they were still in Belgium and they had the relevant identification; even so, Georges was taken away for questioning. Marie-Antoinette and Clémie waited for him for over an hour before he returned – without his sack of potatoes, which had been confiscated by the police. Clémie recalled, in translation from the original French report:

> We now started climbing the wooded slopes of a steep hill, zigzagging to avoid open spaces. After half an hour of climbing, we were in sight of the barbed wire, about 10ft high. But it was not here that we were to pass. We skirted the fence for some distance, until finally Georges gave a grunt of satisfaction. It was still there – a hole conveniently made by some smugglers, and through it we went. We were in France; still the woods. We followed a goat track which took us down into the valley. It was now getting dark. In the distance, we saw the village of Monthermé. Soon we were in the village, and as we entered, we took on the casual air of one of the villagers. Georges had friends in the village, and we were to spend the night there. We arrived at a cottage.[12]

Before entering the cottage, Georges asked his two female companions for their names, which so far he did not know. They gave him false names: Marie-Antoinette was Antoinette Duval, and Clémie was Henriette Dhust. They entered the cottage to see a woman in a light print dress, standing over a stove in a dingy room, which served as the kitchen and living room.

111

'Where are the potatoes?' the woman asked gruffly. Georges explained everything. The woman showed Marie-Antoinette and Clémie to a room which contained the only bed in the cottage. With no sheets, the girls slept in their clothes.

It was still dark when Georges woke them at 4 a.m., and they continued their journey through woods, climbed several hills and finally descended into the valley of the Meuse. At a cottage on the edge of the river, they found a friend of Georges's, who lent them his boat, as Clémie wrote:

> While we anxiously scanned the river up and down, Georges rowed us across; and on reaching the opposite bank he hid the boat under the overhanging branches of a tree, ready for our return journey. We were glad to reach the shelter of the woods again. With our arms held out in front of us to avoid low branches and to push aside the bushes, we continued our journey. It had rained overnight, and soon our shoes were wet through and our cloaks sodden. Suddenly we heard voices. False alarm! It was some woodcutters. From them we learned that there was a sentry ahead, and so we made a detour to avoid him.[13]

They reached the outskirts of Charleville. The girls tidied each other's hair and Georges cleaned their shoes. Charleville was full of German soldiers and the only way to avoid their attention was to blend in with the local people. With the help of a young local child, they were taken to the house of Abbé Bierry, whom they knew and believed would help them. Clémie dismissed Georges and arranged their rendezvous for eight o'clock that same evening for the return journey. It was still only 9 a.m., leaving them all day to meet with local contacts to set up the Charleville post.

The Abbé was surprised to see them and enquired after their families. He said that he could not play an active role in the network himself because of his busy religious duties, but Henri Domelier, the editor of the local newspaper, would help them.

Marie-Antoinette and Clémie met with Domelier, who told them that he wished they had come sooner as he had wanted to do something for his country for a very long time. He suggested that the girls pay a visit to Monsieur and Madame Grafetiaux who owned a large pharmacy in the town. Madame Grafetiaux provided them with a change of clothing and took them into a back sitting room, where, as Clémie recalled, 'we held a council of war'.

Marie-Antoinette and Clémie spent several hours with the couple and discussed the plans for the new train-watching post and recruitment of itinerant agents to report on all German divisions moving in and out of the region. It was agreed that Domelier would be the chief of the Charleville Platoon and Madame Grafetiaux his assistant. They were responsible for finding the necessary agents to mount four train-watching posts at Charleville that would control all German troop movements passing through in the direction of Sedan, Rethel, Hirson and Givet. A man called Paul Martin was enlisted as the courier from Charleville to Gedinne because he knew the route over the frontier so well, having already smuggled across refugees. He was to take the first batch of reports to Lucien Voltèche, a forester working for the White Lady in Gedinne. Voltèche found a suitable hiding place in the woods between Gedinne and Monthermé, where the reports could be deposited and collected. On their return to the Ardennes, Marie-Antoinette and Clémie arranged for a courier to operate from Gedinne to Conneux Castle.

Before the girls left on their return journey with Georges, Madame Grafetiaux prepared a substantial meal. After several exchanges of 'Good luck!' the girls were off with Georges towards the frontier. They took a different route by foot, which was easier for Georges to navigate in the dark night. They followed the course of the Meuse and passed through Nouzon. The route was not without its dangers as, at one point, they had to wade through the fast-flowing river to avoid a detachment of German troops (Georges had failed to find the place where he had hidden the boat). The round trip of sixty miles each way was accomplished in forty-seven hours, which was an incredible feat for two such young women.

A Second Mission

It took time before the first reports reached Thérèse at Conneux Castle from Charleville, because the recruitment of agents had taken Domelier and Madame Grafetiaux longer than expected. Nonetheless, it was a breakthrough when they finally arrived; they were the first reports to reach SIS from the Charleville region since the early part of the war. The reports were dispatched by Thérèse to Landau in Holland. A telegram of congratulations was sent to her on the quality of the information received.

For the first month, operations between Conneux Castle and Charleville flowed smoothly; but then the courier service broke down. The courier Lucien Voltèche went twice to the letter box in the woods and found no reports. There were no details for the leadership on what had gone wrong. Thérèse knew that the best way forward was to dispatch someone personally to Charleville to restart the post.

Clémie and Marie-Antoinette volunteered to undertake a second expedition.[14] They left Conneux Castle and arrived at Clémie's family estate in Gedinne to find a German air force unit billeted there. The girls befriended the non-commissioned officers and, from one of them, learned the details of a new German fighting plane. As this NCO was leaving for Charleville the following day to bring back supplies, they asked him for a lift in his truck, on the pretence that they were visiting relatives. He agreed to hide them in the back of the truck, knowing that any patrol would not search it. He drove them to the outskirts of Charleville and they agreed to meet him at the same place the next day.

Clémie and Marie-Antoinette recruited Louis Crépel, the mayor of Nouzon, who was also a close friend of Monsieur and Madame Grafetiaux. He travelled frequently to Charleville on business and he agreed to become the courier between Charleville and Nouzon. The section from Nouzon to Gedinne was undertaken by Lucien Voltèche. The mission was a success and communications were once again established.[15] The Charleville Platoon functioned intact from then until the Armistice in November 1918.

Thérèse de Radiguès once commented, 'The feeling of danger hanging over our heads night and day did not dishearten us, far from it, it seemed that the greater danger became, the more enchanting was our work.'[16]

Frontier Passages

The unexpected arrest on 26 January 1918 of Alexandre Neujean, the chief of the Belgian police in Liège and head of counter-espionage for the White Lady, was a reminder to the leadership that the network could be broken at any point. He was Chauvin's father-in-law and knew the inner workings of the leadership. He sent out coded messages from Namur prison which reassured Dewé and Chauvin that they had not been compromised.[17] His arrest had come about because Mathilde Bidlot, a courier who had helped French POWs to escape in 1915, had been arrested. Her work with POWs had only just come to the attention of the secret police in 1918 and, during their interrogations of her, it became apparent that she frequently visited Neujean. For this flimsy reason, Neujean was arrested.

Repeated interrogation of them both failed to reveal any espionage activities, despite Bidlot being a courier and the owner of a house in Nivelles where the network was experimenting with a new wireless sending set. She served a prison sentence for aiding French soldiers. Neujean, meanwhile, was deported to Germany. The loss of Neujean as head of counter-espionage was a heavy blow, because he had insider information on police raids in his role as chief of Belgian police in Liège.

Emile van Houdenhuyse, a courier, was arrested on 1 July 1918, while carrying some instructions in code from Brussels to Ghent, which were intended for the chief of the Ghent Platoon.[18] He was stopped and searched by two secret police officers, who found a rolled-up envelope in his possession. He gave them a cover story about how an unknown woman had walked up to him outside the Hôtel de Ville in Brussels and paid him 20 marks to deliver the envelope to her friend in Alost. The officers showed him the secret message, but he protested that he had no idea what was in the sealed envelope. The least he could hope for was a reduced sentence at his trial. In the end he was sentenced to ten years' hard labour. What the secret police had failed to discover was that Houdenhuyse was on his way to a letter box being run by a coachman from livery stables that were frequented by German officers who kept their horses there.

Another serious incident with the secret police occurred at Maeseyck, a frontier town between Belgium and Holland. For two years, two Dutchmen, Mr Tilman and his son, had been earning large sums of money by smuggling food and goods that were rationed in Holland into Belgium, where food was even scarcer. Every night they took a great risk as they rowed across the Meuse with their boat weighed down with provisions. It was a perfect route for the White Lady to smuggle out its reports to Holland. From March to October 1918, the White Lady gave the Tilmans their intelligence reports – around 250 sheets of thin tissue paper rolled up inside ten rolls – to take across in their boat. The frontier couriers started to complain about their bulkiness and the increasing difficulty of smuggling them into Holland without detection.

This route worked for seven months, until the secret police sent a plainclothes officer into the area. He noticed the boat crossings. One night, the officer stepped out of the shadows and arrested the Tilmans as they were unloading their contraband. The boats were searched and the reports were found. It was the secret police's largest ever haul; they realised that they had uncovered a major spy organisation and decided to focus on Liège, as Landau recalled: 'The city swarmed with secret agents. The White Lady had to be broken up at all costs. But this concentrated effort had come too late. Even if Dewé and Chauvin were caught now, the organization could still go on working. It had become a hydra which would have taken months or even years to destroy.'[19]

The White Lady continued until the Armistice without a single further arrest.

Post 49 and Intelligence

Many of the White Lady's intelligence reports do not appear to have survived or been declassified; however, some reports do exist for Post 49 and its flying squad, Post 249, dating from January to November 1918. They offer an insight into the kind of information this observation post sent back to British intelligence. They also indicate just how significant a region was being covered by Post 49, led by Thérèse de Radiguès. Large numbers of German troops and especially field artillery regiments passed through Ciney, near Conneux Castle, from January 1918 until the autumn.

One of the earliest reports from Post 49 in January gave details of German field artillery regiments moving into Ciney. Field Artillery Regiment 97 had arrived in Ciney from Ypres; their ammunition was depleted to just one cannon, and many of their soldiers were wounded. They continued in retreat. Later, Field Artillery Regiment 266 arrived in Ciney from Laon. The original intelligence report reads in translation:

> At Ciney, a horse station was set up, coming from Serbia . . . On the trucks and cars is painted a grenade. They lodged in Leignon, then left on Oct. 2 for Ciney. The trucks were empty and looked like new. They [the latter] would have come from Brussels and will go to the front.[20]

This information enabled British intelligence to establish which troops were in retreat, and which reinforcements were being sent in a particular direction on the front line – and was thus crucial in enabling Allied forces to prepare for fighting in those front-line areas. During spring 1918, the Germans began their last major offensive action, in which they moved vast numbers of troops by train, night and day, throughout occupied Belgium, northern France and Luxembourg. All German troop movements from more than fifty train-watching posts that passed through all junctions in Belgium were sent to the British Secret Service. A temporary reprieve in arrests meant that the White Lady could function at maximum efficiency just at a time when intelligence on the enemy was most needed.

Another report provided details that Field Artillery Regiment 46 had arrived in Ciney and a small airfield with two hangars was about to be built in Chacoux. It gave details of the arrival of new planes at other nearby airfields, and the column of the Field Artillery Regiment III in Falmagne and Falmignoul. It went on to say:

> This regiment was [last] here in May. It has since taken part in the battles of July 16 and 18; they had 130 killed and a large number of wounded; abandon almost all their cannons; the soldiers say that the lines of the horses were cut to save themselves . . . They must regroup here and believe they will stay only 15 days and return to Laon. It is said that the soldiers of Gemchenne are called to the military tribunal of Namur to explain the death of their leaders. The demoralization of the troops is extreme, they declare that they will not fight any more.[21]

During August and September 1918, there were reports from Post 49 of large-scale German losses of men and artillery, as well as precise details of logistical supplies and the army's kitchen being transported in wagons. The soldiers who were resting and regrouping spoke of waiting to make a new advance, of losses on the front line of infantry who had 'suffered enormously and are still at the front', and also of losses sustained by the German cavalry.[22]

A report in August gave information on the movement of Field Artillery Regiment 97, which was replenished by new soldiers from Germany, and by some who had recovered from previous injuries.[23] The soldiers spoke about how they travelled 30 to 40km a day and had already covered 200km in total. They were heading for the front line via Alsace; others were going to Russia and the Eastern Front. They had only enough ammunition for three months.

German soldiers of Field Artillery Regiment 63 had arrived in Ciney, having walked for two days on foot because of a train collision. Several were wounded. They were without guns, had sustained huge losses in the fighting and were described as extremely tired. There were signs of an army starting its retreat. German officers asked the local mayors how many men could be housed in their respective villages if the civilian population was to be evacuated; in total 180,000 troops would need to be accommodated.[24]

One report sent from Post 49 read:

Artillery troops arrived in the region during the last weekend and during the beginning of this one. They are rather demoralized and small in number . . . These troops have come from the Marne, the majority came by road, according to their statements. Here is what they [the German soldiers] say: 'We were ready to attack, when suddenly we were, at the same time, overflown by multitudes of enemy planes which strafed us, bombarded by an atrocious artillery fire; we only had time to flee, walking on heaps of dead and wounded of ours, it was appalling and frightening.'[25]

In a report coming from Post 249, information was given about the bridges across the Meuse being mined and about the installation of barbed wire some 500m behind the river.[26] This had been carried out by a civilian workforce.[27] The gun installations were deserted from Aiglemont to Lumes, in the Ardennes area of northern France. A munitions depot at Lumes was empty. This provided the White Lady leadership and SIS with indications that German forces had left that region.

German soldiers continued to arrive in September 1918. It was a war-weary army that was struggling physically and with morale. The soldiers asked the local people for a well-sealed room to be able to practise the use of gas.[28]

There were troop trains every day now, indicating a full-scale enemy army on the move. Their slow progress across Belgium was catalogued by the White Lady. These trains were travelling at a reduced speed due to the sheer volume of traffic on the lines.

Council of Female Leaders

During the final weeks of the war the White Lady leadership instructed its posts to send reports with precise details of the German armies in retreat. Just as those armies had originally been transported by train to the front lines, so too in retreat they would be moved back to Germany by train. But even though the army was withdrawing, it did not mean that the German secret police were any less of a threat.

Recent arrests indicated to the secret police that they had uncovered a major espionage network. The Germans threatened to deport the entire male population to Germany and an unknown destination.[29] It did not happen in the end, but Dewé and Chauvin could take no chances. They took the decision to appoint a reserve board or 'female council' that consisted solely of women who would take over the command of the White Lady if they themselves were arrested.[30] In addition, all battalions and companies of the network were asked to put women in place as reserve leaders. The main board of the White Lady would be taken over by Juliette Durieu, who had aided the breakout of Creusen and Fauquenot from prison, as commander; Thérèse de Radiguès as deputy commander; Laure Tandel as deputy commander should Radiguès be compromised; as well as Emma Weimerskirch, Marie Delcourt, and Julienne and Anne Demarteau.[31]

One of the leadership's dispatches in these final days mentions the women taking over and also provides instructions for the posts on what to do if the German army was in retreat, as was beginning to be evident in October 1918. It reads in translation:

Received your very interesting report for which we thank you. It is requested that you immediately set up a railroad post on the line furthest travelled by the [German] troops. Have the railway reports made according to the model received . . . Here are some special notes: in case of Armistice continue to work and send reports. If the men are removed the ladies must take the direction, so consequently initiate them into the service; stay [in post] as long as possible; in the event that one is cut off from all transmission one must continue to operate and hide the information. If the armies withdraw it is better to march with them to be able to continue to render service. We look forward to your reports, which today are of paramount importance.[32]

Instructions were issued by the leadership, once again reiterating the use of women: 'In the last moments of the occupation, it is expected that you will hold out for as long as possible at the post and will surround yourself with female agents from now on so that the service will continue to operate without any interruption in the event of the evacuation of the men. It will also be necessary to create more posts to the north as the Germans retreat.'[33]

The new railway posts were remunerated at between 400 and 500 francs per month. Intelligence reports were to continue to be transmitted to Dewé and Chauvin for as long as possible. Codenames of the new agents were to be sent encrypted in a message to the leadership in Liège. Even in the final stages of the war, the network's operations continued to be critical, as indicated in some final instructions: 'Advise everyone to be calm and cautious because your intelligence posts are currently the most important on the front and a halt in your operation would constitute a real disaster for the Allies.'[34]

Dewé later wrote:

The women have played a considerable role in our organization. Their intellectual assistance was absolutely essential to us. They have been mixed with all the manifestations of the life of our Body; they occupied the highest functions, as well as the most elementary. We have enshrined this situation in our internal organization, by placing them indifferently in all positions, and in our activity, by entrusting them with the most delicate and dangerous missions.[35]

The women displayed courage and heroism, and it is no exaggeration to state that SIS's network could not have functioned or succeeded without them.

Chapter 8
WE HAVE DONE OUR DUTY

By October 1918, the battles which had once raged on land, air and sea were reaching their final stages; only a month later, the Armistice was signed. In this final phase of the war, the importance of the White Lady did not diminish. Its agents sent eyewitness reports to British intelligence, telling of a German army in retreat and withdrawal back across Belgium and towards Germany. Detailed reports were sent to Landau. Particularly valuable were those from Thérèse de Radiguès's Post 49, which described the arrival of a large number of German troops in Ciney. The reports included details of the German regiments in retreat and tales from German soldiers on the state of the war. One German soldier described how they 'had to flee before the English on the night of September 28th, abandoning arms and cannons'.[1] These soldiers aspired to peace and said that many of their troops were resting behind the lines, and no longer wanted to be posted to the front. Information like this signified to British intelligence that morale was lacking, and affecting an army's willingness to fight.

War had taken a heavy toll on the Belgian people living under occupation. Agent Jeanne Cleve told a British intelligence officer that the population was destitute and starving, living mainly on cabbage and turnips.[2] She had not eaten a potato for fifteen months, nor any meat for almost two years. Many of the people of Charleroi were walking around the town barefoot and dressed in rags.

Agents in Rochefort and Jemelle reported how German officers had given orders for Belgian civilians to evacuate hotels, castles and schools in readiness to receive wounded German soldiers from the front lines. Other intelligence reports noted the locations of blown bridges, gun emplacements and mines, which regions had been evacuated by enemy troops, and where the German forces continued to resist by defending their positions. There were details too on the names of Belgian villages that had been looted and burned by an army in retreat. A report by Post 49 noted, 'On 13th [October] trains carrying French, English and American wounded came through Jemelle from ambulances in the vicinity of Charleville. The population was able to bring them food.'[3] Ten days later, medical staff started to arrive in ambulances at Rochefort from Charleville, Sedan and Rethel. Various German field artillery units continued to retreat and pass through Ciney, with their troops saying they were ready to surrender. There were other reports of forty-five German companies stationed around Charleville who mutinied and refused to leave for the front line. News of a demoralised German army in retreat was important information for British intelligence and the Allied commanders.

A total of 212 wounded German soldiers were brought from the front line to Dinant. Other reports from the White Lady observation posts noted the large numbers of men on the move, along with columns of horses, and the movement of Russian and German prisoners of war. The Germans were moving their heavy guns and 200 howitzers, which were towed by tractors from Charleville towards Nouzon. This was a German army in withdrawal. After four years of slaughter and bloodshed on the battlefields of Flanders, the war was nearing its end.

On 11 November 1918 the Armistice was signed and war was over. In towns and cities across Belgium, there were scenes of jubilation as crowds danced in the streets and sang the Belgian national anthem. In Liège, the centre of the White Lady's wartime espionage operations, there was celebration too. However, dangers still lurked under the surface from those trying to instigate political unrest. This was evident in the city of Seraing, in the province of Liège, where red flags hung in the streets amid an atmosphere of socialist revolution as workers went on a general strike. German forces were required by the terms of the Armistice to evacuate the occupied territories, including Belgium, within fourteen days. It was a monumental task to move the troops, equipment and wounded men back to Germany.

The agents paid a price for their operations with the White Lady. In total it was estimated that 1,200 secret service agents in France and Belgium had been imprisoned during the war.[4] Over 100 agents of the White Lady were shot by the Germans or died in prison.[5] More than 400 were condemned to death, but the sentences were commuted to penal service. Many of the women were taken to Siegburg prison in Germany, where they endured brutal interrogation, periods of solitary confinement and long sentences of hard labour. Their spirit of resistance did not diminish – they refused to make ammunition for use against the Allies, and were punished for it. They displayed extraordinary bravery, and even though they must have been terrified, they would not be intimidated by the occupation regime.

Jeanne Delwaide, who spent over a year in Siegburg prison, said, 'We have done our duty – as good British soldiers – our patient labour was not in vain.'[6] She was recognised after the war with the award of an MBE from the British.

For those men and women remaining active in the field behind the German lines, the security measures put in place by the Belgian leadership enabled the network to function very effectively until the end of the war, with relatively few other losses.

Unfinished Business

After the Armistice, the work of the White Lady was not yet done. It was required to continue to observe and report on the German armies in retreat across Belgium, to ensure those armies were in compliance with the terms of the Armistice. The observation posts reported on the troops evacuating from all previously occupied areas of Belgium and northern France. The roads were cluttered with columns of German transport and vehicles, horses and other animals, and the field kitchen of a once vast army. One report from Post 49 noted that the large-scale movement of equipment included on one occasion 110 horses and chariots, 900 sheep and 2,000 horned animals.[7] Late in November 1918, Post 49 made its final expedition to the border with its intelligence reports.[8]

At Conneux Castle, the occupying German officers had left. In their place came up to seventeen British officers from the liberating forces, who were quartered in the castle. After 16 November 1918 their numbers were increased by the arrival of officers from the 66th (2nd East Lancashire) Division who had seen fighting in the trenches in Flanders. After the Armistice, the division was stationed in the Namur region and some of its men were accommodated in five rooms set aside for them in Conneux Castle. Marie-Antoinette de Radiguès recalled how they socialised with the family, hung flags in celebration of the victory and attended a local dance.[9] Thérèse's friends, the Villermonts, also had British officers billeted in their castle.

The British officers were still in Conneux Castle for Christmas and New Year 1918/19. On Boxing Day, Major General Hugh Bethell, who commanded the division, was invited to lunch at the castle. In turn, he invited the family to a ball at Leignon on 2 January 1919, attended by eighty officers and five generals. Marie-Antoinette de Radiguès commented on how the women wore their pretty dresses for the occasion. 'The supper was exquisite,' she wrote. 'It was served by the officers and the orderlies: slices of foie gras, ham, paté then turkey, smoked meat, cakes of several kinds, chocolates, oranges and tangerines.'[10]

Her account offers a rare snapshot into joyous celebrations and the happy side of civilian life for these families in the aftermath of war, after four difficult years of suffering and occupation.

Landau Meets the Officers and Agents

On New Year's Day 1919, Dewé and Chauvin wrote to the leaders and agents to express their thanks and admiration for their work. One of these letters survives in the archive of the Tandel sisters, Laure and Louise, to whom Dewé and Chauvin wrote that their posts in the western part of Belgium were 'among the very best in the country'.[11]

As soon as it was safe to do so, Henry Landau crossed the border into Belgium to meet the men and women who had been the hidden faces of SIS's clandestine wartime operation. He had been communicating with this network and its members but, with the exception of Dewé, had never met any of its individuals face to face. He made his way to meet all the leaders and battalion and company commanders at an address that he had only committed to memory. It was, he later wrote, the most dramatic moment of his life:

> As I entered the room where they were gathered, Dewé and Chauvin rushed forward to greet me. I was overcome by their fervent expressions of welcome and loyalty. Quickly they introduced me to the others in the room. I found myself in the presence of a group of warm hearted, sincere, though somewhat austere people. There were three priests, and an equal number of women; the others were college professors, engineers, lawyers and members of the professional classes.[12]

There was one final task, and that was for Landau to make good on his promise to the Belgian leadership and agents to be recognised in a military capacity. He had originally told them that the British had agreed to their military status, women and men alike, but this was not true: Cumming knew nothing about it. The request was made trickier by the fact that women had no combatant role in the British army at that time, and therefore there was no mechanism by which they could be recognised or given awards. Landau could hardly admit to the White

Lady leadership and agents that he had lied to them three years earlier, so he kept quiet, working behind the scenes to inform Cumming and get his retrospective approval. He was hopeful that military status would be granted because the White Lady had delivered astonishing results for Cumming in the war. Regarding the women, Landau told Cumming that they should receive military awards as soldiers because 'they ran exactly the same risks as the men'.[13] In his words, they were 'as brave and efficient as the men' too.[14] Cumming agreed.

British intelligence honoured the request and more than 3,000 awards were given to the Belgian agents. Their names were published in the *London Gazette* in 1919. Lambrecht was posthumously awarded an OBE and received a mention in dispatches by Field Marshal Sir Douglas Haig. Walthère Dewé and Henri Chauvin were awarded a CBE, and Thérèse de Radiguès an OBE (later MBE) and the Knight's Cross of the Ordre de Léopold (1922). Marguerite and Marie-Antoinette de Radiguès received an MBE, and the Tandel sisters an OBE.

On 31 March 1919, Haig received the main commanders of the White Lady at Ham-sur-Heure-Nalinnes in the Belgian province of Hainaut, and thanked them for their weekly wartime intelligence reports. In his speech, he said that they had made a significant contribution to the success of military operations. In May 1919 the leaders were received by King Albert I of Belgium, who asked them to convey his congratulations to all members of the network and expressed the importance of their work. At a special ceremony in Liège on 31 January 1920, Major General Sir William Thwaites (Director of British Military Intelligence) conferred various awards on members of the White Lady on behalf of King George V. Many were also decorated by the French and Belgian governments.

The Organisation after the War

There was further important work to do in the immediate aftermath of the war. On 31 January 1919 Thérèse de Radiguès had been called to

Liège by Dewé, and in her absence from Conneux Castle, her husband and daughters continued to socialise with the British officers billeted there. Dewé wanted no remembrance or glory for himself for the clandestine wartime work, but felt it important to record the activities of the agents. Thérèse was tasked with organising all paperwork and files of the White Lady network that had been in the headquarters, and also creating a collection of testimonies from the agents and couriers.[15] She asked each of them to provide a typewritten account of their activities for the White Lady. These testimonies were typed in French, signed by the agents and then counter-signed by Thérèse as a witness. She oversaw the compilation and collation of all reports, which formed a substantial historic record of the organisation behind German lines during World War One. The archive is catalogued today under its original French name, La Dame Blanche, and is split between the IWM in London and the State Archives in Belgium.

From 1919 to 1922 a commission was established and chaired by Dewé.[16] It was to safeguard the official archive and make the necessary legal decisions on its status and future. Aside from Dewé, its members are known to have included Thérèse de Radiguès, Laure and Louise Tandel, Victor Moreau and Juliette Durieu, among others.[17] At a general meeting of the commission in Brussels on 7 February 1922, the president of the War Archives Commission of the Belgian State was in attendance. He was there to take possession of the archive and oversee its transfer to the Belgian state by no later than Easter 1923. It was agreed that the papers and documents in the archive would remain secret for at least thirty years. After that they would be released publicly, but with consideration to any documents of a confidential nature being retained for longer. A legal document to this effect was signed by members of the commission on the date of the meeting. The agreement was executed by Dewé on 28 April 1922 and the archives were formally transferred to the Belgian State Archives.

With the archives of the White Lady secure, members of the commission resumed their civilian lives. Dewé was offered a prominent post in the Belgian cabinet by Count Lippens, but it would mean moving from Liège to Brussels, and he decided instead on a quiet life in Liège with his wife and their four children. Dewé spent the inter-war years with his family and surrounded by his books, with time to enjoy some study. He was also viewed as a possible director of the Belgian Telegraph and Telephone Authority, but again, he did not wish to leave Liège. Dewé went on to work in restoring telecommunications in the province of Liège.[18]

Thérèse de Radiguès returned to her family life at Conneux Castle. All her sons survived the fighting; Louis, Carlos and Jean arrived back home on 29 November 1918. Xavier did not return to Conneux Castle until 1921 because he had signed up for six years of military service, and fought in the Congo and then Burundi (East Africa). Thérèse was widowed in 1927 and moved from Conneux Castle to 41 avenue de la Couronne, Ixelles in Brussels.

With duties finished in Holland, Landau was posted to Berlin as the British passport control officer – a cover for his work for SIS. He did not enjoy the job, due to administrative problems and competing Allied intelligence missions there.[19] With personal financial difficulties too, he resigned in 1920. In 1923 he immigrated to America, where he worked as a teacher. He died in Mexico on 20 May 1968.

Legacy of the White Lady

According to intelligence officer Sigismund Payne Best, the Germans never discovered the true scale of the SIS network in Belgium, northern France and Holland during World War One. Instead, they believed that the main sources of intelligence to the Allies came via pigeons carrying messages and men in hot air balloons.[20]

The achievements and legacy of the White Lady are underappreciated and, given its importance in securing vital information from behind the German lines, it should figure more in intelligence histories. It should be given due recognition and prominence for being the most successful network of the British Secret Service in Belgium in World War One.[21] It was said to have provided SIS with over 70 per cent of all intelligence gathered in the war from neutral countries, and a staggering 95 per cent of intelligence from occupied countries.[22] For instance, the recipient of all those reports, Cumming, wrote in July 1918 to the leaders of the White Lady:

> The work of your organisation accounts for 70 per cent of the intelligence obtained by all the Allied armies not merely through the Netherlands but through other neutral states as well . . . it is on you alone that the Allies depend to obtain intelligence on enemy movements in areas near the Front . . . the intelligence obtained by you is worth thousands of lives to Allied armies.[23]

Cumming's assessment might be accurate, but it and others like it should be tempered with the caveat that they may have been exaggerated in order to boost morale, or made by interested parties keen that their own involvement with the White Lady was put into the spotlight.

Nevertheless, it is an immense legacy. Importantly, much of the initiative and inspiration for this clandestine work came from the members themselves who, motivated by patriotism and their Roman Catholic faith, and with no formal training, developed a highly successful intelligence-gathering operation behind the German lines for the British Secret Service.

And we must not forget that the White Lady – La Dame Blanche – could not have succeeded without its predecessor, the Lambrecht Service. Even though it had consisted of only forty agents and a few observation posts, the Lambrecht Service laid the foundations for what was to follow in the Michelin Service and the White Lady. The leaders and agents continued after Lambrecht's execution, learned from their mistakes and picked up the pieces of a shattered network to begin again.

The symbolism of a ghostly white lady who hailed the end of the German ruling dynasty turned out to be true. The White Lady network delivered on its name. Through its intelligence operations, it did indeed help bring about the demise of the German occupation in Belgium, and the Kaiser's dynasty did not survive after 1918. The White Lady was a trailblazer, and established a model that would be resurrected in the next war.

1. An awe-inspiring memorial to the White Lady (La Dame Blanche) intelligence network of World War One and its leader Walthère Dewé. A finger to the lips in a 'hush' gesture, the figure is sculpted in white stone on the exterior wall of the Chapelle Saint-Maurice on a hilltop in Liège. The chapel is the last resting place of Dewé.

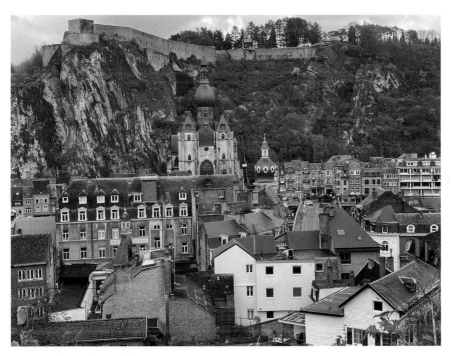

2. The city of Liège became the central operations location for the White Lady in World War One and the Clarence Service in World War Two. It was the birthplace of the first network's principal leaders, Dieudonné Lambrecht and his cousin Walthère Dewé.

3. Dieudonné Lambrecht, the founder in December 1914 of an intelligence network for the British behind the German lines in Belgium. He was its principal leader until shot by the Germans at the Fort de la Chartreuse, Liège, on 18 April 1916.

4. Walthère Dewé with his wife Dieudonnée. He took over as leader of the network after Lambrecht's execution. In 1917 the network was renamed La Dame Blanche. Dewé went on to lead the successor network, the Clarence Service, in World War Two.

5. An original map showing the regional sectors where each battalion and company of the White Lady operated across Belgium. It depicts the areas where agents were also sent into France, the Grand Duchy of Luxembourg and Germany to gather intelligence and spy on German forces.

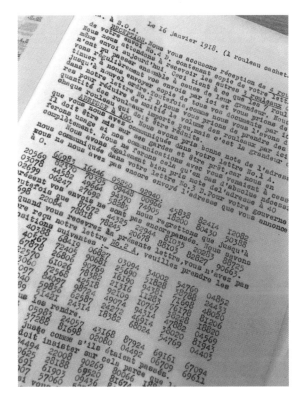

6. A code used by Post 49 of the White Lady in 1918. Messages were frequently written in code and smuggled over the border into Holland by couriers, where they were delivered to Richard Tinsley at the clandestine headquarters of the British Secret Service in Rotterdam.

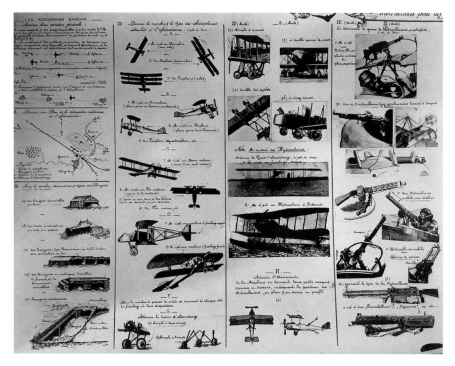

7. An example of an information sheet that was issued to the White Lady agents to enable them to identify military information on the ground – in this case, the types of German aircraft and how to identify hangars, some of which might have had an unusual construction to camouflage them.

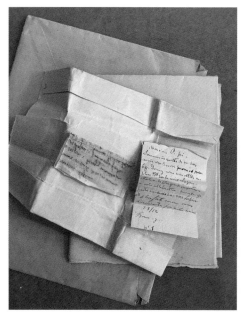

8. Original tiny messages written by hand. The messages were folded so small that they could be concealed inside ordinary objects, like the button of a jacket, a broom handle, a bicycle valve or in a clod of earth.

9. Thérèse de Radiguès, one of the leaders of the White Lady and Clarence Service. She founded Post 49 for the White Lady, which covered the Ardennes and southern Belgium, and sent agents into the Grand Duchy of Luxembourg.

10. Conneux Castle near Ciney. From here Thérèse de Radiguès secretly ran a sector of the White Lady while German officers were billeted in the castle. They did not suspect that she was working for the Allies. Her husband Henri and their daughters Marguerite and Marie-Antoinette operated as agents of the White Lady. Marguerite was later in a recruitment squad that consisted entirely of women whose role it was to expand the network.

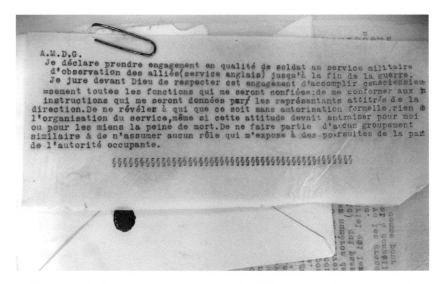

11. The oath of allegiance. On enlisting in the White Lady, the women and men swore an oath of loyalty in which they promised to 'enlist in the capacity of soldier in the Allied military observation service until the end of the war … [and] not to reveal anything concerning the organisation of the service, even if this stance should entail for me the penalty of death'. The members of the network were given military status and ranks.

12. The Boompjes, Rotterdam. From an office along here, Richard Tinsley worked as director of the Uranium Steamship Company. This was a cover for his real work for Mansfield Cumming, head of the British Secret Service. Rotterdam was the perfect base from which Tinsley and his intelligence officers could coordinate and run covert intelligence networks in and out of German-occupied Belgium, Germany and other European countries. Henry Landau arrived here in July 1916.

13. German intelligence headquarters in Rotterdam in World War One. German counter-espionage and Field Police units hunted down members of clandestine networks and resistance groups who were working for the Allies. Networks were broken up and their leaders arrested, along with couriers and agents. Some were shot by firing squad, while others faced long sentences in St Gilles prison in Brussels or Siegburg prison in Germany.

14. The Fort de la Chartreuse, Liège, where Lambrecht was shot on 18 April 1916. Other agents of the White Lady network were shot there after arrest by the Germans, including Elise Grandprez on 8 May 1917 and brothers Louis and Antony Collard on 18 July 1918. Elise had run a letter box and worked as a courier. Using invisible ink, she had written her secret reports on packing paper, box covers and bookplates.

15. Remnants today of the high-voltage electric fence which the Germans constructed along the Belgian–Dutch border in 1915. Dubbed 'the wire of death' by Belgians and the German army, its entire length was guarded by a combination of sentries, mounted patrols and police dogs. Passeurs and spies were undeterred by it and found ingenious ways to get through, some by using long rubber boots, sleeves and gloves to prevent themselves from being electrocuted.

16. Villa des Hirondelles at Wandre on the banks of the river Meuse. This house served as the regional secretariat for the White Lady and the final place for typing the regional intelligence reports before dispatch to Henry Landau in Holland. The site was the subject of a security breach in March 1918 and several members of the network were arrested.

C'est vivre, que mourir;
mourir alors qu'il fait bon vivre;
mourir pour le but de la vie,
qui est Dieu et sa Justice.

Louis Collard.

Janvier 1918.

Par amour pour Vous
et pour ma patrie, ô mon Dieu,
j'accepte avec joie et avec bonheur
le sacrifice que vous me demandez.

Antony Collard.

Le 17 juillet 1918.

17. Brothers Louis and Antony Collard, who successfully established a train-watching post on the strategic Longuyon–Sedan railway line and into occupied France. Their sector also penetrated the German-occupied Grand Duchy of Luxembourg to gather intelligence. They stayed at the Villa des Hirondelles and it was here that they were arrested by two members of the German Field Police in plainclothes. The brothers, who were only in their twenties, were shot at the Fort de la Chartreuse in July 1918.

18. Madame Jeanne Goeseels, who operated at the Villa des Hirondelles. She was arrested at the same time as the Collard brothers and endured brutal interrogations, but did not give away the names of those operating in the network. She was sentenced to death by the Germans, but this was commuted to imprisonment. She enlisted in the Clarence Service in World War Two.

19. Madame Tutiaux, who worked for the Paulin Jacquemin platoon of the White Lady in 1915. The platoon operated in the Ardennes and coordinated the clandestine missions of airmen who were landed into the region. Women made up approximately a third of the White Lady network and took the same risks as the men. They operated invisibly and in plain sight as agents, leaders of sections, couriers and keepers of safehouses.

20. The farm cottage of Monsieur and Madame Tutiaux, from which she operated as a courier. Her husband also worked for the White Lady and coordinated the intelligence reports for the region.

21. One of the safehouses used to hide agents of the White Lady. Many of the safehouses were run by the women.

22. Stewart Menzies, chief of SIS (MI6) from 1939 to 1952. It was during his time as 'C' that the Clarence Service operated in German-occupied Belgium. The Clarence Service was later described as 'the highest among the networks of military information of all occupied Europe'.

23. Hector Demarque, pseudonym 'André Clarence', was co-leader of the network with Walthère Dewé. He was recruited in May 1940, and the Clarence Service was named after him. He operated initially from Liège, where he recruited Belgian businessmen, and they used their contacts to gather industrial and economic intelligence on the German war machine. His house served as one of the network's many headquarters until its move to Brussels.

24. The seal of the Clarence Service used on official documents of the network. It depicts the legend of St George slaying the dragon in a triumph of good over evil. The symbolism mirrored the Clarence Service which, through its work, was defeating the occupying forces of the Nazi regime.

25. Ruth Clement Stowell, who worked with Frederick Jempson, the head of the Belgian desk at MI6 in London. She was an agent handler who trained agents, organised the parachute missions and dispatched agents into Belgium. She was also responsible for the Luxembourger agents and their secret missions into the Grand Duchy of Luxembourg. She is a prime example of the hitherto hidden roles of women in such covert operations. Luxembourg honoured her work by making her Chevalier of the Order of the Oaken Crown.

26. The certificate for Alice Matthys, who enlisted into the Clarence Service as agent number 3385. The certificate was given to all members on their enlistment. It depicts the primary work of the network – its parachute missions, clandestine radio communications and observation posts that watched the movement of German troops across the Belgian railways.

27. Walthère Dewé, pictured here with Marguerite de Radiguès and her nephew Yves at Château Ostin in 1942. It was one of the safe havens used by him. Dewé, who operated under the codename 'Cleveland', spent most of the war in hiding from the Gestapo.

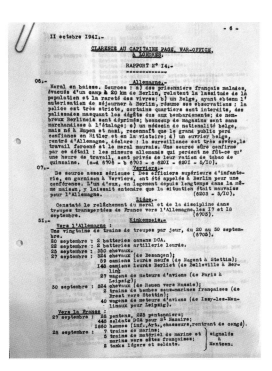

28. An intelligence report from the Clarence Service for Major Page (Frederick Jempson), dated 11 October 1941. It provides details of events on the ground as collected by the network's agents in Belgium and Germany.

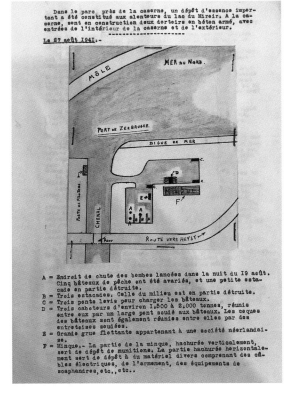

29. Another example of a Clarence Service report for Page from 1941, which includes a diagram of the port of Zeebrugge. These reports could each run to twenty or thirty pages and included hand-drawn diagrams, sketches and photographs of key sites behind the German lines.

30. The personal record for agent Francine Blondin ('Lulo'), who enlisted in the Clarence Service on 17 December 1943. It notes that in July–August 1944 she provided details of the location of V-1 installations in the region of Calais and Boulogne in northern France, and the transport of V-1s by train in the Arlon and Halanzy area of Belgium.

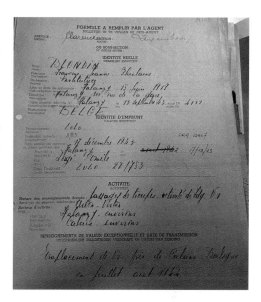

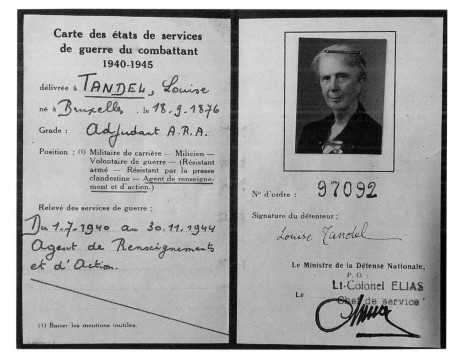

31. The identity card for Louise Tandel. She and her sister Laure both served in the White Lady and the Clarence Service. In World War One, Louise was manager at the head office of the White Lady in Brussels, from which she set up new observation posts west of the city. In World War Two, the sisters recruited agents and operated a safehouse and a place from which radio operators could transmit their messages.

32. *(left)* Thérèse de Radiguès, a founding member of the Clarence Service with Walthère Dewé in September 1939. In her seventies, she was the oldest member of the network. The main headquarters moved from Liège to her house in the Ixelles district of Brussels. She headed and ran a sector, and her agents, many of them women, went on to deliver V-weapon intelligence for the British Secret Service.

33. *(right)* Rue de la Brasserie, where Walthère Dewé was fatally shot on 14 January 1944 by a German officer while fleeing arrest, after leaving the house of Thérèse de Radiguès. On learning of his death, MI6 sent a telegram to the Clarence Service which read, 'The British and Belgian governments deeply moved by the death of our friend, an admirable patriot … [and] irreplaceable leader.'

34. *(left)* Memorial plaque to Walthère Dewé near the entrance to Chapelle Saint-Maurice, Liège. He is one of Belgium's greatest heroes and one who left an immense legacy in the history of MI6.

PART II
THE CLARENCE SERVICE

Chapter 9
THE CLARENCE SERVICE

On 3 September 1939, fifty-nine-year-old Walthère Dewé was contacted by a British Secret Service agent whose name was given as 'Daniel'. His real identity was never disclosed. That morning Britain had declared war on Nazi Germany after German forces invaded Poland two days earlier. War had increasingly been anticipated throughout the 1930s, especially after Germany expanded its territory and invaded Austria on 12 March 1938, annexing it the following day. The Sudetenland was taken for the Nazis in September that year, and then on 15 March 1939, Czechoslovakia was invaded, thus further expanding the borders of the Third Reich.

With Europe at war again, MI6 had an important mission for Dewé and the old guard of the White Lady. He was asked to establish an intelligence network in Belgium, just as he had in the last world war. It was to be the direct successor of the White Lady and modelled on it. As before, it was to have military status, but be modernised where necessary, and its spycraft would be modified for a new era.

By now the original leaders of the White Lady were in their sixties and seventies, but they had the expertise to successfully revive the old network. MI6 issued a directive to form two MI6 networks that came to be called Clarence and Mill. These two networks went on to gather an impressive volume of both operational and strategic intelligence from behind German lines. They succeeded precisely because they were the direct successors of the White Lady and operated with many of the same leaders.

Although Belgium was neutral in September 1939, 'Daniel' told Dewé that MI6 was under no illusion that Germany would not seize the country again. Preparations had to be made. The new network was to be formed immediately to act as an early-warning system across Europe. Its task was to gather information for MI6 on the situation in Belgium and its borders, as well as penetrating agents into Germany to collect intelligence. The network would be divided into sectors covering defined geographical areas or regions in which agents would operate. Each sector was established and overseen by a chief who also recruited agents, couriers and operators of safehouses for their sector, and themselves distributed and organised radio, arms and explosives.

On the same day that Dewé received the communication from 'Daniel', he contacted Thérèse de Radiguès, now seventy-four years old and living in Brussels. Her personal file notes that she was recruited on 3 September 1939 as agent number 4.[1] She was to be the oldest member of the network and its co-founder with Dewé. A woman already known for her indomitable spirit as the head of Post 49 in the previous war, she served in the rank of captain, using the pseudonym 'Madame Frère', and as the network developed, was placed in charge of the department for safehouses and meeting places. This involved arranging shelters for hiding agents who had been compromised, organising safe meeting places for the staff of the Directorate (the committee that ran the network), conducting negotiations for the network, ensuring the establishment of various posts for radio broadcasts, and liaising over suitable areas for parachute operations. She went on to run her own agents, among them her daughters Marguerite and Marie-Antoinette and son Jean.[2] Thérèse's grandson François de Radiguès comments, 'My grandmother was a strong character, fiercely patriotic, and a fearsome figure to be reckoned with.'[3]

Having mobilised Thérèse, Dewé then contacted Herman Chauvin and Father Jean Des Onays, his former co-leaders in the White Lady, and Arsène Scheurette. Together with Dewé and Thérèse, they formed an initial steering committee and reached out to other veterans of the White Lady. This led to the appointment of a board of directors and a committee.[4] The board consisted of eight members, nine from 1944, five of whom were women.[5] Their weekly meetings were held in Thérèse's house in Brussels.[6]

On 4 October 1939, Dewé was received by King Leopold III of Belgium to discuss the new clandestine network. Leopold told him that as head of state he had to comply with Belgian neutrality, which had been declared in 1936.[7] Nevertheless, he said to Dewé, 'When you leave here you are as free in your actions as when you arrived.'[8] This was a clear endorsement for the network to go ahead and work secretly on behalf of the country. SIS had already agreed with Dewé that if Belgium were occupied again, his network would work exclusively for SIS. There had been changes at SIS since the days of the White Lady. Hugh Sinclair had taken over from Cumming as chief in 1923. After Sinclair's death in November 1939, he was succeeded by Stewart Menzies, who served as 'C' for the duration of the war.

The network was initially known as Corps d'Observation Belge, and not until Hector Demarque joined it in 1940 was it renamed the Clarence Service. More about that later. Its unique circular seal, used by the Clarence Service on all its official documents, was of St George slaying the dragon. Two mottos were used on it: 'God and my Right' at the top, and 'Union makes Strength' at the bottom. It symbolised the strong union between an England at war and an enslaved Belgium.

An Early-Warning System

From the autumn of 1939 onwards the network made preparations to provide an early-warning signal of an imminent invasion. Observation posts at Malmédy, Eupen, Calamine and St Vith were set up to report on developments on the ground. The city of St Vith was an important post because it was located on Belgium's eastern border; from there it was possible to monitor and identify German troops if they started to amass near the frontier. In addition to the observation posts, and as part of that alert system, agents were regularly sent deep undercover into Nazi Germany to monitor events and report back on military installations, fighting units and equipment. During this early part of the war, they penetrated as far as Leipzig, Nuremberg, Cologne, Frankfurt and Bonn to monitor Germany's changing military strategy and whether its army was on the move and intended to expand further beyond Germany's borders.[9] Agents in another section of the network developed contacts at the German embassy and consulate in Belgium, to gain the confidence of German diplomats and surreptitiously pick up political and military information that could prove useful.[10]

Other early preparations by the Corps d'Observation Belge included setting up four locations for sending radio transmissions to SIS, at Liège, Brussels, Marche and Namur. The equipment, which included antennas and transmitters, was brought from England. 'Daniel' of SIS tested the ones at Liège and Marche, and possibly Brussels too (although this is not recorded). He did not have a chance to visit Namur. It was anticipated that young Belgian men would be away fighting and unable to operate the stations, so it was decided that the transmitting stations would be operated by women and the messages would be sent by them or by priests. With the emergency of war, it was also decided that there was no time to train them in the full Morse code alphabet; rather, they learned a simpler code for sending messages made up of groups of five digits.[11]

Around October 1939, Dewé received a visitor. He was a Dominican priest by the name of Father Paul and was none other than Edmond Amiable, one of Dewé's agents from the White Lady, who in 1917 had undertaken a mission to set up the Hirson Platoon. Amiable had been ordained into the priesthood and was ready to serve his country again. His experience with the White Lady proved valuable for this network, as he carried out intelligence missions between Fourmies and west of Sedan in the Ardennes region of Belgium, and along the French–Belgian border. He had a number of loyal friends from the days of the White Lady network whom he could recruit. In the autumn of 1939, 60 per cent of intelligence received by French commander Joseph Georges (French General Headquarters) came via Amiable's agents in Belgium.[12]

By late April 1940, signs of the German intention to invade Belgium were already being picked up by the small number of Dewé's agents involved in the early-warning system. Since January 1940, Dewé had been given messages, almost on a daily basis, with information that a German invasion would occur and it would be devastating. Immediately prior to the invasion, French troops in the Dinant–Longuyon region were reported by Dewé to be too weak to repel a German advance; and the German armies would be able to push through the Ardennes. These warnings were sent to the relevant Belgian, British and French authorities, which today raises unanswered questions of why the German advance was not halted and whether any measures could have prevented another German occupation.[13]

On 7 May 1940, André Mentior, a Liège industrialist and agent of the Clarence Service, was sent into Germany to spy on the movements of German troops on the Aachen–Cologne–Barmen–Wuppertal railway line and along other lines. He gathered the information, but found himself unexpectedly caught up in the movement of German troops for the invasion.[14]

German forces crossed the Belgian border on 10 May 1940 and began their advance across the country for a second time in less than twenty-six years. That same day, Mentior successfully crossed into Switzerland, taking with him information for the Belgian Legation in Berne. He was received there with disdain by the Belgian minister, who vented his anger to Mentior that Britain and France were dragging Belgium into another world war. Mentior was sent away. He arrived at the French embassy, received a warm reception and was given a visa to travel to Paris. He arrived in Paris with his information for French intelligence.

In the coming days, the Blitzkrieg ('lightning war') saw the rapid advance of German troops across Western Europe to occupy the Low Countries, the Grand Duchy of Luxembourg and much of France. Denmark and Norway had already been invaded the previous month. There had been other warnings coming from the network's observation posts. Just two days before the invasion, on 8 May 1940, Dewé's agents reported that the Germans were felling trees and destroying dense hedgerows along the Belgian frontier. All warnings appeared to fall on deaf ears within Belgian and French official circles.[15] It is not for this book to examine why the intelligence from Dewé's agents was apparently not acted upon, but the following day, 9 May, his network's headquarters was receiving hourly telephone reports that the army of the Third Reich was on the move – columns and columns of troops and equipment. That same day, MI6 man 'Daniel' arrived in Liège and met with Dewé. He received a first-hand account of the information from Dewé's agents on the German military advance. In spite of all Dewé's warnings in the weeks and months beforehand, it was too late. The invasion could no longer be prevented. The first German troops moved across the Belgian border hours later on 10 May 1940 and began nearly five years of occupation.

Thérèse de Radiguès's daughter Marguerite later described that day. She was married and living with her husband Georges Clérinx at Château Ostin, Villers-lez-Heest. She wrote:

On the morning of 10 May, we were awakened by the commotion of the artillerymen stationed in Ostin, then before five o'clock, our Thérèse came to us in a panic to tell us that the Germans had entered Belgium and Holland. After the first moment of disbelief, the radio confirmed the abominable truth. By nine o'clock, paratroopers had descended into the region, and our soldiers had dispersed into the countryside looking for them. The Boche planes were already flying over Ostin. Georges was walking around, wandering, to my great despair, with his nose in the air, and searching the sky with his binoculars.[16]

Marguerite went on to recount how she and others distributed cigarettes and coffee to Belgian soldiers in the nearby battery. The following evening, around 6 p.m., the castle was violently shaken by two strong explosions from bombs that had fallen in the woods behind the vegetable garden.[17] Marguerite and Georges soon had to flee the advancing German troops, leaving Ostin by car and staying in temporary places, and for a time in France. They were able to return to the castle before the end of July 1940, to find it had not been reduced to ruins. They lived there during the German occupation of Belgium and undertook clandestine operations for the network after it became the Clarence Service.

Many senior Belgian figures in authority had also fled to France or England with the advance of German forces. The Belgian government eventually went into exile in London; there, the Belgian Security Service worked with MI6 on clandestine operations. Again, MI6 was heavily reliant on intelligence from behind the German lines in Belgium. Dewé and thousands of courageous women and men of Belgium once again served their country whilst under the boot of the occupying forces.

German Occupation

By the evening of 12 May 1940, German forces had reached the river Meuse. It took a matter of days before the German army fully occupied the country, and this afforded Dewé and fellow engineers enough time to destroy the provincial telephone network. Dewé departed for Brussels and met with Colonel F.A. Blake (the British military attaché at the embassy) and with 'Daniel' for one last time. Colonel Blake soon found himself trapped behind enemy lines and made his own arduous secret escape from the country.[18]

British, Belgian and French troops were still holding a fortified region – the bridgehead of Antwerp, Koningshooikt, Louvain, Wavre and Gembloux. On 15 May, Dewé learned that orders had been given to blow up the service's central office in Brussels, but with Allied troops still holding the bridgehead, he felt this action to be premature. He made telephone contact with Major General Ernest Wiener, commander of the army divisions, and secured his permission for the central office not to be blown up.[19] The German army had not yet reached this area and Dewé believed that people should remain in their civilian posts. With his expertise as chief telegraphic engineer in Liège, he travelled to Ghent, Bruges and other northern regions to restore telecommunications where these had gone down and, with his colleagues, ensured that the Belgian army still had its means of communication. The Germans prepared to attack Belgian positions on the canal between Ghent and Terneuzen.

During the afternoon of 18 May 1940, and without an official mandate, Dewé sent a letter to the Belgian minister of communications, with a copy for the defence minister (both were then abroad), and informed them that he was taking over command of communications in the remaining unoccupied areas of Belgium.[20] He had instructed his agents to remain in their respective regions and they were now under his exclusive orders. In taking this action, Dewé revealed himself to be a practical, visionary leader who was prepared to do what was necessary to protect his country and who had the required technical expertise. Other key administrators of government departments had fled with the advancing German army, and so his action in taking over communications safeguarded those lines for the Belgian military units still defending the last unoccupied countryside and towns of Belgium.

On 22 May, Dewé was appointed chief of telegraph, telephone and radiotelegraph communications in the rank of general by Major General Ernest Wiener, Belgian chief of signal troops at General Headquarters. Just eight days later, Wiener was taken as a prisoner of war and transferred to a camp in Germany until 1945. As chief of communications, Dewé personally visited the areas under German bombardment to ensure his orders were being carried out, and 'managed to avoid the premature withdrawal of agents and the untimely destruction of the installations; and rendered invaluable services to the allied armies manoeuvring in Belgium by helping to maintain essential connections until the end'.[21]

On 28 May 1940, Belgium capitulated to German forces. The network's board immediately made its two transmitter stations in Brussels and Liège operational to enable messages to be sent to 'Daniel' at MI6 in London. The two stations operated until the end of January 1941, after which they went down and the connection with SIS was temporarily lost. Although transmissions were being received by SIS until January 1941, SIS had not sent any confirmation back on that or whether the information was useful. It was difficult not to receive any responses from SIS in this period, but Dewé was experienced enough to keep running the network along familiar lines.

For Dewé, there was an additional personal danger in this war. In 1934, Henry Landau, who had coordinated the White Lady for SIS from Holland, had published his memoirs in the United States. As the network's leader, Dewé's name appeared throughout the book. Copies were still available after the outbreak of war in Europe in September 1939. It could have serious consequences for Dewé, who could now be identified and was at risk of being hunted down by the Germans. As soon as German forces moved over the Belgian border in May 1940, Dewé had to go into hiding. He adopted the codename 'Cleveland' and carried on as the network's chief, operating from his various hiding places, and moving location every few days.[22]

But if Dewé was already compromised, why did MI6 go back to him? Because their relationship went back to the previous war, and Dewé was a highly experienced leader who had already operated in the same role for SIS/MI6 in the White Lady. After the outbreak of war on 3 September 1939, Germany did not occupy Belgium for another nine months; and although occupation was anticipated, it was not a foregone conclusion. And so why shouldn't MI6 call on Dewé to restart the network? He had the knowledge and the connections to bring together an initially small organisation at war's outbreak – one that would become much larger after May and June 1940.

The more pertinent question is, perhaps, why did Dewé decide to continue after the German occupation? He still took up the role of chief knowing that he would be facing all the added complications and danger. Available sources do not answer this, but it must be borne in mind that, just as with World War One, he believed it to be his patriotic, sacred duty as a Belgian and a Roman Catholic. And there was every chance that the Germans may never discover his hiding places.

Leading Figures

Within a week of being appointed chief of telegraph, telephone and radiotelegraph communications, Dewé got in touch with his old contacts in the trade. He recruited Jean-Louis Demarque ('Saturne'), a retired civil servant of the Telegraphic and Telephone Company, who enlisted as agent number 18 and, on 18 June 1940, created a section that concentrated activities in Brussels.[23] He headed the observation service and typing section, and oversaw safehouses in his sector. Later he recruited his brother, Georges, who set up locations from which the network's radio transmissions could be sent and provided storage space for documents.[24]

Jean Demarque's thirty-six-year-old son Hector was formally recruited on 28 May 1940, appointed a co-leader with Dewé of the whole network, and given the pseudonym 'André Clarence'.[25] The network, which had originally started under the name Corps d'Observation Belge, changed its name to the Clarence Service, named directly after Colonel Hector Demarque. Hector operated initially from Liège and recruited Belgian businessmen, who in turn used their contacts to gather industrial and economic intelligence about the German war machine. Demarque's house served as one of the network's many headquarters, as well as a hiding place for weapons and explosives and a safehouse for Belgians wanted by the enemy.

The Clarence Service soon moved its main headquarters from Liège to Brussels and operated primarily from the house of Thérèse de Radiguès in the Ixelles district, the same district where Hector and his father also lived. A second SIS network called Mill (see Chapter 11) was formed in 1941 and under the same directive from SIS as the Clarence Service. Both were the direct successors of the White Lady.

Enlistment in both networks was voluntary and an oath of loyalty was sworn, usually in front of Walthère Dewé and Thérèse de Radiguès. As with the White Lady in the previous war, military ranks were given to the agents. Thérèse's grandson François de Radiguès commented:

My grandmother spoke little about the war and kept all its memories in her heart, praying for the living and for the dead. Those who wanted to join the White Lady and later the Clarence Service had to take an oath on the Bible and the secularists did so by raising their right hand in front of my grandmother and Dewé. Pseudo-resistance fighters who wanted to monetise their information were systematically rejected. My grandmother centralised all information which was transmitted to the English.[26]

Female members of the board of directors were given their own assignments, often alongside their regular day job. Forty-five-year-old Rose Houyoux worked at the Royal Museum of Art and History. She was recruited to the Clarence Service on 28 May 1940, the seventh person to be enlisted, and was allocated the number 7.[27] She used the pseudonym 'Isabelle' and became a member of the secretarial section. Between May and August 1940, she was responsible for the encryption and transmission of Clarence Service messages from her home, sheltered compromised agents, and transported radios and mail around Brussels. She then became chief of the important Littoral sector that oversaw intelligence from the 65km-long coastline of Belgium. Her agents would later deliver intelligence on Hitler's secret weapon programme.

Violette Verhoogen ('Clotilde') was enlisted as agent number 2. She was curator at the Royal Museum of Art and History and a colleague of Rose. She received, coordinated and analysed all reports relating to traffic by rail, road and river.[28] She drafted the weekly traffic reports for the Clarence Service and led one of its sectors with her own agents – mainly women who ran the letter boxes in Brussels. She became head of the intelligence section responsible for the observation of the railways. Her elder sister Germaine was also recruited to this sector by Rose on 1 November 1941; among her many agents was Henri Lavachery, who ran a letter box and operated as a courier.[29] Another of her agents, Marthe van Bomberghen, had houses in Anvers and Brussels. She was recruited on 1 September 1940 and ran a letter box and acted as courier until the liberation of Belgium in September 1944.

Baroness Germaine de Menten was Dewé's personal secretary and secretary to the board. She was fluent in French, English and Italian and was recruited by Thérèse de Radiguès. Both women lived in the Ixelles district of Brussels and they were known to each other.[30] An aristocrat and the daughter of the first Belgian officer to be killed by the Germans in 1914, Germaine typed the weekly intelligence reports for London, and carried out many liaison assignments between Brussels and the heads of the local sectors of the Clarence Service. She operated under the pseudonyms 'Miss Picot' or 'Frédérique' and had a clandestine radio transmitter installed in her home for use by the radio operators.[31] She later ran a sub-sector of agents that brought in valuable V-weapon intelligence (see Chapter 15).

Dewé's immediate family was involved in the clandestine work: his wife, their daughters Marie and Madeleine and their son Jacques. The exception was the eldest son, also called Walthère, who had been taken prisoner by the Germans in May 1940. He remained in a German POW camp for the rest of the war.

Thirty-seven agents who had been in the White Lady readily joined the new network.[32] They included Franz Creusen, a member of the board of directors of the Clarence Service, who became one of the first agents to be arrested by the Gestapo in 1940.[33] He had already served twenty-three months in a German prison for his part in the White Lady in the last war and now he found himself incarcerated again, this time for fifty-six months in prison, before being transferred to a concentration camp. He was liberated in May 1945, along with Nicholas Feller, another agent who had been arrested in 1940.

The Tandel sisters joined the Clarence Service, having been central figures in the White Lady. Sixty-five-year-old Laure and sixty-three-year-old Louise enlisted in the network on 1 June 1940, among the earliest members, under new service numbers 14 and 15 respectively.[34] They both used the pseudonym 'Mademoiselle Latour', but with different first names. They lived together and used their home as a radiotelegraphic and radiotelephone transmission site. They undertook leadership roles and risked their lives in sheltering many parachutists who had been sent by MI6 (which was known to them as the 'Page Service').[35] The sisters were responsible for informing the Clarence Service committee as soon as parachutists had arrived safely in the country. They were affiliated to the General Services department of the Clarence Service and ensured that the chiefs, Dewé and Demarque, were able to keep in regular contact with their operatives.

The sisters personally enlisted other agents into the network; among them was Paul Janssens ('Pélissier'), whom they recruited in 1941. He served until liberation and headed the intelligence-gathering around St Ghislain. He worked as a civil servant at the shipping department of the Ministry of Public Works, and regularly provided information for the Clarence Service on inland shipping in Belgium and Germany, as well as details of the transport of material for enemy fortifications and airfields.[36]

As agent handlers, Laure and Louise received military intelligence from their various agents on German troop movements around Brussels and other regions of Belgium; on aerodromes and German air force activity; and on the movement of boats on canals. Both women were recommended for promotion to the rank of lieutenant.[37]

During the course of the war, in addition to officially recognised agents, there were other women and men who aided the Clarence Service. They are named in folders for each sector of the network, including the couriers and operators of safehouses and letter boxes.[38] Each folder, with the sector's leader written on the outside, contains individual forms (often only one or two pages) which give personal details, including name and address, date of birth, parents, civilian occupation, date of enlistment, network identity number, and their role (agent, courier, letter box). Often at the bottom of the first page there is a brief description of their contribution (e.g. V-1 installations around Calais) or their areas of operation (Brussels, coastal, Calais), or simply military and political intelligence. These personal notes were created as part of proposals to have them recognised as agents, but many of them did not receive that official designation. The form includes specific personal achievements that they carried out for the network, often handwritten at the bottom, rather than typed. These personal forms give us today effectively a database of the Clarence Service and all those who helped it.

From the SIS end, a 'Major Page of the War Office' coordinated with the Clarence Service under SIS's Belgian desk. The leaders of the Clarence Service did not know Page's real name, nor that it was the British Secret Service that was running its operations; which it did from 'Room 900 at the War Office'.[39] Over eighty years later, it has not been possible to establish the precise location of Room 900, which may have been in a requisitioned building near Whitehall or in MI6 headquarters at Broadway Buildings. Its whereabouts remain somewhat mysterious.

Major Page

'Major Page' was the cover name for Lieutenant Colonel Frederick John Jempson, who headed the Belgian section of MI6.[40] Dewé never knew his real name. From March 1941 until the liberation of Belgium in September 1944, all weekly reports from the Clarence Service were sent to 'Major Page' in London. These reports survive today in the Imperial War Museum.

Jempson was born in Battle, Sussex, in March 1894. He had little formal education and joined the Metropolitan Police on 25 May 1914, aged twenty; his previous occupation was listed as 'footman'.[41] He was released temporarily in 1918 to serve in the Artists Rifles and was discharged into the reserves as a private on 29 January 1919. He rejoined the police, serving as an ordinary policeman, and on one occasion accompanied a senior officer to arrest a suspected spy. The officer was impressed with Jempson and sent him across to Special Branch.[42] After the Artists Rifles, he had then served in the Spanish Civil War, spying on communist elements in Spain. As a result of his experiences, he was sent to Paris around 1935 and became fluent in French. By 1939, he was the logical choice to head the Belgian desk of MI6.[43]

Working with Jempson at MI6's Belgian desk was Lieutenant Ruth Clement Stowell. They were answerable directly to Claude Dansey, the deputy head of MI6 and the man said to hold the real power.[44] As well as coordinating with the Clarence Service from the London end, they oversaw agent operations into Belgium and Luxembourg.

Ruth Stowell

Ruth Clement Stowell (née Wright) is one of the hitherto unsung heroines of the Belgian operations. She was an agent handler who trained and organised the agents who were parachuted into Luxembourg on secret missions.[45] Her duties included liaison between MI6 in London and the intelligence networks in occupied Belgium and Luxembourg.[46] She was born in India in 1913. Her father worked in the district office for the Indian Civil Service and died a month before she was born. Her mother was a remarkable woman who realised that Ruth should be as independent as possible. She sent Ruth to Cheltenham Ladies' College, then to France. She was a natural linguist and learned French. Afterwards, she took a shorthand typist course in London, before marrying a cousin.

Ruth answered an advertisement in *The Times* that had been placed there by the Arabist author and traveller Freya Stark. In 1938, they travelled to Aden on a great journey; Ruth was to be Freya's assistant and write up her books. After a few months, Ruth and Freya had an argument and Ruth found herself without employment. She called at the British embassy in Yemen and asked for work. She was told there were no vacancies, but she could work in the codes and cypher section.

When war broke out in Europe, Ruth was sent back to England on a troopship, and was soon posted to Bletchley Park. Ruth was a linguist and after a couple of months her fluency in French became known, and she was invited by one of the Bletchley Park officers to meet his colleagues at the St Ermin's Hotel, near St James's Park, London. At that lunch, she was informed that there was a vacancy on the Belgian desk that also covered the Grand Duchy of Luxembourg, and this was when she joined Jempson to run the Clarence Service with him.

While working at MI6's Belgian desk, Jempson interviewed the Belgian nationals who would become agents, and Ruth prepared all their training and their missions ahead of being parachuted behind the German lines into Belgium and Luxembourg. Her son John Scarman comments, 'She ensured that the agents were kitted out correctly; their clothes with Belgian labels, and ensured they had a Belgian haircut before their mission. She was meticulous in her attention to detail and checked their watches, shoes, clothing and went over a strong cover story.'[47]

Ruth was also responsible for the Luxembourger agents who were being sent back on secret missions into Luxembourg. She organised their training and had total oversight of their missions behind the German lines. Her son John says, 'She had no training for the job; it was exhausting work, with a lot of tragedy. So often, she would have to stay up all day and night during an agent's mission to wait for news of its success.'[48]

The contributions of women like Ruth in agent-handling and intelligence operations have been largely undiscovered or under-reported in histories of the war. She was absolutely pivotal to the success of MI6's Belgian and Luxembourg operations, and now she can receive long-overdue public recognition for her part in the success of the Clarence Service from the MI6 end.

Belgian Intelligence

On the London side of the Belgian operations, a close working relationship existed between MI6 and the Sûreté de l'État, the Belgian intelligence service, which operated in exile from 38 Belgrave Square and was headed by Fernand Lepage. In general terms, Lepage liaised with Jempson and Stowell over Clarence Service agents, their missions and intelligence-gathering.[49] Another key figure at these headquarters was Lieutenant Jean Nicodème, chief of the Belgian section for transmissions and communications. He had been a prisoner of the Germans in 1940, escaped and made his way to England. He returned to occupied Belgium in December 1940, but decided not to stay. He and three others – a group nicknamed 'the wise men' – were smuggled out of the country. They were led across the line of the Somme, and then over the Belgian border by Jean North ('Joseph Dubar'), a brilliant leader and guide of Dewé's network. They crossed the unoccupied zone and arrived in Montpellier in the south of France, from where smugglers took them to the Pyrenees and across into Spain.

On arrival in England, Nicodème was taken first to the Belgian military base in Tenby in Wales, before being called to London by Lepage. Nicodème oversaw aspects of the Belgian Secret Service operations with MI6. He organised the training of agents in conjunction with MI6, personally saw agents off on their parachute missions, and demonstrated a concern for their fate. He was deeply affected by news of agents being lost in action.[50] He was engaged in overseeing the collection of intelligence, and collaborated with MI6 and oversaw the recruitment of men for intelligence sectors of Clarence or as radio operators. In this work he was aided by Serge Lebrun and Pierre Deschamps, who worked in his section. Correspondence between Nicodème and MI6 survives in declassified archives in Belgium, in which letters sent by MI6 are headed from Room 900 of the War Office.[51]

Many other resistance networks were operating in Belgium from 1940, including Zéro and Luc, led by Fernand Kerkhofs and Georges Leclercq respectively, but those are not the focus of this book. These two organisations were not the direct successors of any networks in World War One and could not draw on direct experience, unlike the leaders of the White Lady.

The Special Operations Executive (SOE) that operated out of Baker Street in London sent agents into Belgium, but this was a totally separate organisation from Clarence, and currently declassified files reveal no overlap between the two of them.[52] There was tension and bitter rivalry between MI6 and the Belgian section of SOE. MI6 did not share its information or operations with SOE, including its missions in Belgium. MI6 disliked SOE's modus operandi, which drew attention to clandestine activities by disrupting enemy communications and conducting sabotage behind enemy lines. These actions came disturbingly close sometimes to MI6's own discreet clandestine operations; often they provoked Gestapo raids in the areas where MI6 was operating. This brought with it the risk of both SOE and MI6 operations being compromised.

September 1940 to January 1941

Observation posts were set up across Belgium to gather information on the German army, its defences and military installations. Agents were dispatched into northern France, especially operating along the coastline, and had already been sent over the border into Germany. As the war progressed, they were sent deeper into Nazi Germany, again with the task of collecting information on Axis forces, military capability and new weaponry. The observation posts provided an extraordinary volume of detailed military intelligence across the war that will be covered in subsequent chapters. Between September 1940 and January 1941 Clarence was hampered by lack of funds, and initially had no guarantee of reimbursement from British intelligence if its agents used their own money. That would change during 1941.

One of the earliest MI6 missions into Belgium was carried out in September 1940 and called 'the Richard Mission'.[53] It was a mission in which Captain Jean Ducq, who was already known to Dewé, was dispatched to London with a numerical code (already agreed with 'Daniel') for communications between Clarence and SIS. He was also carrying fifteen pages of documents detailing the current military and economic understanding of the German forces. Rather than carry them on his person and risk them being found, the documents were photographed on Leica film, which was hidden in two tiny waterproof boxes.[54] The documents included suggestions for passwords and the names of places in Belgium in code. The contents were verbally communicated to Ducq, in case the waterproof boxes did not reach London. It took Ducq four months to arrive in the UK, having made a journey via Vichy France, Algeria and Morocco. He arrived in London in January 1941, by which time the content of the documents was already outdated.

An essential priority for MI6 was to re-establish radio transmissions with the Clarence Service. Jules Delruelle, an engineer operating under the codename 'Aristide', succeeded in doing so after a secret mission at the end of 1940.[55] Delruelle had been recruited by Dewé in Liège in September 1940 and given agent number 10. In the middle of December 1940 he left Belgium for Spain, having memorised thirty new codewords for MI6.[56] The network periodically changed its codes for security and these were committed to memory, not written down, and passed on to those who needed them.[57] Delruelle arrived at the British embassy in Madrid and successfully delivered the code to the military attaché, and secured a small amount of money for the Clarence Service before the main funds could be sent from London. It was because of this particular mission that a regular courier route was established from Belgium via Vichy France to Spain.[58]

Spain became an important route for clandestine activities between Belgium and London. Intelligence reports were smuggled via Lille, Paris, Bordeaux and down to Biarritz, then into Spain. Madame Blaise of the network was involved in part of this line as she took the reports and correspondence as far as Jura, where they were picked up by another courier and taken via the US ambassador in Switzerland to Vichy France, who dispatched it to London (the US was still officially neutral at this point, and did not enter the war until December 1941).[59] It was a long chain of events, but demonstrates the circuitous route that sometimes had to be taken to get information out of Belgium to London.

In addition to this, engineer Gérard de Burlet established another mail line to London through Spain. He met weekly with Dewé and Demarque to brief them on important intelligence and other matters of relevance to the network. He operated in the regions of Brabant and Liège, where he installed radio equipment, operated the radio, and couriered documents and radio equipment to wherever they were needed. This included taking mail and film on various occasions to Vichy France, then to Dax, from where it was sent to England. He recruited other technicians, all of whom provided valuable technical assistance to the network. One of them, Maurice van Gijsel, headed the photographic department of the Clarence Service and operated in and around Malines (Mechelen).[60] He undertook numerous activities; he was responsible for constructing and repairing the transmitting devices and installed antennas. He acted as a lookout during transmissions, as well as collecting military, political and economic intelligence.

Intelligence for MI6

According to the files currently available, during its operational period, the Clarence Service sent 872 radio messages and smuggled out more than 160 reports, including photographs, sketches and maps.[61] This material offers an overview of the information being provided to MI6 and includes photographs of key military sites, the coastline, ports and military installations, and positions suspected of being German radio communication sites. Reports covered all of this and more, comprising information on troop movements, identification of troops, munitions, weapons, location of factories and production, German communications and headquarters. Much of the photographic intelligence was sent to London as microfilms, hidden in a tiny box about the size of a matchbox and half the depth.

MI6 could not station intelligence officers in Paris or Rotterdam to receive the intelligence reports, as it had in World War One, because Holland and half of France were under German occupation by June

1940. Links had to come direct from England. Intelligence was smuggled back to Britain via the couriers who operated between Belgium, France and Spain. Eventually, ninety-two couriers operated along these routes.

As the new year dawned in 1941, direct radio contact between Clarence and London still had not been established. It was the most pressing concern. MI6 began to plan a number of top-secret missions that would see a number of Belgian parachutists leave from RAF Tempsford, Bedfordshire, in blind drops behind the German lines.[62] RAF Tempsford was the airfield where many SOE agents also left for their missions into occupied Europe.

The missions by the Belgian parachutists were to be a turning point in establishing direct contact between MI6 in London and Clarence headquarters.

Chapter 10
THE PARACHUTISTS

On the night of 12–13 January 1941, agent Jean Lamy ('Dewar') parachuted into Grandménil, near Manhay in the Ardennes.[1] He was the first of a number of operational agents to be dropped by MI6 into Belgium from the beginning of 1941.[2] Lamy's background as a ship's wireless operator was useful to the Clarence Service. Now, he brought with him a transceiver to enable Clarence to send and receive messages, and became Dewé's personal radio operator. His mission established the Clarence Service's first radio contact with MI6.

During the few weeks that he was operational for Clarence, Lamy transmitted 130 messages to London. He was convinced that his transceiver could not be detected, and in this he was naive. He used the equipment for long periods of time, which risked detection by the Germans. Sure enough, on 26 March 1941, the Gestapo raided his hiding place while he was carrying out a transmission. He broke off what he was doing and threw his codebook in the fire, but it was too late, and the secret police retrieved it. He was taken away, beaten up and horrifically tortured, then transferred to St Gilles prison. Threatened with his parents being killed if he did not transmit messages back to London on behalf of the Germans, he was coerced into transmitting around seventy-five messages to MI6 while under the enemy's control.

Lamy realised that the Gestapo must know his real identity and probably that of other agents, and so he warned London that he was transmitting under duress by deleting certain words in the transmissions. Twice he transmitted the word 'danger', but this was believed by London to be an error. During six months of intense interrogation and torture, Lamy did not betray the name of a single agent.[3]

On 10 January 1942, Lamy was condemned to death. But he was transferred to Germany the following month and survived the war. He returned home on 12 May 1945, dying a few years later as a result of his treatment in captivity.

Lamy's arrest was a disaster. It broke all radio contact between MI6 and the Clarence Service – something MI6 had tried to establish for nearly a year.

By May 1941, all other resistance networks in Belgium had collapsed, and would not be up and running again until 1942. The Clarence Service and Mill were the only MI6 intelligence networks still able to operate in the country.[4] The urgent priority for MI6 was to re-establish radio contact with Clarence.

Gestapo Raids

Lamy was not the only agent who suffered at the hands of the Germans. The network faced dangers, too, from the German Field Police and the Abwehr's counter-espionage section, which hunted down spies and operatives working for the Allies. Working for the Clarence Service was more dangerous than working for the White Lady in the last war because of the absolute brutality of the Gestapo. All agents knew that if they were arrested, they and their whole family would be tortured and executed. Dewé understood that not only agents but their families too were making a total commitment to the Clarence Service.

On 22 July 1941, the Gestapo mounted their first raid on Dewé's house. He was in hiding, and no compromising material was found. His wife Dieudonnée was interrogated but she gave nothing away.[5]

They returned in August 1941 and again in September and October. On each occasion, Dieudonnée stayed calm under pressure and did not give away the network, nor did she lose her nerve during long interrogations. She was quick-witted and gave the Gestapo false leads, which sent them on their way.

Dewé remained under suspicion and continued to lead the network in hiding, only appearing occasionally for meetings with his co-leader and other members of the board of directors. He moved around the countryside staying with reliable contacts, while recruiting agents and expanding the organisation. He rarely saw his beloved family during the conflict – a separation that pained him, but he knew that he had to do his patriotic duty.

Agent Marble

In July 1941, a new agent, Captain Paul Jacquemin ('Marble'), left England and was parachuted into the Ardennes to restore radio contact for MI6.[6] He was forty-two years old, having been born in 1898 in Lives, Belgium. He became a civil engineer, geologist and expert on mines. Just prior to the war he was working in Liège, and before that had spent time in Italy, Yugoslavia and Mozambique. He was injured on landing and arrived a couple of days later in Brussels, where he was sheltered by Monsieur Chapeau (director of a Belgian company).[7] Jacquemin's mission was to find a radio operator and set him up at an address from which he could send transmissions, then establish his own intelligence sector for Clarence.

Once he had recovered from the injury sustained during the jump, Jacquemin established himself at 29 rue de Toulouse in Brussels. He recruited a telegraph operator called Eugène Capron to transmit under his supervision from a villa in the town of La Louvière, in the Hainaut province of Belgium. Jacquemin's mission succeeded in restoring radio contact between Clarence and MI6 after the silence since Lamy's arrest.

Jacquemin travelled to familiar regions of Liège and Charleroi to identify sites for Allied bombing missions. Several times a week, his cousin, Rachel Machorot-Valat, couriered his messages to La Louvière for Capron to transmit to London. Between August and 8 October 1941, Capron transmitted thirty-seven messages to London.[8] Nine messages were sent back to him from MI6, one of which authorised the network to borrow funds, with a guarantee that the money would be reimbursed by London at the end of the war.

On 3 October the Germans raided Jacquemin's home in Brussels. No documents were found because these were being hidden by his cousin. But when Jacquemin returned home from Liège on the 15th, Gestapo officers were waiting for him. The transmission station at La Louvière had been discovered. Jacquemin was arrested and taken to St Gilles prison, where he suffered torture and interrogations until January 1942, when he was transferred to Germany. He gave nothing away. There was no news of his fate; MI6 received a cable from Clarence on 10 February 1942 which simply stated, 'Still no news from Marble.'[9]

A year later, there were rumours that Jacquemin had been shot.[10] This was confirmed to be true – he was shot in Germany in 1943.[11] It is thought that Capron, who had been captured during October 1941 (transmitting his last message to MI6 on the 8th), had given him away under torture.[12] Capron was executed in Essen on 28 May 1943.[13]

Despite the loss of her cousin, Rachel Machorot-Valat offered her services to the British.[14]

Agents Student and Frantz

On 8 September 1941, Paul Godenne ('Student') was dropped into France, near the Belgian border, with a code for Dewé's co-leader Hector Demarque and a radio transmitter for the network.[15]

Dewé and Demarque were unsure of Godenne, finding him nervous and potentially unstable. They became more concerned when he failed to locate and retrieve his parachute for two weeks, having hidden it on landing. Godenne handed over the wireless set and taught the new code to Hector, but decided not to stay in Belgium and went to unoccupied France to live with family. The new transmission station at 51 boulevard de la Cambre in Brussels was nevertheless named after him, and Demarque's wireless operator took over the codename 'Student'.

The content of cables between MI6 and its networks are rarely available to historians, either because they are in closed MI6 archives or because they have not survived. Some of the cables sent by 'Student' are among the 872 radio messages between the Clarence Service and MI6 surviving in the archives, and can provide an insight into the kind of information they relayed – which often pertained to practical matters in network operations. One example reads: 'Please excuse delay in resuming broadcasts interrupted fifteen November. Delay caused by need to equip various operating locations to track enemy spotting. To this end we will continually alternate locations of our broadcasts. Each place has received a name that we can give you if you deem it useful.'[16]

An extract from another cable from 'Student' gives insight into the spycraft being used: 'Could make micro-photographs if you could communicate to us composition of the sensitive layer for micro-photography. This information can I think be obtained at the following address *Watson and Sons Opticians* three hundred and thirteen High Holborn London.'[17]

In February 1942, Captain Nicodème wrote to 'Major Page' requesting more radio operators.[18] A number were sent into Belgium, but an officer and radio operator were also landed in unoccupied France to enable agent 'Sabot' to concentrate exclusively on intelligence-gathering.[19] On 3 March 1942, with the help of the Tandel sisters, parachutist Gérard Waucquez handed Demarque two radio transceivers.[20] The supply of intelligence improved in this period, such that by April 1942, the Air Ministry in London wrote that reports coming out of Belgium had 'added very considerably to the picture of the German night fighter organisations'.[21] The War Office commented on the accurate, comprehensive railway information being regularly provided by

MI6 sources, which 'very frequently provides important confirmation of troop movements reported by other agents'.[22]

On 28 May 1942, Joseph Leblique ('Frantz') was parachuted into Belgium. He is one of the very few parachutists whose names we know. Information about 'Frantz' is scant, as it is for the others, but it is important to place their names on record; more information about them, and others as yet unknown, may emerge with the continuing declassification of files. 'Frantz' brought with him a reserve code for the Clarence Service and details of undisclosed plans. While trying to return to England afterwards, he was arrested by the Germans.[23] He did not reveal anything during interrogation and the network remained unbroken.

Intelligence Reports

The weekly Clarence Service intelligence reports for this period cover an extraordinary amount of diverse information and provided MI6 with an impressive overview of the situation behind enemy lines.[24] Looking at specific examples of this kind of intelligence can provide an understanding of precisely what sort of information was being collected, where it was obtained, and the level of detail that was of interest to MI6.

Most reports average five to six full pages, and they give detailed information from various regions of Belgium about the German army, navy and air force, and the transportation of goods, fuel and resources along roads, canals and rail networks. They contain current information on military troops and their movements and equipment; ports, shipping, barges and the construction of U-boats; airfields, planes, ammunition depots, enemy parachutists, new weapons, transport and communications; and factories, production and tanks. As 1941 progressed, the Clarence agents started to append drawings, diagrams, maps and photographs of locations. Intelligence reports were coming in from Clarence agents who had been sent into Germany, and these gave similar details of military and industrial installations inside the country, including Berlin.[25]

The first extant Clarence Service report is dated 20 February 1941. Nothing survives among currently declassified files prior to this date. This first report provides an account of the considerable damage caused by the Royal Navy in its recent bombardment of Ostend, including details of the destruction of an enemy seaplane base and U-boat hangar there.[26] The report mentions that the airfield at Maele had been abandoned; six trains carrying bombs had arrived at the Maria-Aalter airfield; a main gasoline depot was located along the railway line between Ghent and Zelzate; and there was considerable activity at the airfields of Wevelgem and Poperinghe in the construction of new shelters. This kind of information provided the Allies with key military targets for their bombing missions.

In the second report, dated 6 March 1941, there was confirmation that the Maele airfield near Bruges would soon be back in operation.[27] The enemy planned to use Condor aircraft in an offensive against Britain. On the Wevelgem line, south-west of Courtrai, there were sheds camouflaged with mesh, which stored a large stock of incendiary bombs. A secret meeting was held there on 28 February from midnight until 4 a.m. Sixteen new hangars were seen on the eastern edge of the railway line and five running along a farm on the Brussels–Liège line. The construction of new sheds and hangars was underway at Brunthen, near St Trond. There was intelligence that seventy-three heavy German bombers were due to arrive in April. On 27 February, Clarence Service agents had seen a significant number of German infantry troop movements between Termonde, a village in East Flanders, and Malines, a city between Brussels and Antwerp.

By mid-March 1941 information was sent to London by the Clarence Service that the headquarters of Luftwaffe command was located in the Residence Palace, rue de la Loi in Brussels, and this headquarters was to move to an unknown destination within three weeks. The headquarters for aviation transportation of troops was identified on the same street at number 75. A 4km-long column of cavalry, infantry, weapons, artillery, twelve anti-aircraft guns, 150 howitzers and approximately 2,400 men was observed on 15 March, all heading from Tervuren (a Flemish town about 30km from Brussels) towards the city of Tienen.

As in the previous war, observation posts provided valuable military intelligence about the railway network and the troops being moved, giving an insight into the next offensive on a particular part of the front line. Between 26 February and 4 March 1941, 120 trains were counted along the Namur–Charleroi line, all heading for Namur and carrying rolling stock, cars, trucks, closed cattle wagons and food supplies. Around sixty-five trains passed through from 5 March, most of them carrying guns and anti-aircraft cannon. The following day, there was a report that two wagons loaded with 2m-long torpedoes had left Gusselies, near Charleroi, heading in the direction of Tamines, in the province of Namur. Approximately 9km north of Brussels, tank wagons carrying gasoline had been seen, and 8km west of Ghent, there was a large deposit of munitions in the woods. Its precise location was given in the report.

Clarence Service agents operating in Germany sent back details of gas depots located in the centre of Nuremberg; these occupied the entire length of a street.[28] It was noted that 98km north-east of Berlin there was a POW camp holding only Belgian prisoners. Other intelligence reports said that Hitler intended to withdraw the majority of his troops behind the Siegfried Line and maintain only a thin line of troops in Belgium. His aim in doing so was to provoke a British attack and draw British troops into the region, so his forces could then launch a surprise lightning strike on them.[29]

According to German naval officers, Rotterdam was their largest construction and repair centre in spring 1941, but owing to congestion of ships in all the shipyards they were looking for space elsewhere (places like Ostend, Bruges and Ghent).[30] With this information Clarence Service agents could report back on when or whether ship repairs expanded to those ports. Agents provided feedback that the Allied bombardment of the port of Wilhelmshaven between 16 and 23 March

1941 had been effective. Germany was still in negotiations with the USSR to obtain wheat for Belgium. The difficulties were said to be great because Germany reserved 40 per cent of the quota of cereals for itself. Russians demanded the supply of Belgian machinery and tools but Germany refused to give the raw materials necessary for their production and construction.[31]

Industrial and economic intelligence was collected. The directorate of Belgian Railways had refused a German company, Siemens, an order for the telephone installations at the Belgian stations. The reason given was preference for a Belgian firm.[32] There were reports of a mutiny of German soldiers in a house at Tubize on 15 March 1941.[33] The information was precise: they had left early in the morning for a training exercise in the countryside, but had been given meagre rations at breakfast and the previous day. They returned to the same paltry food in the evening and became violent towards their superiors. The latter brought in the German police, and the soldiers reacted by throwing hand grenades. One officer and an NCO were killed, several soldiers were injured and the premises was damaged. This serious incident led to the imprisonment of the mutineers.

A few days prior to this report, Clarence Service agents had learned that a Union flag had been raised in defiance at the top of a large 40m-high rock called La Chandelle de Chaleux, near Dinant. The location was inaccessible except to experienced mountaineers. The Germans were unable to climb it, and had to resort to tearing up the flag with their machine-gun fire. A few days later, on the night of 29–30 March, an English flag was hoisted at the top of Collegiate Church in Dinant. At 8 a.m. the next morning the Germans called on firefighters to have it removed. Twenty-eight civilian hostages were taken.

Voluminous quantities of similar intelligence continued to flow from the agents. Reports became gradually longer and with more annexes of illustrations and diagrams of sites mentioned in the reports, to provide an astonishing level of pictorial detail.

Summer and Autumn 1941

By August 1941 agents were picking up rumours that an invasion of England would be mounted with the support of German paratroopers.[34] Preparations for it were underway, with 5,000 paratroopers arriving in Namur from different areas of Germany. Buildings were being prepared to accommodate them. From another agent in Liège, there were details of over 2,000 new German recruits being trained in the Ardennes. Agent Clotilde reported on the large movement of troops by road for two days from France towards Charleroi.[35] It is rare for the agent who has supplied the intelligence to be named in a report.

The agents provided ongoing accounts of Allied aircraft that had been shot down, including news of English planes brought down over Liège on the night of 5–6 August 1941.[36] The pilots were buried secretly the next day at dawn. A bomber was shot down by enemy fighter planes near Marche-en-Famenne, in the Belgian province of Luxembourg. Three crew died, one escaped and ran off, and two, including a colonel, were taken in and saved by Clarence Service agents.[37] Another English plane was shot down near St Trend. One airman was injured and taken prisoner, while the others escaped to Liège. There were further details of aircraft shot down elsewhere in the Namur province, with confirmation that the aircrew had been buried locally.

New details were provided on the construction of U-boats in Hamburg, as well as boats being painted. The enemy had installed an anti-aircraft barrage along the line of Mons–Charleroi–Bierwart and Maastricht – precise locations of these were provided by the agents. They observed the gradual transport of troops from Flanders and Pas-de-Calais across several months, mainly by sea along the coast from Dutch ports and using Canal Albert. They discovered steelworks at Quiévrain and foundries in La Croyère, near La Louvière; these were the Germans' main production sites for automatic weapons. There were detailed drawings of enemy defences and installations along the Belgian coast between Knokke-Zoute and Zeebrugge.[38] One agent provided details of the thickness of reinforced concrete, the number of cannons mounted along the wall, the billets of artillery officers, supply stores, repair workshops for cannons and guns, and stores for engineering equipment. A diagram in this report indicated camouflaged hangars and munitions depots at the Zeute aviation field. There was a workshop for aircraft repairs hidden in the woods.

During the summer of 1941 there were almost daily reports of military activity at Zeebrugge and Ostend, including the movement of boats, the launch of two bombs which landed in the sea, the location of ten armed boats at moorings, and news of a tanker loaded with 3,000 tons of fuel which was then unloaded into gasoline tanks. In Ostend on 23 July, six U-boats, armed trawlers, a destroyer, small cargo ships and anti-aircraft boats were in for repairs. These details helped to keep track of enemy losses and damage to their naval capability. Another large tanker entered the port of Zeebrugge on 1 August. Subsequent reports continued to give lots of details on defences, enemy movements, boats, the location of guns and depots, the loss of Allied aircraft, enemy naval troops and fortifications by the enemy. Details were provided on the defences of Brest along the French coast: shelters with 2m-thick concrete roofs led down to the harbour.[39] These concrete structures were camouflaged with grass. In the harbour, minelayers were very actively at work.

On the night of 31 August–1 September, two British airmen, Sergeant Leonard Arthur Warburton and Sergeant John William Hutton, were shot down in Hasselt. They were taken in by local people, moved to Brussels by an agent, handed over to the Comet Line, and were making their way back to England. The other personnel in the aircraft were safe, but their whereabouts were unknown. Scattered throughout the reports are details of British aircraft losses, and crew who had survived being shot down. Many Belgians gave them shelter and smuggled them on to the Comet escape line in Brussels.

Occasionally the network's agents brought news of the fighting on the Russian front. German forces had invaded the USSR in June 1941, bringing the Soviet Union to the side of the Allies. The United States' entry into the war in December 1941 was still almost six months away. A Clarence Service report noted that 'according to a reliable source, the losses suffered by Germany in Russia preclude an end to its Russian campaign during 1941. With a poorly prepared winter campaign, Germany could not resume an offensive until Spring 1942 and in military circles it is believed that Germany could not invade England before 1944.'[40] This is important data because the year previously Britain had been on high alert over a possible German invasion. This intelligence supported British views that Germany was increasingly unable to invade England because its resources were heavily committed on a second front.

The train and road networks continued to be a valuable source of information. During the last week of August 1941, a convoy of horse artillery came from Normandy on the Mauberge–Mons–Charleroi–Namur roads.[41] The infantrymen were described as tired. On 16 September, a heavy anti-aircraft train, consisting of twenty-one wagons of equipment and 160 young German soldiers, headed for St Nazaire, a fortified harbour on the French west coast. In the week immediately prior to this, a total of 120 troop trains moved across Germany with arms and equipment. The new young recruits from these trains were stationed in Belgium and northern France. Heading from Mentzen to Germany on 17 September 1941 were four trains with aircraft equipment and parts, and in the following days, infantry trains, vast quantities of ammunition, and fourteen trains transporting tanks, planes and trucks.

A continuous stream of information continued on the enemy's construction of runways at aerodromes, aircraft hangars disguised as farms, munitions depots and planes that had been identified in various locations. By the end of September, it was being reported that twenty trains a day were moving towards Germany, with heavy artillery batteries, 350 horses and fifty-nine new heavy trucks heading for Stettin, for example.[42] A transport of 324 horses moved from Rouen to Russia for fighting on the Russian front, and by early October reinforcements were arriving in France: 500 soldiers were sent to St Nazaire, and 1,860 infantrymen returned from leave for stations in France. More German soldiers were moved into Namur, Liège and Luxembourg. All this is only a tiny snapshot of the volumes of information being sent to London by the Clarence Service. This was a vast army constantly on the move.

From September 1941, another SIS network was formed directly out of the Clarence Service and using personnel who were already in the network. It worked in parallel with Clarence as a sister SIS network, but was run independently of it. It was much smaller, having a total of ninety-four recognised agents.[43] It too gathered intelligence on the railways and German military capability, and provided information on German defences along coastal regions. It was overseen from the SIS end by 'Major Page' and Ruth Clement Stowell at the Belgian desk. Although not stated in the available files, it is highly probable that it could have continued, increased its agents, and taken over if the Clarence Service was compromised and had to cease operating.

Its name was Mill.

Chapter 11
MILL

Captain Adrien Marquet was older than most Clarence Service agents when at forty-eight years old he was dropped by plane, near Cerfontaine, in the province of Namur, on the night of 12–13 August 1941. He was given the codename 'Mill' and he was to establish a new network which would be named after him. His companion, radio operator Lieutenant René Clippe ('Millstone'), broke both of his ankles upon landing.[1] Marquet hid him and went for help, approaching a local farmer, Léopold Revelart, with a cover story that their vehicle had been involved in an accident and his friend was hurt. Revelart sheltered them and he himself was shortly recruited to Mill. Nearly 1,500 men and women joined as agents and couriers of Mill and collected intelligence for SIS.[2] The organisation quickly expanded right across Belgium and watched the enemy's railway network.

Mill covered the whole of Belgium and its frontier regions, as well as France, Holland and the Grand Duchy of Luxembourg.[3] Mill sent thousands of pages of reports to London, encompassing military intelligence across coastal and inland defences; the movement of special German troops; the German communications network; military installations and anti-aircraft positions; the movement of troops and goods by rail, road and water; and the location of ammunition dumps and fuel depots. Reports also outlined details on aerodromes and types of aircraft, including single-engine fighters, twin-engine bombing planes, and the number of raids seen leaving the airfield.

From the files of individual agents, we know that Mill provided precise information on general activities right across the Belgian rail network, details of suspected spies and traitors, and updates on Allied sabotage operations.[4] It collected the same kind of information as the Clarence Service across the rail network and elsewhere behind the German lines, with radio transmissions reporting on the number of wagons on trains, Axis troop movements, what trains were carrying and the direction of travel.[5] The quality of military intelligence transmitted by weekly reports was said to be always excellent.[6]

Marquet and Clippe

Marquet had begun his wartime career as an agent of the Clarence Service under the pseudonym 'Parent', recruited by agent Anatole Gobeaux in 1939; the latter was a veteran of the White Lady.[7] Marquet was originally from Liège, but had lived in Charleroi, then in Brussels for twenty years. He was a fervent anti-Nazi and staunch patriot, and having worked for a short time in the Clarence Service, he left for England in the spring of 1940, where he volunteered for special missions and was taken up by SIS. He was an electrician and engineer by profession, with valuable technical skills for a mission back inside occupied Belgium.

Thirty-four-year-old Clippe was married with two children, an expert in Morse code who, prior to his recruitment by SIS in May 1941, operated from the Evere airfield, Brussels. He was evacuated in summer 1940 and served as a wireless operator on Belgian ships until he was recruited by SIS. He established the first wireless communications between Mill and London on 28 September 1941. The month after Marquet and Clippe landed in Belgium, the Clarence Service transmitted a message to Page at the War Office:

On 7 September we received a visit from Mill who arrived safely around 12th [August] with his pianist [codename for radio operator] and two pianos [radio transmitters]. We regret that neither of these two pianos is for us. We strongly urge that we be provided with two similar instruments with or without an operator as soon as possible. We have instructed Marble to make you certain proposals on the subject. We would like to point out that Mill and Marble have presented themselves here with an old password. New codewords sent back.[8]

SIS knew that Marquet and Clippe's mission had succeeded. They went on to recruit agents, couriers and people to run safehouses and letter boxes. A network of dedicated and courageous couriers took information across the country and over the border, many of whom were women.[9]

Telecommunications

Mill used the services of seven radio operators.[10] Mill's role in telecommunications with SIS in London led to the engagement of specialised teams to develop a unique long-distance transmission system. A report later stated that it was 'one of the rare networks that used specialised devices to transmit intelligence to London by phonics'.[11] Mill was one of the earliest clandestine networks to use such devices – no specific technical details are provided in the files on them.

A major triumph by Mill was the setting up of a clandestine telecommunications network in a disused station in rue de Louvain in the heart of Brussels, codenamed 'Centrale'. It was set up by Marquet and assisted by René Clippe, Hervé Close and Jean Denis, a chief inspector of the SNCB (Belgian State Railways). Although the technical details are still undisclosed, secret listening equipment was installed on the telephone lines of the SNCB. It captured the transmissions of all German orders concerning the movements of troops and equipment across the railways, without the Germans ever suspecting that their communications had been compromised. In effect, this gave Mill a timetable of all enemy railway transport in real time. It meant that every movement of German troops was known forty-eight hours before it happened. It was real-time intelligence. Hundreds of messages were telegraphed by Mill to SIS in London, with Clippe alone sending 600 messages. This achievement prompted Marquet's promotion to the rank of major on 1 September 1942. It was said to be 'one of the most brilliant achievements of the secret war'.[12]

The recruitment of Jean Denis for major railway intelligence work demonstrated huge foresight on the part of Marquet. As early as 15 September 1940, Denis established a sector of agents to watch the borders and a larger sector for observation of the railways, working largely on his own for several months. He recruited and trained agents and organised a nascent network until he met Marquet and joined Mill. Denis was a technical advisor in civilian life, a major contributor to Mill's railway intelligence picture.

In one account, he wrote, 'From around September 1941, the records of all military rail traffic collected by us, controlled and centralized, were transmitted to Mill. Surveillance was exercised on all rail lines and at all French–Belgian border points from Quiévrain to Mariembourg.'[13] He established a secret office in Brussels where remote radio broadcasts were carried out, without being tracked. From September 1942 the Namur–Givet line was taken under his sector; by this point he was able to control and centralise all reports on German military traffic from Germany to France and vice versa, as well as internal traffic in Belgium. Other information collected for Mill included updated plans and weekly reports on the Florennes airfield; plans of the emergency runways at Cerfontaine, Mettet and Erpion; and plans and photos of various military installations in Entre-Sambre and Meuse, German communication posts, and aircraft tracking centres.

As well as setting up 'Centrale', Denis established a secret office in Brussels in April 1944 where remote radio broadcasts were carried out, without being tracked, and where he ensured a telephone connection with Mill's main provincial agents. He proved to be one of the most valuable members of Mill.

Agents

Women were as essential to Mill as they were to the Clarence Service. Again, they became heads of sectors, operated as couriers and ran letter boxes.

Forty-three-year-old primary school teacher Adjutant Yvonne Collet was recruited to Mill in September 1941 and operated the letter box for Mill headquarters.[14] She established a letter box at her home in Ixelles, to centralise information and collate letters from the couriers. Material arrived daily for her letter box until she was betrayed and arrested on 29 October 1943. She was deported to Germany and died in Ravensbrück concentration camp. Her personal agent file describes her as courageous.

Forty-year-old Germaine Crabbe was a primary school teacher working for Mill out of Brussels.[15] She joined at the same time as Collet and operated as a courier of intelligence reports until her husband's arrest and deportation to Germany. She was the primary courier between the main letter box in Brussels and the network's sectors.

The work of Mill's agents could overlap with the escape lines, in particular the Comet Line that ran out of Brussels. Numa Bouté ('M.2'), a school inspector, was chief of a sector for Mill around Antwerp, Hainaut and Tournai. He went on to expand it to parts of France that bordered Belgium. While working for Mill, he helped Allied escapers and evaders and sent radio messages to London of the airmen shot down in his area. He collected evaders from the home of Joseph Dumont in Leuze and escorted them to Baroness Jamblinne de Meux in Brussels.[16] The baroness was arrested by the Gestapo and may have talked during her intense interrogation, because Bouté himself was arrested on 29 October 1943. He was deported to Germany on 11 March 1944, with no trial, and he died in Elrich camp in March 1945. Bouté's deputy, Germain Wallez ('M.3'), a tax inspector, took over as head of the sector. By now the sector was conducting surveillance of roads through Chapelle to Brussels.[17] Wallez's personal file includes lists of all the agents and couriers in his sector.[18]

Another agent, Marius Salveniac ('Vigor'), created a sub-section of Mill that concentrated information on coal, chemical plants, airfields and electrical installations of the Belgian railways.[19] He provided plans of a complete rail network (Renouvellement Voie Ballast), and the hydraulic electrical installations of the Belgian State Railway. He operated around the region of St Ghislain, and provided excellent industrial and economic information and reports on the rivers behind the German lines. He placed one of his agents in a post that controlled rail traffic at Mons Station. He was arrested on 17 February 1944 and believed to have been released on 6 September 1944.

Agents working for Mill's other sectors reported on Allied sabotage of trains and the rail network, as well as raids on stations. The personal agent file of Robert Mathieu of Hornu contains lists of Mill agents and which railway stations they were working from. Some were signallers in their day job and therefore well placed to help the Mill network.[20]

Gérard Marchard proved to be another valuable agent, because he went on to discover an experimental field in Poland for the V-2 secret weapon. He worked around the province of Namur, had been a prisoner of war from 1940 to May 1942, and possibly escaped (although his file does not say). He was recruited to Mill in Namur in August 1942.[21] In March 1944 he gave information on Messerschmitt factories and a powder factory near Leipzig which were bombed by the Allies fifteen days later. He undertook the sabotage of railway factories and locomotive repair workshops in Salzinnes, and in the course of the war rescued more than thirty Allied airmen. Women operated in this sector too, among them Andrée Leruth of Namur, who was described as 'an excellent agent'.[22]

Second Lieutenant Pierre Kauten organised the sector in the Luxembourg province.[23] He had a doctorate in law from the University of Liège. After arrests of Mill's Liège agents, he reorganised the sector and improved its performance; it went on to report on troops, fortifications, ammunition depots and radio detection equipment in the Mogimont region. Other agents acquired plans of German installations and battle plans.

The risks undertaken by agents of Mill were as serious as those of the Clarence Service network. German counter-espionage units were determined to break up any network suspected of operating for the Allies. Captain Jean Dardenne was one of the agents who lost his life because of his operations for Mill. He ran Mill's propaganda service, which was named Porcupine-Mandrill.[24] A young lawyer with no savings, he was married with a ten-year-old daughter, operated around Hainaut and was head of the Charleroi sector. He was arrested by the Germans for espionage on 1 November 1943 and held in prison in Belgium for a month, during which time he diverted the attention of his interrogators away from the network and thus prevented further arrests of Mill agents. He was deported to Germany on 30 November 1944, with no trial, and died in Dachau concentration camp.[25] A letter of condolence was sent to his widow by the Belgian Security Service.[26]

Intelligence Gained

Mill was in regular communication with SIS and, according to 'Major Page', 'transmitted valuable information'.[27] A glimpse into the importance of what was gathered can be found in some of Clippe's radio messages which survive in the personal file of agent Jean Denis. A cable of 10 March 1943 gave the movement of German troops, including the movement of infantry from Holland to France.[28] In another for 9 April 1943, it was reported that between 1 and 3 April 1943, thirteen trains were loaded with equipment and moved to France via Mouscron; and then from 3 to 6 April, the cable stated, '24 loaded German trains to Flanders, Antwerp, Ekeren . . . Waas.'[29]

Another cable from Mill to SIS on 8 June 1943 stated, 'from 21 to 27 May, passage of 18 Tiger tanks towards France, destination Tergnier and Plouarnel. These transports accompanied by SS troops; equipment painted yellow, plus two tanks and pebbles.'[30] For 20 August 1943, there were 'reports of various special transports from Rotenhafen to Brest, St Nazaire and La Pallice, carried out in the greatest secrecy'.

During 1944, Clippe was promoted to the rank of captain and maintained communications for Mill until 5 June 1944, when he was arrested and held in St Gilles prison.[31] SIS communicated to Marquet, 'We hope the full extent of his [Clippe's] work is not known to the Germans and that he will not be shot . . . Truly a magnificent example of tenacity and loyalty.'[32]

The Mill network was another example of how the White Lady paved the way for intelligence-gathering in Belgium in the next war. Like the Clarence Service, it operated along the same lines, developed the same organisational structure, and learned from the successes, failures and experiences of the White Lady. According to Marquet, Mill had around 1,500 members, nineteen of whom died for their clandestine operations.[33] The number of officially recognised Mill agents (IAA) after the war was ninety-four.[34] The network was not crushed by the Germans and 'proved to be one of our best services'.[35] It functioned successfully until the end of the war.

Chapter 12
A VAST WEB

A vast web of agents and couriers now operated for the Clarence Service and Mill across Belgium. They were incredibly effective networks that continued reliably to send intelligence to MI6. The volume of information and sheer detail of the Clarence Service reports give an insight into how valuable they were behind the German lines. The first such report of January 1942 provided MI6 with details of the movement of troops and equipment by night.[1] In the same report is the following technological information, in translation:

> Flénu-Mons: in the Flénu construction workshops there is a large depot of bombs of all kinds. One of our agents is keeping a special watch on it and is able to give us a regular report on the movement of projectiles entering and leaving the depot. Although activity has been low in recent months, it has been possible to deduce from the observations that this depot supplies the German airfields in the north and west of Belgium and in northern France. Transport of devices is done by trucks or wagons, interspersed with wagons of coal to try and disguise it.[2]

In February 1942, Jempson at MI6 headquarters received intelligence from Clarence Service agents on the first known German radio 'direction-finding station for controlling night fighters'.[3] Another report the following month located the first directional wireless communications station in Belgium.[4] The information was passed to chief scientist Professor R.V. Jones, head of the scientific section of MI6. Clarence Service agents were dispatched on several missions into Germany and Nazi-annexed Austria, from where they brought back information of military value and details of factories in Germany and Austria.[5] One agent, an engineer by occupation and known only as 'Alexandre' in the files, worked undercover in the Böhler factories and had access to various plans, which he copied. In May 1942 he brought back information that the workforce had increased from 4,000 workers to 16,000 within just a year. This indicated a major scaling up of production and signified the importance of the site.

Another agent reported on a flying school at Paderborn in Germany, which was also hiding other military activities. During the day, the hangars housed bomber aircraft and in the evenings the aircraft were moved to a light hangar in the woods on the edge of Paderborn.[6] The hangars were covered with camouflage nets. It was observed that during the daytime, the planes were loaded with fuel, ammunition and bombs by the students of the flying school; then they were hidden in the woods in case of an Allied airstrike on the main hangars during the night. It was noted that this depot was full, with over 3,000 tons of bombs of between 125kg and 2,500kg each and a large quantity of incendiary bombs. Of particular note was the presence of roughly ten concrete torpedoes, containing an undisclosed toxic substance. The report included an annexe with a plan of the depot.

Regular details continued to be sent to London about the artillery and horses being moved with German troops across Belgium. Report 75, for example, consists of twenty pages of intelligence plus diagrams, photographs and maps.[7] From 28 November to 3 December 1942, one train with thirty to forty wagons was observed along its entire route, passing through Tongres and travelling along the Namur–Luxembourg line. It was reported:

On the Meuse and Sambre lines only trains carrying equipment and materials for companies and for fortification or supplies for the German army, ran to France. Towards Germany there were trains carrying new automobile equipment (especially Renault) and various commercial material ... From Belgium, the second tranche (21 trains) was reported transporting troops from Flanders to Germany, mainly via Muyzen, Hasselt, Hamont ... Towards Flanders, a stream of 12 empty trains passes from Hamont to Meirelbeke.

Reports in this period continued to provide information on German activities in the regions of Brussels, Liège, Namur, Zeebrugge and Ostend. Details were given of an Allied bombing raid on Cherbourg, France in December 1942, in which the airfield's radio-telegraphic facilities were destroyed. Thirty-seven of the post's forty-two occupants were killed in the raid. These eyewitness reports afforded important confirmation of whether a raid had been successful or not, which would have been difficult to verify by any other means.

The Gilles Group

During 1942 Antoine Delfosse, who would become minister for justice from October of that year, was tasked with setting up a secret committee within Belgium that represented the Belgian government-in-exile and could liaise with London. He turned to Dewé for help. Delfosse and Dewé visited Thérèse de Radiguès and together they started a committee known as the Gilles Group, which was chaired by Charles de Visscher, a renowned jurist at the University of Louvain who secured the support of other influential figures on the committee.[8] The Gilles Group had two primary focuses: first, direct communication and liaison with the Belgian government-in-exile in London; and second, the rescue and smuggling out of Jews who were in hiding in the country. The first goal was to inform the Belgian government-in-exile about the situation within Belgium, including the morale of the population, and actively to support the resistance. This information aided the government-in-exile in its work with Britain's Political Warfare Executive to direct psychological warfare against the enemy in Belgium.[9]

The group's work in rescuing Jews is little known and is another example of the demarcation between espionage, intelligence-gathering and rescue becoming blurred, just as it did with the escape lines for Allied airmen and soldiers. An arrangement was made by the Belgian section of MI6 to drop diamonds by parachute to fund the group's rescue missions. Madame Blaise negotiated a price for the diamonds with Antwerp dealers to convert to funds for their clandestine work. Visscher and Walter Ganshof were the most active members on the committee until June 1943, when Ganshof had to flee Belgium. Transmissions from London to the committee came via a Clarence Service radio operator who was codenamed 'Aristide'. His real name was Jules Delruelle and he was an industrialist by profession.[10] The rescue work of the Gilles Group extended further when Dewé made contact with Yvonne Nèvejean, director of the National Agency for Children. Nèvejean and many of her employees worked together with the Comité de Défense des Juifs en Belgique to rescue thousands of Jewish children, and funds were transferred to Nèvejean's agency via the Gilles Group to support their valuable work. Dewé's own wife hid a two-year-old Jewish child, called Serge Robine, for a few months. His parents were friends of the Dewé family.

From his places of hiding, Dewé met regularly in secret with Delfosse, who by now had founded an armed resistance movement of liberation in Liège.[11] Delfosse himself had to flee to England after the arrest of a colleague in June 1942. On 1 September 1942, the Clarence Service received a message from MI6 that Delfosse had safely reached England.

With the increase in Allied bombings in Europe the number of shot-down air crew would also increase, and they would need protection. Dewé knew that even though the Clarence Service was solely an intelligence organisation, it would be impossible for its sectors around Namur and Luxembourg to avoid any contact with the escape lines. There were concerns not to overlap the work of intelligence networks with escape lines because, as in World War One, close contact could mean that if one was compromised, it risked the same happening to the other. Of the forty-three deaths of members of the Clarence Service, several were due to an overlap with other secret networks, including the escape lines. It was a lesson that had to be learned again in this war, to keep escape lines separate from intelligence and espionage operations.

By the end of 1942 there were more than twenty clandestine Belgian networks operating in the country and into France. They were equipped with around twenty-five radio transceivers between them; their operators trained in Britain, then parachuted into Belgium or France.[12] MI6 sent new, ground-to-air 'Ascension' sets to the Clarence Service, and these were used with some success in Belgium.[13] These had been developed by Richard Gambier-Parry's SIS communications section, Section VIII, at Hanslope Park in Buckinghamshire. This new technology enabled agents to speak directly to an aircraft above and did not require the use of Morse code. The sets were much easier for inexperienced operators to use. They operated across short distances, making it harder, but not impossible, for the Germans to locate the transmissions via their direction-finding equipment and vans; they still had to be scattered across different points in a city and in the countryside, and transmissions could be for no longer than fifteen minutes. For security reasons, the volume of transmissions was also reduced. Due to the successful missions by Belgian parachutists during 1941, radio contact between the Clarence Service and MI6 was not disrupted and MI6 arranged to send its own telegrams to the network at set times.

Loss of Agents

Capture by the Gestapo was an ever-present risk for agents of the Clarence Service. During 1942, the network suffered a number of losses, and that included its agents being taken to concentration camps. Elisabeth Plissàrt was one of them; she was arrested in 1942 and died in

Ravensbrück concentration camp in January 1945. That was a fate that also befell Juliette Durieu and her sister Nelly. Juliette was a senior figure in both the White Lady and Clarence Service, having been designated Dewé's reserve commander in the White Lady should he be captured. In 1942, the sisters were providing shelter to the radio operator Jean Brion. He was able to send an estimated twenty messages to London from the sisters' home in Liège. On 16 June 1942, the Germans intercepted one of his broadcasts. Brion and the Durieus were arrested and deported to Germany. The two women died in Ravensbrück in early 1945.

During 1942, Dewé's home was subjected to a number of Gestapo raids, with his wife Dieudonnée continuing to throw the secret police officers off the scent and avoid arrest. It pained Dewé to be separated from his family, only seeing them occasionally and for the briefest periods of time.

As high-value intelligence kept flowing to MI6 in London, the arrest of some of the Clarence Service's key agents was unrelenting. On 9 November 1942, thirty-nine-year-old Jean de Radiguès, son of Thérèse, was arrested at his home on avenue de Tervueren, Brussels.[14] It sent alarm bells through the leadership because Jean knew so much about the leaders' identities and the network's operations, including the activities of his own mother and sisters. The consequences of his interrogation if he broke down could be catastrophic for the Clarence Service. The leadership tried to discover what had gone wrong and whether the Clarence Service was about to disintegrate.

Jean de Radiguès

Jean de Radiguès had been recruited for the Clarence Service by Dewé immediately after the occupation of 1940, with the blessing of his mother, Thérèse. Jean was a veteran of World War One, during which he had lost a lung in the Battle of the Yser in 1914. In 1920 he married Jacqueline de Montpellier d'Annevoie and they went on to have six children.[15] Jean operated as a Clarence Service agent in Belgium and northern France, from where he took messages containing political, economic and military intelligence daily to either his mother or Dewé. Dewé tasked him with distributing funds among the various resistance organisations because of his civilian employment as a director of the Belgian Bank Company, which enabled him to travel, but also because of his connections. The bank had its headquarters at 61 avenue Louise in Brussels and from there Jean acted as liaison between its board of directors and the German occupying authorities. It meant that he had frequent contact with various German services.

On one occasion, when Jean was away from the bank, a Luftwaffe officer arrived to deposit something for safekeeping, during which he mistakenly removed another package from a vault. It happened to contain details for a Clarence Service radio station named Student IV.[16] It is not known whether the officer realised the significance of the package, because it did not lead to the bank being raided by the German authorities. However, a more serious situation developed shortly afterwards that led to Jean's arrest, and the incident occurred because he had set up his own network for escapers.

On his own initiative, Jean helped some friends to leave occupied Belgium for Britain or the Congo.[17] He did not wish to burden the Clarence Service leadership or agents with requests for volunteers, so he organised and ran the escape line independently from his intelligence work. Anyone working for both an intelligence network and an escape line, albeit separately, would potentially risk both if caught. To obtain false identity papers, Jean contacted Baron Jean van Campenhout, a veteran of the last war and a civil servant who was already in contact with the bank. He provided the false papers to Jean when needed, and escorted escapers over the border.

In the autumn of 1942 Campenhout informed Jean of his plans to travel to London to create a new intelligence network. Jean had in his possession some documents that needed urgent couriering to London, and this afforded him the ideal opportunity to smuggle them out.

Among them were reports and material intended for the eyes of eminent Belgians currently residing in exile in London – Georges Theunis, former prime minister of Belgium and currently governor of the National Bank of Belgium, and Paul Henri Spaak, another former Belgian prime minister who was working with the Belgian government-in-exile.[18] Dewé gave consent for Jean to hand over the documents to Campenhout, including a note addressed to 'Major Page' of SIS/MI6.

While in possession of the envelope that Jean had entrusted to him, Campenhout was arrested by the German Field Police. During intense interrogation, he gave up Jean's name and revealed that he was an agent for the Allies.

Jean was arrested on 9 November and taken to St Gilles prison, where he was held in solitary confinement for five months. He underwent several interrogations across a prolonged period of time, including severe torture, but did not break. His courage in protecting the network from discovery safeguarded the liberty and perhaps lives of the Clarence Service's operatives and leaders.

Behind Closed Doors

During Jean's time in prison, his wife Jacqueline obtained permission from the German authorities to send him linen and provisions once a fortnight. The box she used had a false bottom and that was how Jean, who was incommunicado, received news from home. Jean went to trial on 21 April 1943. Jacqueline wrote in her diary:

> Jean must be tried at the Palais de Justice behind closed doors. We are forbidden to attend the judgment. I will go to the Palais de Justice early in the morning to see Jean, whom I haven't seen for five months, and to find out what happened to him . . . At the end of the session, I have the children attend so that they see their father as he leaves the hearing. When the group of condemned leave the Palace, heavily surrounded by soldiers, we are forbidden to go near

them. But Olivier (10 years old) passes like a little rat through two soldiers; through the cordon and manages to embrace his father. The Germans are furious and he is delighted.[19]

At the closed hearing, the court called for the death penalty seven times for Jean's actions, which were listed as being against German state security, sabotage on arms depots and other military sites, distribution of propaganda leaflets, the organisation of the passage of escapers, and being the author or intermediary of documents containing information for the British. The closed court concluded that he was an agent of a foreign power. The accusations were read out in German, without an interpreter present. His lawyer was not permitted to attend his trial or read his file. With such an indictment, Jean's fate was sealed. The court condemned him to death and he was returned to prison to await his fate.

In his memoirs, Jean remembered:

During the first six months, I suffered days of exhausting length, of slow minutes one after the other in abandonment, idleness, monotonous isolation [solitary confinement]. From April to September 1943, I shared a cell with other comrades in Saint Gilles [prison] as a death row inmate. Every week, friends left, some to the firing squad, others to Germany. The time of interrogations was replaced by that of painful separations and the anguish of execution.[20]

Jean's friends and contacts rallied into action to save his life and improve his conditions. Jacqueline wrote in her diary, 'I am terribly impressed how many friends came to my rescue – how many steps were taken from all sides and in all places to save my poor Jean. From then on the restrictions in the prison were less severe [for him]. Jean was in the cell with others and allowed to see us. A visit granted to me every 15 days . . . Painful interviews.'[21] As reflected in this last comment, despite the relief, prison visits were obviously emotionally fraught.

On 2 October 1943, Jacqueline was called into the office of a German officer, who informed her that Jean's execution had been postponed because an appeal for clemency had been received from several high-level Belgian personalities, including royalty and diplomats.[22] The German military command ordered the postponement of Jean's execution. But, three days later, while the appeal was being examined, Jean was deported to Germany and detained in the prison in Sonnenberg, then Wolfenbüttel and Magdeburg. He would be incarcerated for three years.

Jean believed that what had sustained him through all this horror was his Roman Catholic faith. He kept strong and felt the presence of God daily in captivity. On 27 April 1945 Soviet troops liberated Brandenburg prison in Görden, where Jean was then being held. The majority of the prisoners were transferred to Oranienburg concentration camp, then being used as a displaced persons' camp, but Jean's poor health meant he was not well enough for the journey. He remained in the Brandenburg prison under Russian jurisdiction until 22 June 1945, when he was deemed well enough to return to Belgium.

Expansion of the Web

Behind the German lines in Belgium, the clandestine fight was quietly carrying on for British intelligence. Protection of the leadership was paramount and Dewé continued to move every few days to different safehouses, often sheltered by women of the network. He was a practising Roman Catholic who attended mass every morning, even though he was in hiding. He was known to have been hidden by Thérèse de Radiguès and Alfred and Thérèse Liénart in Brussels, and Sylvie Arnaud in Liège. He had numerous safehouses in or near Ciney, with Georges and Claude Pirlot-Orban; at Château de Masogne with Baron Henri de Moffarts and his wife Marie-Antoinette (née de Radiguès); and in Ostin with Georges and Marguerite Clérinx (née de Radiguès, daughter of Thérèse and sister of Marie-Antoinette).

The year 1943 saw personal tragedy for Dewé when, on 14 January, his wife suffered a heart attack and died. Dieudonnée was fifty-nine years old. Dewé was devastated. She had been his rock and support. Since the start of the war, he had only seen her for short periods of time because he was residing in various safehouses. He risked his own safety to attend her funeral. After her death, Dewé handed over the running and coordination of the network's parachute operations within Belgium to Hector Demarque so that he, Dewé, could concentrate on expanding the network. He returned from the funeral to the safehouse where he was then sheltering, now with a single focus – to expand operations right across Belgium and deeper into Nazi Germany. A vast and complex web of Dewé's agents criss-crossed Nazi territory.

That same month, January 1943, an unnamed officer at MI6 headquarters in London made a complaint that reports from Belgian sources were taking up to three months to arrive and were therefore diminished in usefulness.[23] The quantity and quality of intelligence being gathered for MI6 was not in question, but delays of between a week and a fortnight between the actual gathering of information and this material making it into intelligence reports were unavoidable. However, the kind of information being gathered by the Clarence Service – about troop movements, or intelligence on new weapons, technology and defences – was still valuable when it arrived. The logistics of moving an army, including its equipment, field kitchens and supplies, were complicated and took time. Within the framework in which the Clarence Service was operating, its intelligence was not so time-sensitive or obsolete when it was received in London. It still enabled MI6 to gain a panoramic overview of the German war machine. Claude Dansey, MI6's deputy chief, was so impressed by the accuracy of the Clarence Service reports that he told the leaders it was 'a great work'.[24]

It was during 1943 that MI6 finally managed to smuggle dollars into Belgium to fund Clarence. The debt of 800,000 francs which had been accrued by the network since its beginnings was paid into a bank and the debt was cleared by MI6.

By early May 1943, news reached Frederick Jempson, head of MI6's Belgian section, that all his courier lines between Belgium and France had broken down. This was due to arrests in France at the various collecting and forwarding centres in Paris, Lyon and Toulouse. He asked Hector Demarque to open a new route through Sweden, but in the end very little intelligence came out via this route.

Supplies were still being delivered to Belgium via special parachute drops. Jempson wrote to Captain Nicodème with a list of items dropped by container into Belgium during April and May:

> Wireless sets and accessories formed a considerable part of the consignment and the shape of these packages when introduced into the cylindrical containers severely limited the quantities of the 'vivres' [smaller items] that could be added. Thus, it happened that certain articles required by our agents could not be sent, or at best in small quantities only; for example, tea and coffee which were in large round tins. It is hoped that a greater variety of vivres and larger quantities may be included in the next consignment.[25]

This is a rare item of MI6 correspondence in the Clarence Service archives. So little evidence exists from the MI6 side because the Secret Service files remain closed. It is a window into the kind of supplies being sent in support of the Belgian operations.

Radio communications remained a key focus for MI6 across the war. These operations were supported by new parachutists being dropped into Belgium. During the night of 13–14 February 1943, Jules Stercq ('Player') was parachuted into the country with $10,000 for the Clarence Service and charged with a special assignment.[26] He was to introduce a new type of device for transmitting and receiving messages.[27] On landing he made his way to report to Laure and Louise Tandel, who sheltered him. His transmitter was dropped near Morhet (in the Belgian province of Luxembourg) on 19 April 1943 and then taken to Sint-Martens-Latem, near Ghent, where a new broadcasting station was established. Seventy messages were broadcast from there between the beginning of July 1943 and the end of March 1944. Stercq oversaw the functioning of this station and was charged with the organisation of various parachute drops of food, equipment, weapons and funds. He was a member of the management board of the Clarence Service at this time and formed a reception department to oversee and coordinate the arrival of parachutists.

In March 1944 Stercq had to cease his activities on doctor's orders after contracting pulmonary tuberculosis. He died of the illness in a sanatorium in Switzerland on 27 April 1948.[28]

Agent Fortune

Radio operators remained an essential part of the success of the network, but their task was fraught with the constant risk of being located by the enemy's mobile van detectors. Marcel Verhamme ('Fortune') had been working as a radio operator for the Clarence Service since his recruitment and narrowly missed being caught by the Field Police on 31 May 1942, while sending an urgent message from the house of Henriette Dupuich at 25 rue Edmond Picard.[29] She was one of the earliest leaders of the Clarence Service and had also been a member of the White Lady. Agent 'Saturne' (Jean-Louis Demarque, father of the Clarence Service leader Hector Demarque) was keeping watch on the street while the transmission took place. He had noticed a tracking van and a car travelling at high speed towards Dupuich's house. Demarque rushed to the house and rang the doorbell three times (the agreed signal for danger). Verhamme immediately halted the transmission. However, contrary to agreed security protocols, Henriette opened the door to Demarque. Rather than stand on the doorstep and draw attention to himself, he entered.

The vehicles stopped outside the house next door. The Germans had clearly not managed to pinpoint the exact address that the transmission had issued from. They alerted the Field Police, who arrived a few minutes later and began a search of the neighbourhood. Fortunately, Henriette's house escaped their attention and the day was saved for the network on this occasion.

A few months later, on 27 August 1942, Verhamme was broadcasting from the house of Frédérique (Baroness Germaine de Menten) in Brussels when he was the subject of another security scare. On this occasion, Hector Demarque was keeping watch in rue de l'Aurore in Ixelles, within sight of the base from where the detection vans left, pretending to be waiting for a tram. He had already instructed Verhamme not to transmit for longer than five minutes. Within two minutes of Verhamme starting his message to London, a tracking van pulled away from the headquarters. Hector had opportunity to alert Verhamme this time, but it was conclusive proof to Hector that the vans were picking up transmissions within the city. After this, broadcasts were limited in Brussels, and preference for transmission bases was given for houses in the countryside where there was more time to get away should they be detected. Verhamme duly relocated, and one of the places he then transmitted from was the home of the Tandel sisters. With some narrow escapes, he had thus far succeeded in transmitting messages to MI6 for over a year.[30]

The following year, on 21 July 1943, when Verhamme was broadcasting from the home of the Cambier sisters (Valentine, Marguerite and Jeanne), the transmission was identified by a German direction-finding van; its crew alerted the Field Police. Verhamme was given warning by one of the network's watchers and he was able to leave the house unseen. Two officers arrived and questioned Valentine and Jeanne, both of whom remained calm, and luckily, the officers omitted to search the premises.

Once the men had left, Valentine packed up the radio transceiver and retrieved the messages concealed in the special hiding place in the house. She exited the back of the property with the radio transmitter and messages, climbed through a hole in the garden hedge and cut across the fields to chaussée de Waterloo. From there she took a tram to Schaerbeek and went into hiding. Hector Demarque picked up the equipment and messages from her at the safehouse a short time later. The Field Police officers returned to the Cambier house for a second time and mounted a full search, but found no evidence.[31]

Verhamme and another operator, 'Gabriel', had to go into hiding. Verhamme was sheltered by a couple named Liénart; Dewé was also residing with them at the time. 'Gabriel' was given shelter by fifty-three-year-old Clotilde Coppens at 59 avenue du Parc in Brussels. She had enlisted in the Clarence Service the previous year.[32] She was a key figure on the organisational side, as she had formed a secretariat and offered her home for the daily administration and meetings. Every week the number of couriers working in all sectors of the network was recorded. She herself was a courier and ran a dead letter box from her home. She recruited other members of her family and friends.

The Field Police hunted for Verhamme and 'Gabriel' and visited their relatives for information on their whereabouts. On 22 July 1943, they arrived at the home of 'Gabriel's' mother; she told them that he was travelling. Verhamme's family also received a visit, but it is not known what they told the officers. Against Dewé's advice, Verhamme decided to visit his family a week later and was arrested. The Field Police were watching the place.

Verhamme had achieved so much for the Clarence Service prior to his arrest. Between October 1941 and July 1943, he had transmitted 200 messages to London and received 150 messages back from MI6. From prison, he assured the network that he had given nothing away during the interrogations. Yet the Germans' success in discovering the locations from which radio operators were transmitting rendered those places unusable at any point in the future. There was no question of the Clarence Service ceasing the radio transmissions, but new locations had to be swiftly found.

'Gabriel' had managed to evade the Field Police, but on 6 August 1943, he telephoned his mother to check if she was well. The Germans were at her house too. Despite the Field Police holding a gun to her head during the phone call, she gave her son a coded message to warn of danger and he survived. She was arrested, then released a month later for lack of any evidence against her.

Verhamme was sentenced to death and shot at the Tir National in Schaerbeek, Brussels – the site of many executions in both world wars – on 16 November 1943.

Agents Ghis and Sohngen

In March 1943, the Tandel sisters recruited André Didier ('Ghis') as an agent and observer.[33] He was a teacher in Uccle and lived on the same street as the Tandels. He provided regular military intelligence on the regions of East and West Flanders, Brabant and Antwerp, including reports on German defences, troop movements by rail, road and sea, buildings being used by Axis forces and the clandestine passage of Allied pilots via the escape lines.

Didier recruited another agent called Albert Sohngen, who joined on 1 April 1943.[34] Sohngen had a different background to the majority of other agents. He was originally German, born to a German father and Belgian mother. After his parents' divorce in 1923, he returned to Belgium with his mother and lived in Brussels with his grandmother. At the outbreak of the war, he was mobilised by the German army and employed as a draughtsman at a cartographic office in the Breskens region. It is not known how he crossed paths with André Didier, but having been recruited into Clarence and while still serving in the German forces, Sohngen provided plans and locations of German defences and other structures in the coastal region of Belgium. He gathered intelligence on the deployment of German troops and the state of their morale. He was permitted regular leave to visit his mother and grandmother, which did not raise any suspicions from the German army. He used these opportunities to meet Didier and pass him information. As liaison officer Didier passed the coastal plans and information to Laure and Louise Tandel.

Didier was arrested by the Gestapo on 20 January 1944 and deported to Germany on 12 August 1944, where he was sentenced to death. His sentence was later commuted to eight years' hard labour. He spent time in Flossenbürg concentration camp, but after March 1945, all trace of him was lost and his fate is unknown.[35]

Sohngen's own work for Clarence appeared to end after Didier's arrest. Possibly he was suspected of having betrayed Didier, although there is no evidence that he did so. In August 1944, Sohngen was arrested in Paris by a resistance movement and sent to England, where he was held in a POW camp until the end of the war.[36] During the time that he operated for Clarence he had provided vital intelligence on the coastal areas of Belgium, and given precise and detailed operational plans on all German offensive and defensive military action. He had also provided information on the location of dummy and camouflaged forts, as well as of minefields.[37]

The arrest of radio operators and agents by the Germans was ongoing, but nevertheless the parachutists who supplied them continued to be dropped into Belgium for the remainder of the war.[38] On the night of 15 August 1943 another agent, codenamed 'Serge', parachuted into the country, along with two containers for the radio operator network 'Student'.[39] The containers contained Belgian francs, dollars, cigarettes, sugar, butter, coffee, tea, dried milk, chocolate, tins of corned beef and sardines, soap, wireless sets, socks, pullovers and shoes. Further parachute drops were organised from London, all received by a Clarence reception committee on the ground. One drop into Freux-Ménil included weapons, devices and food.[40]

Alongside the work of the radio operators, agents were dispatched yet deeper into Nazi Germany, reporting back from locations (captured in the Clarence Service intelligence reports) as far afield as Hamburg, Nuremberg and Leipzig. They continued to collect regular military intelligence, including technical information and reports about the removal of uranium salts to Germany.[41] In July 1943 there was reporting of German troop manoeuvres.[42] One agent working in a German head-quarters near Breskens, just across the Dutch frontier, reported back on minefields and the nature of German forces along the Belgian coast. A contact in the Belgian oil company provided useful industrial intelligence on petrol and resources, vehicles in use, German communications and the Belgian railway system. Other agents provided verification on the results of the RAF bombing of German cities, among them

Hamburg, Düsseldorf and Cologne; and the location of installations at Zeebrugge and Ostend, as well as German defences at Knokke. The reports were accompanied by an increasing number of black-and-white photographs of relevant sites observed by agents. The written and visual evidence on German anti-aircraft defences, gunners, aerodromes and gun emplacements, and a vast array of other material, provided the most comprehensive and valuable picture possible behind the German lines.

Chapter 13
WOMEN OF CLARENCE

From the beginning of the war, women were embedded right across the Clarence Service network. As in World War One, the German forces did not expect women to be engaged in such work and so they were particularly useful. Only a fraction of their contributions can be told here.

Crucially, as with the White Lady, Clarence Service women were given military status like the men and received a military rank as members of the British military intelligence apparatus – all this while British women still could not enlist into combatant roles in the regular British forces. Women again stepped up and played their part as heads of intelligence regions, leaders on boards and in various departments of the Clarence Service: they operated as couriers, keepers of records and liaison agents, analysed and typed up intelligence reports, sheltered agents and provided safehouses for the documents, and ran sub-sectors of the network.[1]

Walthère Dewé was primarily sheltered in the houses of Clarence Service women, and sometimes in the homes of married couples. His two daughters, Madeleine and Marie Thérèse, had enlisted in the network. Marie Thérèse served as an agent and courier for her father, and also as a courier for the Comet Line. For the latter, she organised contacts in Limbourg for airmen and evaders and escorted them to Tongres, working from the family home in Liège.[2] She handed them over to Aline Dumont ('Michou') of the Comet Line, who arranged for them to be taken on to Brussels.[3]

Prominent amongst the Clarence Service women was Thérèse de Radiguès, who recruited agents from the very beginning of this war. From her house in Ixelles, Brussels, she ran a large sector of the network that had five sub-sectors.[4] The majority of her agents were women, but not all. Some of her agents created further sub-sectors and reported back to their individual heads of section who, in turn, sent their reports to Thérèse.[5] Among those recruited by her were Thérèse Plissàrt, her sister Elisabeth and Louisa de Marotte de Montigny. The work was not without its risks: all three women were eventually arrested by the Gestapo, taken to St Gilles prison for interrogation and deported to Germany.[6] As we will see shortly, it was some of Thérèse de Radiguès's female agents who delivered on the highest-priority intelligence for MI6 – Hitler's secret V-weapon programme.

Thérèse's married daughters Marie-Antoinette and Marguerite had enlisted into the Clarence Service, just as they had served previously in the White Lady. Marie-Antoinette's husband, Baron Henri de Moffarts, was also a member of the clandestine network. Marie-Antoinette had been recruited by Dewé personally on 1 May 1943, undertook liaison work for him and provided refuge for agents.[7] She assisted her husband in collecting military intelligence in the region of Ciney.[8] The baron had been recruited by Abbé Knood, and all the information and supplies he collected, including the pigeons dropped by parachute for the network, were passed to Knood.[9]

Marguerite and her husband, Georges Clérinx, were living at Château Ostin at Villers-lez-Heest. The couple had leased the estate from the Eggermont family, who were also involved in the Clarence Service. The castle became a hub of clandestine operation in the region.

Château Ostin

Marguerite had been a Clarence Service agent since August 1940. She provided intermittent shelter for Dewé, especially during 1942, and aided her husband's broader clandestine work, the precise nature of which is not disclosed.[10] Marguerite kept a diary of life in Château Ostin during this period.[11] It presents a rare insight into daily life on the country estate – who visited and when, ordinary events, such as attending mass conducted by a local priest, and accounts of a seemingly ordinary life – but it also contains references to the couple's wartime activities. After the D-Day landings in Normandy on 6 June 1944, and in preparation for the eventual liberation of Belgium, Marguerite and Georges hosted in the castle a section of the General Staff of the Belgian Secret Army (Zone IV), commanded by Colonel Roger Librecht. The colonel set up a command post inside the castle.

With the Germans snatching any youths they could find to serve in the German army, Yves de Radiguès and his brother Charles arrived at Château Ostin to hide. They decided to join the Secret Army – Yves as a dispatch rider, Charles as a decoder.[12]

The clandestine operations at the castle were betrayed by a radio operator after he was captured and horrifically tortured during interrogation by the Gestapo. Under intense duress he gave away the name of the person who was receiving his message: 'Charles . . . at the castle of Ostin'.[13] On 17 August 1944, the castle was raided and the men were arrested, including fifty-two-year-old Georges Clérinx and Colonel Librecht.[14] Marguerite wrote in her journal that day, 'How can I describe my consternation, my anguish when I saw the whole group of men surrounded by these vile Gestapo agents . . . I went back to get cigarettes . . . shortly afterwards Father Olivier arrived in the courtyard. He had remained hidden in the bushes.'[15]

Marguerite went to a nearby farm to warn the rest of the network. The telephone was cut off. The women gathered in the kitchen there and talked over the events of the day, before Marguerite went to the chapel to offer prayers for the men. She was convinced the Gestapo would return and raid the castle the next day. She couldn't sleep and was up at midnight, tidying the room that the colonel had stayed in. The Gestapo did return and searched Charles's room, but not the colonel's, which was surprising to Marguerite. The women around Marguerite's circle tried to ascertain when the men would be released and were informed that if they were innocent, they would return. In the following days, the women prepared parcels for them. One of them, Lil de Radzitzky, left for Namur with seven parcels.[16]

In spite of the arrests, clandestine activity continued at the castle until the end of the war. On 22 August 1944, Marie-Antoinette arrived with a typewriter from a legation. Marguerite commented in her diary, 'it was dangerous. I was able, despite my upside down head, to put a good bag of potatoes and vegetables for Mother in the car as well as some greengages and tomatoes.'[17] The typewriter had come from Brussels, but it is not known from which embassy. Antoinette delivered the vegetables to Thérèse in Brussels.

The men who had been arrested at Ostin were eventually deported to Germany. All except Colonel Librecht perished in Mauthausen. Charles de Radiguès died on 22 October 1944 and Georges Clérinx on 21 December 1944.[18]

Couriers

The vast majority of the Clarence Service couriers were women, ranging in age from sixteen to seventy. Effectively invisible to the enemy, they could move unchecked around the countryside and towns. One of them was Olga Leclair, who was recruited by her agent husband, Richard Hoornaert, in Ostend in June 1943.[19] She went on to head a sub-sector of at least sixteen agents, and oversaw her own husband's missions. She collected military intelligence and acted as a courier between her husband and Marie Levez. On one occasion in September 1944, when another courier refused to courier reports because the situation had become too dangerous, Olga did it herself.[20] The train on which she was travelling was attacked at Ghent by troops of the Belgian Secret Army; several casualties were sustained. Olga managed to take the mail and reports onwards by road to their destination. It turned out to be urgent intelligence for the British on enemy troop movements in the region of Nieuwpoort (Flanders) and Ostend. In October 1944 she provided information about the movement of enemy tanks in Knesselare in East Flanders.

The female couriers frequently ran a dead letter box as well, like Second Lieutenant Clotilde Coppens, who displayed remarkable courage when she was carrying a large number of reports from the countryside and was stopped by a German patrol.[21] Her calmness saved her from being searched by the field officers, the consequences of which could have been very serious for the whole network. Every week she undertook a count of the number of couriers working in all sectors of the network. She was extremely active in many other activities for the Clarence Service, sheltering those members of the board who had to go into hiding, and using her home for meetings and the daily running of the organisation. She actively recruited other members from among her family and friends and was totally devoted to the cause. After the war she helped collate the network's papers and archives.

Henriette Dupuich was one of the original board members of the Clarence Service, and had been an agent of the White Lady.[22] She was recruited in 1940 as agent number 3 and lived in Ixelles. She was chief of a sector with her own agents and couriers, specifically tasked with military, economic and political intelligence.[23] She was also commander of Clarence Service's prison department, which monitored the fate of agents in jail and provided welfare to them. Later she helped support and shelter compromised agents in her own home.

Thérèse Liénart used her maiden name van de Put, and collected military, political and economic information, often operating alongside her husband, Alfred Liénart. Both had been recruited by Miss Poswick in October 1941.[24] They provided shelter in their home for compromised agents. Their duties extended beyond intelligence-gathering. Thérèse was another of the keepers of the network's archives, while her husband organised couriers and dead letter boxes, safeguarded the funds and provided safehouses.

Adjutant Simone Anspach, a fifty-three-year-old hotelier by profession, was recruited by Dewé in Liège. After her enlistment as agent number 19 on 10 May 1940, she made her hotel available as a safehouse, where Dewé sheltered at times and held numerous secret meetings. She also sheltered evaders in her hotel – another example where rescue work and intelligence overlapped.[25] Anspach used her connections to help expand the network and carried out liaison missions. She narrowly escaped arrest in July 1942 when German soldiers occupied the hotel. She fled and hid in a safehouse in Brussels for the remainder of the war, where she continued to operate as an agent.[26]

Another Liège woman, Mariette Baldauf, operated as a courier after enlisting in 1942.[27] Aged twenty-nine, she transported secret correspondence and letters and conducted espionage until the end of the war.

The Clarence Service was utterly dependent on its couriers, without whom the hundreds of reports could not be ferried across occupied Europe and out to MI6. This underlines their essential role within the network.

The Lena Mission

The secret war of forty-one-year-old Frédérique Dupuich provides a rare glimpse into how some women of the Clarence Service were dispatched on special missions. She spoke French, English, German and Italian and operated under the name Lena Deway. She had to flee Belgium in 1941 and exited via one of the escape lines through France, Spain and Portugal. On arrival in England, she requested to be sent back on a mission into occupied Europe. On 6 June 1944, Captain Aronstein, who was overseeing her training in England and organising her clandestine operation, recommended her for the rank of captain due to the importance of the imminent mission, 'Mission Lena'.[28] In this, she accompanied wireless operator 'Polka' for the Socrates radio network and organised his communications.[29] It was a mission to be coordinated from Brussels that sought to liberate Belgian personnel and

POWs being held by the Germans. She was given 10,000 Belgian francs to set up the mission, as well as false identity papers and details of potential contacts. She was to establish the whereabouts and seek the release of Belgian railway workers who had been arrested after sabotage of the railways and been taken to Germany for forced labour.[30]

The result of her operation is not provided in declassified files. She returned to London and then prepared for a joint SOE/Belgian government propaganda mission.[31]

Roles of Female Agents

The declassified agent files attest to the wide contribution made by women, operating in roles equal to men. In many cases, husbands and wives worked together, such as Second Lieutenant Jean Orban-Englebert and her husband Dr Orban. She joined in September 1940, aged twenty-seven, originally recruited by Dewé in Liège, and operated under the pseudonym 'Madame Blaise'.[32] On several occasions she drove long distances with clandestine transmitters and radio equipment that had been parachuted into Belgium for the Clarence Service. During one of these transports, she managed to save a radio operator from arrest by the Germans by carrying his transceiver for him. She took a great risk because if she had been caught with it, she would have been arrested and subjected to brutal interrogation. Was she naive to think she would not be caught, or did she realise, as proved to be the case, that the Germans would not suspect her as a woman? Jean Orban-Englebert created a covert network of contacts to penetrate the prisons around Liège, keeping a secret line of communication open with the service's incarcerated agents. She was arrested on 6 August 1943, but outwitted her interrogators and was released a few weeks later. She continued her work for the Clarence Service.

Antonina Grégoire ('Beatrice') worked for a year in coordination between the Clarence Service and the Belgian resistance movement, including as a deputy leader of one of the resistance groups.[33] From October 1943 until 1944, she was responsible for an intelligence section of the Belgian resistance that gathered information for sabotage and assassination.

Alice Cheramy was recruited in June 1943 and her role was a liaison officer and courier in the Brabant region, operating under the codename 'Mireille'.[34] She managed to avoid arrest during some very difficult situations. At the end of the war, she was designated agent first class by the Clarence Service chief, Hector Demarque. Jeanne Claessens received intelligence material from couriers, collated the material and then couriered it to two priests at the abbey in Val-Dieu. They were Father Etienne, a travelling agent and courier, and Father Hagues, who sent the intelligence to London. Her day job was as headteacher of a boys' school in Fouron-le-Comte.

Women supported and hosted radio operators – a highly risky venture, as they might all be caught by German radio direction-finding equipment. They also hid agents and Allied evaders who were on the run – another hazardous activity. Fifty-two-year-old Countess Marie Thérèse de Meeus, who lived in Brussels, joined the Clarence Service on 1 March 1943 and went on to shelter the British escaper William Castley and Dewé's son Jacques.[35] She worked for the Red Cross until April 1944. Alice Marlier (née Ceulemans) is listed as agent number 8, so was an early recruit into the Clarence Service. Recruited by Horace Verhoeven, she used codenames 'Mrs Royale' and 'Mrs Dumonceau'. Her house in Saint-Josse-ten-Noode was used for transmissions by the radio operators. She became an editor of intelligence material, then a section head at the network's administration headquarters.[36]

The above offers a snapshot of the diverse range of women's silent, unobtrusive work for the Clarence Service. Their contribution has been hidden for too long by official secrecy. Women proved to be tough, dedicated and utterly determined to play their part in the war, and wanted to serve in a military rank. They were as courageous as the men and ran the same personal risks. It is no exaggeration to say that the Clarence Service could not have succeeded without them. In so many ways, hitherto largely unacknowledged, they were its secret weapon.

Chapter 14
1944

On 9 January 1944, MI6 sent a message from London to inform the Clarence Service that agent Elie Nubourg ('Tweed') would be parachuted into the country in four days. It was received by radio operator Gérard de Burlet. A reply was sent back to SIS by radio operator Jules Stercq ('Player') that the mission was too risky and should be postponed. The network was once again reeling from the arrests of some of its members.

Just two days earlier, on 7 January, Dewé's daughters Marie Thérèse and Madeleine had been arrested during a raid on the family home in Liège, on charges of assisting Allied airmen. It was a week before the first anniversary of the death of their mother, Dewé's wife. The two women were taken to a concentration camp. Jeanne Goeseels, heroine of Villa des Hirondelles and the White Lady, personally notified Dewé. According to her account, when given the news, the sixty-four-year-old leader remained strong and calm. His son Jacques, who had worked as a courier for the network since 10 May 1940, had managed to hide in a cupboard and was not found during the raid. He fled the house and alerted the head of the Liège sector of the Clarence Service, before going into hiding at the castle of Countess Marthe de Meeus in Vyle-Tharoul.[1]

He was then hidden in Brussels by the countess's sister, Countess Marie Thérèse de Meeus.[2]

Further arrests were made on the same day the Dewé sisters were captured. Berthe Morimont (née Lambrecht), a Clarence Service agent and a helper for the Comet Line, was apprehended with her daughters Anne and Lucienne and another agent, Anne-Marie Ferrier. Dewé was concerned that the women might not be able to endure the Gestapo's brutality and might crack during interrogation. They knew intimate details about operations, agents and the whereabouts of Dewé and Demarque, who were hiding in the home of the Liénarts. Key personnel of the Clarence Service were therefore moved to new safehouses and Dewé relocated to a house on rue de la Vanne in Ixelles.

Lucienne and Anne Morimont gave nothing away throughout all their interrogations, and were released from prison due to lack of evidence. Their mother Berthe was transferred to Ravensbrück concentration camp, along with the Dewé sisters and Anne-Marie Ferrier. Berthe Morimont and Madeleine Dewé died in Ravensbrück the following year.[3] Anne-Marie Ferrier survived captivity, as did Marie Thérèse Dewé, who was liberated from Mauthausen concentration camp.[4]

Dewé recognised that the Germans might find him at any time, as the arrest of his daughters confirmed. He believed in an ultimate Allied victory in Europe: the Allies had had successes at El-Alamein in 1942 and Stalingrad in 1943, the liberating armies were continuing their hard-fought advance up through Italy, and the Soviet armies were just pushing into Poland. Dewé was confident that eventually the Allies would liberate Belgium and the rest of occupied Europe. Of the greatest importance to him was the knowledge that if he was arrested at any point now, the Clarence Service could survive because his highly competent and trusted co-leader Hector Demarque had the experience to head it without him.[5] It had become a vast, efficient and complex web across Belgium, whose leaders and agents knew exactly how to continue should Dewé be caught by the Gestapo.

1944

The Phone Calls

By 13 January 1944, it was known that the telephone line of Sadi Carnot, a member of the Clarence Service, was being tapped by the Germans. According to Jean de Radiguès's unpublished memoir, his mother had received a couple of mysterious phone calls after Carnot's line had been tapped, in which the caller claimed to be wanting to warn the father of the Dewé sisters who had been arrested. Jean wrote:

> My mother received a telephone call from Liège informing her that the Gestapo, in search of an Allied airman, had raided the home of Dewé in Liège. His daughters had been arrested; and his son managed to escape. The caller asked that the father be notified. This was done, but the telephone communication had been intercepted by the Germans. Shortly afterwards, another phone call originating from Liège asked my mother if she had sent the message and if she knew Mr Dewé's address. She replied in the affirmative, but immediately had the impression that this call was not normal. Dewé made a quick inquiry which provided him with the conviction that the telephone call had come from the Germans.[6]

Even though Carnot had been discreet, during another call on his line Thérèse de Radiguès's name had been mentioned, and had been overheard by the Germans. Dewé found out and, against the advice of those sheltering him in the safehouse, took the decision to go personally to her house at 41 avenue de la Couronne in Brussels to warn her.[7] He could have sent someone else, but he wanted to do this himself. Thérèse was now seventy-nine years old and the two of them had an unbreakable bond of friendship carved from two wars as leaders operating in the shadows of espionage. Like him, Thérèse had close family members in concentration camps (her son and grandson). Their families had maintained their connections in the inter-war years, too. Dewé now believed her life to be in immediate danger.

Arriving at avenue de la Couronne on foot, Dewé urged Thérèse to disappear for a while. She refused, not believing herself to be in imminent peril. Still extremely concerned for her safety, Dewé returned the following day, 14 January, at around 3.30 p.m. The maid invited him in and informed him that Thérèse was somewhere in the neighbourhood and due to return shortly. As the sirens sounded for an air raid, Dewé hung up his hat and coat and waited in the small sitting room.

The German police were calling at various houses as part of their ongoing investigations into conversations overheard on Carnot's telephone line, and they duly arrived at avenue de la Couronne. The maid opened the door to three officers and told them that Thérèse was out. One of the officers glanced around the hallway and saw an overcoat hanging on a peg. He nodded towards it. 'Whose is that?'

'It belongs to the gentleman waiting for madam in the sitting room,' replied the maid.

The officer opened the sitting-room door and asked Dewé what he was doing in the house.

'I've come to sell coal to madam,' Dewé replied.[8]

The officers took Dewé's briefcase and examined the contents. They were suspicious of Dewé and called the Gestapo on avenue Louise for a car to take him to St Gilles prison for questioning. As they waited for the car, Thérèse returned home to find Dewé standing, very pale, against the door of the drawing room. She was taken by one of the three officers into another room. Afterwards she recalled, 'I heard a lot of noise, doors opening and closing; then screams followed by gunshots.' There were reports from one officer that Dewé had escaped; another said that he had been shot. A third officer entered her home and said that Dewé had been shot on the corner of rue de la Brasserie and avenue de la Couronne. There was much confusion as to what had happened.[9] But within a short time, the truth became clear.

François de Radiguès, Thérèse's grandson, explains what his grandmother said had occurred:

The officers escorted Dewé into the car outside. He decided to flee and got out through the other door and ran. He sprinted to the crossroads of the avenue de la Couronne and the rue de la Brasserie, where he jumped on a tram coming from the place Saint-Croix, but the traffic lights turned red and the tram stopped. Dewé got off and resumed his run. The Gestapo officers shouted 'Halt!' They wanted to take him alive. At that moment, a Luftwaffe officer who was walking up rue de la Brasserie drew his Luger.[10]

Dewé was shot at close range and fell against a house on the pavement of the rue de la Brasserie. An ambulance arrived twenty minutes later. He never regained consciousness and died en route to hospital.

The network learned the devastating news a few days later on 18 January. Hector Demarque took over as the chief of the Clarence Service. The next day, Jules Stercq sent a message to SIS in London informing them that Dewé had died. A telegram was received by return, which read, 'The British and Belgian governments deeply moved by the death of our friend, an admirable patriot ... [and] irreplaceable leader.'[11] MI6 had lost one of the greatest chiefs of its intelligence network and Belgium one of its best sons.

The Germans never realised that the man they had shot in Brussels that day had been the head of the biggest British intelligence network in Belgium.

Thérèse de Radiguès was arrested on suspicion of espionage and taken to St Gilles prison for interrogation. With exceptionally quick wit, she feigned dementia; the interrogators concluded that this elderly woman who did not even know the time of day could scarcely be involved in spying against Germany. She was released by the prison commandant and, with inspirational energy, continued her work as one of the network's principal leaders until the end of the war.

The Gestapo's ongoing enquiries into what was heard on Carnot's line made little progress. The two phone calls made to Thérèse (mentioned by Jean de Radiguès above, although not in other sources) continued to be at the centre of their investigations. The person who had made the first mysterious phone call subsequently said he remembered it having been a young voice that answered the phone. That meant it couldn't possibly have been Thérèse, and she had already been counted out as 'having dementia'. The Gestapo investigated who else was at home at the time; namely, Thérèse's daughters Marguerite and Marie-Antoinette. Marguerite was deaf and unable to hear the ring of the telephone, and so it could not have been her. The Gestapo demanded proof as to whether or not it had been the voice of Marie-Antoinette heard on the line. By the time of the Gestapo investigations into her, Marie-Antoinette was in Paris (possibly on secret work for the Clarence Service). She was arrested on boulevard Flandrin and taken to Fresnes prison, south of Paris, where she was interrogated and held for two months. Her innocence was eventually recognised and she was released.[12] Even Jean de Radiguès was questioned, despite the fact that at the time he was in prison in Germany. He made a note of this particular interrogation in his prison notebooks. He denied any knowledge of his mother's espionage activities, commenting in his unpublished memoirs, 'I don't think they [the Germans] ever learned the name and importance of their victim [Dewé], nor did they manage to unravel the story of the phone call.'[13]

The Clarence Service continued to lose agents, either from arrest or because they simply disappeared without trace. These included two heads of sectors.[14] It was a testament to the fortitude of the remaining women and men that they carried on.

Wireless Operators

Around the time of Dewé's death, the health of radio operator Stercq ('Player') was deteriorating and he was retired from the network. His replacement, Elie Nubourg – whose original planned drop had been postponed for two months because of the wave of arrests of key network members – was parachuted into Belgium on the night of 3–4 March

1944. Tweed's career with the Clarence Service lasted only a few weeks. On 29 March 1944, he sent a message to MI6 about German traffic across the Belgian railways and was arrested that same day.[15] His equipment was taken during a raid of the house of Lieutenant Maud Mary de Cort, from where he was transmitting.[16] He was detained along with his deputy radio operator, Pierre Walkiers, and de Cort, who had provided their shelter.

De Cort was British, married to a Belgian, and had been gathering military information in the region of Ghent, using the codename 'Marie Thérèse', since her recruitment on 10 May 1940. Even though she had a teenage daughter to raise, she did not hesitate to volunteer her services to the Clarence Service as a safehouse and base for transmissions. She was arrested along with Tweed and imprisoned until 2 September 1944.[17] She displayed a defiant attitude, and was reported as 'facing with cold blood and courage the numerous interrogations that she had to undergo, and revealing absolutely nothing of the many secrets that she knew'.[18] After her release, she was promoted to the rank of second lieutenant because of 'the importance of the risks incurred, the long duration of her clandestine activity and magnificent attitude in front of the enemy'.[19]

During his interrogations, Tweed endured torture so severe that he lost consciousness. He gave up a few names of Clarence Service agents and helpers, mainly those in their seventies, believing that the Germans would be less harsh on much older members. That proved to be so, because the elderly members who were subsequently arrested were released two months later. Tweed and Pierre Walkiers were transferred from prison to Flossenbürg concentration camp, where they died.[20]

The only radio operator remaining to broadcast for MI6 was Gérard de Burlet. MI6 urgently needed more radio operators and recalled former agent Paul Godenne ('Student') to the network in April 1944. He had previously been stood down because of fears that he was unreliable. When he had returned to Belgium in 1943 and offered his services again, he had been declined. But the situation was very different in 1944. It was difficult to recruit radio operators in London, so Godenne was given a second chance to work for the network.[21]

D-Day Planning and Intelligence

The importance of the Clarence Service for MI6 intensified further as the Allies prepared for the D-Day landings, an invasion on the Normandy beaches that would be the largest air, sea and land assault thus far. It had been over a year in the planning. In spring 1944, MI6 started to put special plans in place for the Clarence Service in the event that only part of Belgium could be liberated by the Allies. MI6 messaged the Clarence Service on 14 March 1944 that if there was only a partial liberation, the network was to continue, but to be decentralised and subdivided into sectors, each with their own radio networks.[22] Their messages would then be transmitted direct to MI6, rather than via headquarters. All agents were to remain in post and work for the independent sectors.

At this time, the Clarence Service suggested to MI6 that it would like to reorganise communications ahead of the anticipated invasion. As part of this planning for D-Day, Henri (Herman) Chauvin, the sixty-eight-year-old veteran co-leader of the White Lady and an important leader in the Clarence Service, was appointed head of telecommunications and equipment in the Liège sector. He used his knowledge as a highly skilled engineer to devise a more secure system of communication for the Clarence Service.[23] MI6 made its own proposals, designed to speed up the flow of intelligence, and suggested dividing the radio network in Belgium into nine sections, each with a wireless or Ascension operator.[24]

Critical to D-Day planning was the intelligence picture. Intelligence reports from the Clarence Service in the year before D-Day provided volumes of valuable current information on German troops and their movements, Allied bombings and the results of bombing sorties on engine sheds and locomotives, enemy activity at aerodromes, and black-and-white sketches and plans of a range of sites, including the railways and docks.[25] The continuous volume and quality of the intelligence gathered for MI6 was impressive. From autumn 1943 the network was specifically asked for updated information on all defences along the Belgian coast, including whether the Germans had erected metal obstacles below the tide level to prevent any landings, as they had along the French coast. Gérard de Burlet transmitted a message to inform MI6 that the Germans had erected 360 concrete blocks in the Channel, all in the shape of pyramids and with a metal stake on the top.[26] One report and detailed map provided precise information on the coastal defences of Pas-de-Calais on the French coast.[27]

Blueprints of stations and rail lines were smuggled out to London. These are impressive blue-and-white technical plans which unfurl to a length of two to three metres, and survive today in the Clarence Service archive at the Imperial War Museum.

Agent Fernand Pironet, an insurance broker, provided military and industrial espionage on the enemy. He discovered an underground munition depot near Antwerp and Brustem, and camouflaged aircraft hangars.[28] He supplied the Clarence Service with plans of fast patrol boats as well as the citadel of Liège, and the location of the Paris–Berlin underground communications cable.

In February 1944, MI6 thanked the Clarence Service leadership for the latest railway traffic assessment, and wrote, 'The information on military trains in your letter of 3 January 1944 is very useful to us. They allow us to determine without ambiguity the lines to which they relate and whether they are still being used.'[29] MI6 underlined the need for diagrams of a technical nature, as well as information on rail stations and civilian trains.

The weekly intelligence reports from the Clarence Service gave MI6 precise details on the movement of German troops. Even apparently small details mattered. A message of 31 March 1944 from MI6 to the Clarence Service said, 'We have received your reports of bread supplied daily to German troops. This is an excellent way to estimate the number of units stationed in the regions.'[30] Amongst the information required by MI6 were ongoing reports and assessments on the extent of damage from the Allied aerial bombardment of munition sites and gasoline and fuel dumps, as well as details of the transport of oil by the enemy to fuel the movement of troops by road. Where news of atrocities had occurred, MI6 was gathering evidence of war crimes and in this same correspondence to the Clarence Service, it asked the network to try to find out about the execution of Belgian hostages, wanting to know the name of the German officer who had signed the execution order and the officer commanding the firing squad.[31]

Information from within Belgium continued to be valuable ahead of D-Day. It was reported that shortly before May 1944, the Germans had placed protective nets at the points where roads crossed watercourses and near locks.[32] The report is specific in explaining that the nets were not for camouflage, but intended to prevent things being thrown in the water and sabotage of the locks. The Allied bombing of 25 May 1944 around Forest had successfully hit the workshop next to a locomotive shed; four or five engines were destroyed. The turntable, the signals and direct tracks to Ostend had been knocked out and the tracks to Mons had also been cut in several places. This destruction would affect the German supply and reinforcement lines.

With less than two weeks until D-Day, reports were urgently sought by London on the markings on enemy aircraft, the types of aircraft engine in production, the manufacture of special equipment and weapons, the movement of planes, location of headquarters, and the state of the railways and traffic in Belgium and northern France.[33] Sometimes the personal files of agents give brief details of the kind of information that they provided. In the case of Gaston Lebrun, it was data on the fortifications along the Siegfried Line, the locations of camouflaged tanker wagons in secret places, and Axis defences around La Chapelle.[34]

Agents were specifically requested to obtain German documents and plans, technical manuals and German night-fighting equipment. This they did, and today some of these rare blueprint plans of railway stations and ports survive in files at the IWM. The agents who covered the Belgian coastline yielded valuable intelligence, too. Marcel Hermans, who lived near Bruges, operated across Flanders and the Belgian coast, providing exact plans of the coastline that were marked up with German gun positions and anti-aircraft installations.[35] He uncovered the location of German listening posts, and supplied surveys and maps of the moorings on the quays at Zeebrugge and Ostend, as well as the location of military sites near these ports. A hotelier, Joseph de Wilde, provided plans, photographs and military reports on maritime intelligence and deep mines.[36]

The latest information was received by MI6 on the defences in Belgian ports, details on enemy aircraft activity at airfields, and warning of the steady arrival into Belgium of the 1st Leibstandarte Adolf Hitler SS Panzer Division, the elite squad that had begun life as Hitler's personal bodyguard.[37] The division moved to positions north of Paris, along the river Seine, to counter an Allied invasion of Pas-de-Calais. This was another indication, alongside confirmation from Bletchley Park's Enigma traffic, that the Germans had been taken in by the various deceptions by the British Double Cross System, and believed that an invasion was imminent in the Pas-de-Calais area. It meant that by the time D-Day was implemented on 6 June 1944, these crack German troops were held back, awaiting a phantom invasion at the wrong location.

After D-Day

Formal confirmation from MI6 of the successful D-Day landings was received by the Clarence Service two days later on 8 June. MI6 told the Clarence Service that it had to maintain the security of the network and its agents and that its importance was about to increase. Instructions were given by MI6 that all agents were to remain in location as the Allied forces began the slow liberation of France, and were ultimately headed for Belgium. MI6 required reports on all movement of German troops, paratroopers, equipment, planes and lines of defence. In Keith Jeffery's words, MI6 could not 'rest on such intelligence laurels as it had earned by the invasion's success. Although victory over Germany was increasingly regarded as inevitable, sustained stiff enemy resistance on the Eastern and Western fronts left the Allied forces (including SIS) with much to do.'[38]

The Clarence Service reports on the movement of German units on the ground were as critical as at any point across the war. The network sent detailed intelligence reports across a vast expanse behind the German lines – from France, Belgium and its agents in Germany – about the state of German troops, their movements and locations, and (crucially) where that army was in retreat. This was a critical alert system, detailing locations where German troops might be planning to mount a new counter-offensive. Intelligence of a technical nature continued to be gathered, including on Germany's fighting capability. Clarence gave MI6 in London reports from its agents operating in and out of Germany about the jet engine of the Messerschmitt Me-262 fighter and the transport of German infantry and artillery units destined for regions beyond Amiens.[39]

Information was received by London on the results of ongoing sabotage operations behind the lines, including notification that 140m of railway track had been unbolted in Genappe on the night of 11–12 July 1944 and that local resistance fighters had destroyed the power plant there. Other railway lines were put out of action by sabotage, along with bridges and telephone communications. Reports named fake resistance fighters who were collaborators or spies for the Germans.[40] In one case Clarence identified a woman in Arlon who had been recruited as an agent of the German police.[41]

Messages radioed back to London gave precise details of train movements and the transportation of German troops and weaponry. One message stated that fifteen loaded wagons had passed through Montzen on 27 July 1944, en route for Utrecht in Holland. The report continued,

'Little movement of troops during the week ending 30 July 1944. Some departures from Flanders are reported, and a few withdrawals from the Ardennes, destined for Königsberg; the whole not exceeding 5000 men.'[42] It also related that ten trains of infantry had passed through Montzen for Givet, and the same in reverse. Part of another message stated that on 31 July 1944, a transport of German infantry and artillery was destined for beyond Amiens. The following day, up to twelve trains were reported to have moved from Champine to a region beyond Givet and were transporting Leibstandarte troops and a few light tanks.[43]

In many cases, precise times for the movement of troop trains were given to London, and these could be singled out for Allied bombings. Also, one intelligence report stated that on 27 August, work was to begin by the Germans for the defence of the Grand Duchy of Luxembourg.[44] Agent Robert Dupuis brought back information on U-boat construction in Hamburg and aircraft factories at Dessau.[45]

Belgian parachutists and radio operators continued to be dropped into Belgium on new missions. They included Jean-Pierre Bobsang ('Brulage III'), who was parachuted into the Beaumont region of Belgium on 4 July 1944 with a large quantity of supplies, and an undisclosed radio mission on behalf of the Clarence Service.[46] Two others were dropped at the same time, but it has not been possible to establish their names from the declassified files. Brulage III fulfilled his mission 'to the complete satisfaction of his leaders', and sent only a few messages during his time working for the Clarence Service.[47]

According to the official MI6 history, a further six operators were dropped in for the network on 4–5 August 1944, three of whom were trained on the special Ascension sets.[48] One of those agents was Gaetan Vervoort ('Tinsel'), who landed near Sivry on 6 August 1944.[49] A career soldier, he was charged with an important reconnaissance mission in the province of Luxembourg. He was deemed to be an excellent radio operator who ensured ongoing radiotelegraphic communications between the Clarence Service and MI6 in the period after the liberation of Belgium on 3 September 1944.

The final planned parachute mission was due on 28–29 August 1944, when two agents were to be dropped into Belgium. They were François Wanin ('Ribbon') and Joseph Niset ('Oakum'). It was attempted then, but failed for reasons not disclosed. The mission was not attempted again and was finally cancelled on 4 September 1944.

On 25 August 1944, Allied forces had liberated Paris – a major step towards ending the war in Europe. As the Allies pushed towards the Belgian border, the Clarence Service was amassing vital details on a threat that could halt their advance. Hitler was busy covertly moving his V-1 weapons from Germany across Belgium to new locations, to launch devastating attacks on England. But MI6's network of invisible spies in Belgium missed nothing.

Chapter 15
V-WEAPON INTELLIGENCE

The race to locate and attack Hitler's secret V-weapon programme – the V-1 'flying bomb' or doodlebug, and the successor V-2 ballistic missile – would last the whole of World War Two. As we shall see, the Clarence Service would provide some of the most valuable information on these 'vengeance weapons' from behind German lines.[1]

In the face of the Allies' material and industrial advantages and the relentless bombing of German cities by the Combined Bomber Offensive, Hitler intended these wonder-weapons to turn the tide of the war. The V-weapons were to be directed against Allied civilians, inducing fear, lowering morale and wreaking huge devastation on English soil and elsewhere. It was revolutionary technology far in advance of what the Allies could muster at this point, and they recognised that it would be highly valuable as a strategic weapon. Gaining information about its technology, and intelligence about the locations of its production and launch sites, was imperative. It was amongst the highest-priority intelligence required by the Allies.[2]

Scientific research into the development of a rocket had begun in the early 1930s at Kummersdorf, headed by General Walter Dornberger, and continued under his direction at Peenemünde, an experimental base on the Baltic coast of Germany, from 1937.[3] The intelligence picture took some time to emerge. The first references to a secret weapon in British intelligence sources came from U-boat prisoners of war being held in the Tower of London in October 1939, whose unguarded conversations were being secretly recorded.[4] The following month, radar systems and early rocket development at Peenemünde were mentioned in the Oslo Report – an anonymous German document received in Norway and offering to share military secrets – which was sent to MI6, but at that point British intelligence had nothing tangible with which to corroborate the information.[5] Intelligence continued to be gathered on the mysterious programme. In 1942 the RAF flew aerial reconnaissance missions over Peenemünde and the photographs were analysed at RAF Medmenham at Danesfield House in Buckinghamshire.[6] At this time it was not possible to identify anything unusual about the site, but by late 1942 British intelligence knew about a possible German programme to develop long-range rockets because of information from two agents behind enemy lines. According to a Chiefs of Staff memorandum, independent corroboration had until then been lacking.[7]

Confirmation of the V-weapon programme at Peenemünde came from a high-level source in March 1943: Hitler's generals in captivity in Trent Park, North London, whose unguarded conversations were also being recorded.[8] This led to further reconnaissance missions by the RAF in the late spring of 1943, and Operation Hydra was put into motion: the codename for the bombing of Peenemünde on 17–18 August 1943. This was part of a larger Allied operation codenamed Operation Crossbow that aimed at destroying V-weapon sites and the production plant for hydrogen peroxide needed for the rockets.

According to one German general held at Trent Park, in the August attack Germany lost over 700 of its scientists, technologists and workers on site.[9] It set back Hitler's V-2 programme by at least two months, possibly six. It also meant that the first V-1s did not land on London until the early hours of 13 June 1944 – a week after D-Day.[10] Ten were launched, with five failing shortly after launch, but five landed in England; one reached as far as Bethnal Green in East London.[11] Two days later, on the evening of 15 June, the Germans launched more than 200 flying bombs, of which 144 managed to cross into England, with seventy-three reaching Greater London. Thirty-three were brought down by British air defences, but eleven still reached highly built-up residential areas. It gives an idea of the sheer threat facing Britain from these weapons, and if these flying bombs had been operational earlier it is doubtful whether the Allied landings in Normandy could have taken place. This intelligence saved lives.

Hereafter it was a race to disrupt the V-weapons. MI6 was perfectly aware that the programme would be relocated, including the manufacture of parts needed for the V-1s and V-2s. Indeed, that was the case, as proved by the information provided by Clarence Service agents.

Agents of V-1 Intelligence

Intelligence on V-1 and V-2 received from the Clarence Service is to be found in two main sources: the network's radio messages transmitted to MI6, and separate intelligence reports which contain information gathered from its agents. The radio messages are relatively short, usually only a sentence or a paragraph at most, whereas the intelligence reports often run to twenty-five or thirty pages, sometimes more.

Some of the most important intelligence discussed below was provided to MI6 by female agents. Their individual roles in collecting this intelligence can now be appreciated for the first time due to the declassification of their personal files, in which their work in providing V-weapon information is recorded. It is, in fact, unusual for a personal file to note the kind of intelligence being collected; when it does, it indicates the high value of the work. Naming these agents here for the first time is an important part of paying due honour to them for securing such intelligence for the Allies.

In late November and early December 1942, the Clarence Service received some of its earliest information on V-1 bombs from behind enemy lines, thanks to agent Léon Roth.[12] Léon had been apprehended by the Gestapo for his part in a resistance movement that operated between Luxembourg and Belgium. He was sent into forced labour at Peenemünde, where he was able to witness what was going on. In an act of courage, he smuggled letters and material out to his father, Henri Roth. The latter, a Luxembourger, was a Clarence Service agent code-named 'Oscar', a forest ranger by occupation, who was recruited to the Bastogne sector of the network on 1 July 1942 by Adolphe Godart.[13] The files do not record who brought the papers from Léon to Godart, but Godart acted as the courier between father and son, and travelled to the Belgian–German frontier to collect the reports on the testing of flying torpedoes at Peenemünde.[14] Léon's information was amongst the earliest eyewitness accounts from inside the establishment and provided concrete proof of the programme.

In January 1943, Léon provided further information on the testing of new rocket-powered vehicles in Peenemünde. A sketch map of Usedom, a Baltic Sea island, was among the material smuggled out to the Clarence Service in March 1943. There was mention, too, of the Germans launching 'a pilotless aeroplane with a range of 250 kilometres'.[15] The Luxembourgers who were forced labourers at Peenemünde with Léon are mentioned in the official MI6 history, but their names are not revealed. Although Léon's name is absent as well, it is clear that the MI6 history is referring to his work.[16] The information provided by Léon to the Clarence Service was used as part of the intelligence case for Operation Hydra. Léon's legacy deserves to be more widely known.

Clarence Service agents were on the ground actively searching for the V-weapons, able to spy on and discover the locations of installations in Belgium and northern France, observe the trains moving them across Belgium, and uncover the secret factories where their special parts were being manufactured.[17] Section leaders briefed their agents to report on anything that might be relevant to secret weapons, including watching for any unusual structures being transported by rail or road.

During 1943, another agent, Joseph Moutchen ('Bernard'), brought back plans from Germany of a bomb that vaguely looked like a V-1.[18]

He was a Belgian farmer recruited by agent Monique. Drawings relating to the V-1s continued to be smuggled to the Clarence Service. On 4 January 1944 the network produced a report on Peenemünde and V-1s that was based on intelligence from an agent who was working for the Germans and whose job involved travelling in northern France. There he had seen 70m-long platforms, part of the V-1 installations.[19] Another agent observed the same a few days later.

The volume of information increased in July and August 1944 when the Germans started to move the V-1s and their components by train and sometimes road, from Germany across Belgium to northern France. Details of this traffic in the Clarence reports were considerable and included the movement of trains and the precise times and dates they were seen, often by agents during the night, as well as the locations of mobile V-1 launch sites. Their component parts were being manufactured in secret factories in Belgium and Germany.[20] This discovery by the Clarence Service was gold dust for British intelligence and underlines the significance of this network.

The study of declassified files of the Clarence Service enables a fuller understanding and appreciation today of the intelligence picture that the network provided. Taken with all the other sources coming to the Allies, it fed into operations to bomb not only Peenemünde but also other secret weapon sites and installations.

Coastal Sector

A coastal sector of the Clarence Service proved similarly successful in gaining V-weapon material. The sector was created and led by Rose Houyoux, who came directly under the leadership of Thérèse de Radiguès. In 1944, Rose's agents began to report on sightings of V-1s. They identified the locations of V-1 launch ramps and the movement of V-1s by train. Rose went on to create several further sub-networks, one of which comprised 120 agents led by a Belgian engineer, Pierre Vanderveken, whom she had recruited personally. His sector operated across a wide area from Brussels to the coast, and also into northern France and the Dutch province of Zeeland.[21] He and his agents undertook special missions to gather military intelligence in Flanders, Lille, Arras, Boulogne, Calais (including Pas-de-Calais) and Dunkirk, as well as in parts of Holland.[22]

Working in Rose's coastal section was Camille van Welput, a ship owner and a representative in West Flanders for a company based in Liège. He covered West Flanders and the entire Belgian coastline, and identified some of the V-1 launch sites in northern France. His personal file states that he provided information of exceptional value.[23] He reported on the volume of oxygen and acetylene being used in the workshops of Erla Motor Works – in Mertsel, near Antwerp, Courcelle and Courtrai – that were repairing the German Messerschmitt planes. The site had been subject to an air raid on 5 April 1943 by the US 8th Air Force, launched from its base in England. Although the factory sustained considerable damage, it was operational again within a matter of weeks. Van Welput provided a list of the Belgian firms that had priority status to supply oxygen and acetylene for Germany's armament programme. In January 1944 he had given information to the Clarence Service on German fuel depots along the Ghent–Terneuzen Canal, with the quantities of fuel used and the departure times of the fuel trains. He also unmasked the codename of a German spy, Pierre Wertz; precise details of how he did this do not survive in the files.

One unnamed agent of the coastal sector was approached by the Germans in early 1944. He became a double agent and underwent training to work with the German radio operators who were active along the coast. He was known only by his call-sign, '0500'.[24] His identity was kept secret, but his fingerprints were sent by mail to London on 12 March 1944. He was ordered by Demarque to cease all contact with other Clarence Service agents for security reasons.

Daniel Lefebvre, of French origin and a factory manager, operated in one of Rose's sub-sectors. Recruited on 1 May 1944, he located the positions of V-1 and V-2 ramps in northern France and Flanders, and provided details of wider defences along the coast.[25] His file states that during his time as an agent he gave details of the first V-1 mobile site, plus transport of the V-2, in addition to the movement and identification of various German troops. He undertook the clandestine passage of secret documents for the Clarence Service from Antwerp to Lille and Paris.

Agents working along the coastline did not report exclusively on V-weapons: they collected all relevant information for the head of their sector, as in the case of Marie Levez, who was secretary to the head of the Littoral sector, which gathered intelligence along the Belgian coast.[26] Using the pseudonym 'Mariette', she oversaw a sub-section of agents, collected military intelligence herself and operated as a courier. On her personal file it is noted that she 'delivered certain documents in very dangerous conditions'.[27] One of her agents was Jean Balteaux, who discovered information on the V-1 and V-2.[28]

Baroness de Menten

The agents reporting to forty-one-year-old Baroness Germaine de Menten ('Frédérique') were central to the success of the Allied picture of Hitler's secret weapon programme. She recruited her own sub-sector of agents and went on to deliver what is described in her personal file as 'exceptional intelligence' on the locations of manufacturing plants of explosives, as well as information on the V-1, the V-2 and Peenemünde.[29] She dispatched agents into Nazi Germany, including André de Callatay, originally from Brussels, who collected military and economic information. His file states that in March 1943 he discovered the importance of the port of Swinemünde in the V-weapon programme; it was being used to transport materials needed at the V-weapon development site at Peenemünde.[30]

The women in de Menten's Clarence Service section were not confined to a managerial or administrative role, nor did they act solely as agent handlers. Like the male agents, they undertook intelligence-gathering themselves, as well as operating as couriers and in liaison duties. All delivered vital military intelligence, crucially on the V-1, as attested in their personal agent files.

One of these agents was sixty-year-old Thomas Vinaimont, who observed military transport trains along the Herbesthal–Montzen railway line in Belgium. He saw and recorded the trains carrying V-1s and other military equipment, their transfer to other sites and how the Germans were attempting to conceal their existence.[31] A fellow agent, forty-seven-year-old Jean Lefeure, who lived in Tournai, watched the train lines around Courtrai for the movement of German troops. He discovered that there were V-1 launch pads in Mont de L'Enclus, a municipality of Wallonia, in the province of Hainaut.[32] Another agent was Léon Destenay, head of the Belgian branch of Shell, who lived in Liège, undertook military and economic espionage in Belgium, France and Germany and went on to provide the Clarence Service with information on aviation factories in Germany. He revealed the manufacturing by Germany of various turbo engines and parts for the V-1.[33]

V-Weapon Special Reports

As information on the V-weapons increased, a separate section entitled 'Special Reports on the Rockets' was appended to many of the Clarence Service intelligence reports from the summer of 1944.[34] What is now known of the Clarence Service's contribution to V-weapon intelligence comes from agent reports and radio messages sent to MI6.

It is an impressive quantity of accurate eyewitness material that enabled the Allies to track the V-weapon threat and eliminate associated sites via bombing raids. One example, just days before the first V-1 attack was launched against London from the Pas-de-Calais region, came from an unnamed male Belgian agent. Between 4 and 11 June 1944, bad weather and poor visibility had prevented aerial reconnaissance missions over V-1 sites.[35] It was he who reported on 10 June that thirty-three wagons each carrying three rocket-shaped objects had passed through Ghent.[36]

The months of July and August 1944 saw a particularly active period in the amassing of information as the Germans rained V-1s down on London and elsewhere in southern England. Knowledge of where they would be fired from was critical for British intelligence, which relied heavily on Clarence Service agents to ascertain the facts. Some of the V-1 intelligence from this period is known to have been collected by a twenty-five-year-old female agent, Francine Blondin ('Lulo'). She supplied information on V-1 installations at the Pas-de-Calais and the coastal region around Boulogne, in northern France, and the transport of V-1s by train in the Arlon and Halanzy regions of Belgium.[37]

Rose Houyoux's agents were also credited with discovering V-1 launch pads in the Pas-de-Calais region; one of them was fifty-year-old Albert Onghena.[38] On 3 July 1944, one of the agents discovered the location of V-1 launch pads around Dieppe and Neufchatel-en-Bray in Normandy.[39] Another agent, Stéphane Felix Noël, a teacher by profession, located an underground factory manufacturing the V-1s at Meurthe-et-Moselle in the east of France.[40]

On 27 July 1944, MI6 asked the Clarence Service whether the Casale and Claude factories had received an order from the Germans to purify liquid oxygen – a vital part of the secret technology.[41] SIS asked for details of other such sites purifying oxygen, including details of the quantity being produced, times of its transport and final destination.

Troops and equipment, including the V-1s, were being sent by train into France via Belgium. This intelligence led to the bombing of various railway lines by the Allies. The success or otherwise of those raids on V-weapon facilities was reported back from agents on the ground. A detailed report dated 30 July 1944 ran to twenty-eight pages and fourteen annexes, and included details of the disruption by Allied bombing to the rail lines that transported V-1s.[42] It noted that in Courtrai, 'a first wave of planes heavily bombed the railway tracks and the training station; the damage was such that traffic was interrupted for several weeks. At around 23:50 GMT, a second wave dropped all its bombs in the city, causing significant damage and casualties.'[43]

The same report went on to say that traffic had been restored on one track of the line towards Zottegem in Flanders. Around Dinant-Jemelle in the province of Namur, poor morale was observed among the German troops, especially wounded German personnel convalescing in Château d'Ardenne, whose mood was only temporarily improved by news of Germany's use of the V-1.

One Clarence Service report said, 'At Peenemünde they are currently testing V-1s which are 10 metres long, 1.5 metres in diameter and weigh 22 tons. An informant said he heard of a V-1 factory in Salzburg and another in Innsbruck. The transport is done by rail via Paderborn, Soest, Dortmund, Mönchengladbach, Montzen and Druisburg-Herbesthal.'[44]

Intelligence from Clarence Service agents operating in Germany was fruitful. A German informant from Stolberg in the Rhineland region of Germany passed on information that 'the manufacture of wooden wings and fuselages has ceased in the Stolberg-Eschweiler region and surrounding area'.[45] This confirmed that the manufacture of V-1 parts had ceased, but the challenge was to swiftly find out where it had been relocated – a task for the agents behind the lines.

Fragmentary observations on V-1s came from agents in the south of Belgium and Luxembourg. British intelligence could map an overall picture of the changing locations of the V-weapons. Another report stated to MI6 that during the night of 18–19 July 1944, 120 trucks had transported V-1s from Luxembourg across Belgium. A train of flat wagons, each with six flying bombs (V-1s), had passed through Rodange. Two days later, at around midnight, a train with covered wagons, 'which appeared to be more closely guarded than those of the V-1, stopped at Rodange Station, coming from Luxembourg toward Longwy'.[46] The report does not go on to specify what was in the closed wagons, but agents knew it must be significant if it was more heavily guarded than transports of V-1s.

Other trains of the same type had passed through the Meuse valley, but they were said to be few in number and appeared to be on diversion. A train passing through Dinant on 24 July 1944 was reported to 'consist of 36 wagons with the characteristics of a V-1 transport, going from Montzen to Givet. Transport is done by road and rail in the direction of Longwy.'[47] Another report stated:

> The launching of V-1 bombs is confirmed by several sources. About 10 trains carrying these bombs have passed through Montzen, Hasselt, Baisieux, Herbesthal, Liège and Givet between 22 and 29 July 1944. The carriages, special and new, are all attached at Klagenfurt and Villach; or they return empty. One of them was destined for Boisleux, another for Doullens.[48]

A radio message stated:

> Fifteen wagons, loaded, passed through Montzen on 27 July, en route for Utrecht. Little movement of troops during the week ending 30 July 1944. Some departures from Flanders are reported, and a few withdrawals from the Ardennes, destined for Königsberg; the whole not exceeding 5000 men. 10 trains of infantry passed through Montzen for Givet, and the same in reverse.[49]

The Clarence Service's mapping of rail routes used for the transportation of V-1s is impressive. In addition to this, locating the V-1 launch sites became a priority that lasted almost for the rest of the war.

V-1 Launch Sites

Agents of the Clarence Service were instrumental in discovering the majority of the V-1 launch sites in Belgium and northern France. Much of this information was secured from informants who reported to Clarence Service agents that they had it on good authority that there was a ramp in operation at Balgerhoeke. The relevant report went on to state:

> Until now, we had not wanted to give this information because we were not sure that all these agents were not confusing the recent

installation of rail guns moved from Knokke station to Balgerhoeke, with a launch ramp. We have just learned direct from an informant of the Standaert family that there is indeed a launch ramp at this location and operational.[50]

Information was all very well, but it had to be precise. It was often the female leaders of sectors of the Clarence Service who formulated the reports for MI6 and ensured the accuracy of detail.

In July 1944, another worker saw flying bombs being fired from two ramps between Fruges and Hesdin in France. V-1 launch ramps were spotted approximately halfway between Auxi-le-Château and Doullens, and in the Watton Woods. Around Herseaux there was a large underground storage of V-1s. Numerous reports were received on V-1 testing in these places, including those stating such tests had taken place on 19 July, at around 9.30 p.m. GMT. Several such tests were repeated every half-hour until at least 1 a.m. GMT and subsequently at intervals during the night.[51] After further V-1 tests were completed, the launch of V-1s began from new locations in the region of Watten and St Omer, and also at Lille, Roubaix, Tourcing and Mouscron. There were rumours of new launch pads being built at Howardies and Valenciennes.

At the same time as the Clarence Service was reporting on V-1s, it began to pick up information on the movement of V-2 rockets, the successor to the V-1 doodlebug. Clarence Service agents provided some of the first notifications to MI6 on the movement of V-2 rockets. One such report read, 'On 19 July 1944: arrived in Brustem, a special weapon – the V-2.'[52] Brustem was near present-day Sint-Truiden in the Flemish province of Limburg.

August Reports on the V-1

The Germans were particularly active in the movement of V-weapons towards the end of August 1944 and in the days around the Allied liberation of Paris. A radio message sent by Brulage on 25 August stated that the launch of V-1 flying bombs was confirmed by several sources.[53] Agent Burlet wrote up the subsequent report for SIS on the transport of V-weapons during this period. By this stage of the war, the Germans were in disarray in some regions behind the lines, and their direction-finding vans had ceased to operate in many regions of Belgium. Brulage operated without being caught, at a critical time when SIS needed the information on the movement of V-weapons. Two days later a message reached London conveying that between 1500 and 1600 hours, a train carrying a V-1 for the German air force had been confirmed. It had been loaded at Klagenfurt, so it seemed there was a V-1 factory close to the town. The message went on, 'Mysterious works, often including a 50-meter-long concrete track, by 10 to 50m wide, are in progress in the woods and near a reservoir. Located at one of the two woods about 1km north of the border post of Abeele, south of Poperinge.'[54] These were urgent-priority bombing targets for the Allies.

Report number 161 contains a diagram of a pilotless plane (that is, a V-1 flying bomb). It is not clear which agent supplied this. The same report includes a message sent by the radio station 'Student' on 29 August 1944 stating that an informant had spoken about a V-weapon structure 50m in diameter. Another came from a German worker who reported the existence of a V-1 factory in Salzburg.[55] A separate message sent on the same day noted that a train of twelve wagons carrying V-1s had entered Belgium two days earlier, and it had already been on the move for several days. Analysis of this comment might enable British intelligence to work out where it had come from – almost certainly from within Germany – and hence direct its agents there to look for V-2-related sites. There was confirmation too that the V-1 test launches that had been carried out at the end of July around Bruges and Thielt had since been abandoned.[56]

The next report in August consisted of thirty-six pages and twelve annexes. It mentioned that according to accounts from several agents, a train comprising forty wagons loaded with V-1s had been destroyed by Allied bombing on its route from Alost. The report catalogued further damage caused by the bombing of train lines, towns and various installations.[57]

The following report was equally lengthy and had a section on new weapons.[58] Details were given of V-1 trains crossing Belgium around 15 August 1944 and it was noted that Klagenfurt was the loading station for the V-1s, leading to suspicions of a nearby V-1 factory. Information from informants, never named in the reports, continued to be productive. One of them reported that the V-1 weighed 12,000kg. Another informant, described only as a German, had participated in the V-1 tests in the Baltic. A worker returning from Germany reported that there was a factory making V-1s in large numbers, but he did not have the exact location. According to another informant a factory near Willebroeck gas works in Belgium used only German workers and this was the liquid oxygen factory, crucial for the V-1, that other informants had spoken about.[59]

The agents were uniquely placed to deliver intelligence on the precise routes and timings of the V-1 trains. One train was reported as consisting of twelve wagons of V-1s; this was seen at Hasselt at 5.16 a.m. on 19 August 1944.[60] Other trains were said to have special wagons, and others still carried ordinary goods. Several observers saw a train consisting of forty-two wagons that was carrying V-1s and had a convoy for protection. The results of Allied bombing and sabotage by resistance groups were also recounted. Trains were reported to have been diverted due to the Allied bombing of Visé. Between 14 and 16 August 1944, one train was left in a siding at Jemappes, then left for Paris, travelled towards Tournai, but was unable to reach Tournai because of sabotage on the railway track. The last surviving intelligence report is dated 20 August 1944.[61] There are no declassified reports after this, nor for 1945, even though Clarence Service agents continued to operate beyond autumn 1944.

It is no exaggeration to say that the work of Clarence Service agents on V-weapon intelligence provided the Allies with reliable eyewitness information that could not be secured any other way with such accuracy. Their operations across a vast geographical network prevented the V-weapons from tipping the war in favour of Nazi Germany. It was an incredible achievement.

Chapter 16
LIBERATION

On 2 September 1944, radio operator Burlet received the latest instructions from MI6 in London. As soon as the Allied forces' tactical operations came closer to a particular sector of the network, the Clarence Service was to dispatch an agent across the lines to link up and liaise with British and American intelligence officers.[1] All intelligence material that the agent was carrying was to be handed over to Allied intelligence officers. On the morning of 3 September, Demarque sent a message to SIS via Burlet that the Allies had made such a rapid advance that he was not sure he would be able to notify the chiefs of his sectors in time. He therefore sent the details of his radio operators and contacts direct to SIS.

On the same day, just a few hours before the liberation of Brussels, Demarque sent a message to the Belgian government-in-exile from the Gilles Group. It was transmitted by Burlet and informed the government that non-military individuals would be assuming roles in government as soon as German troops had withdrawn, to enable stability to be swiftly brought to the country.[2] That evening, the first liberating troops of the Guards Armoured Division entered Brussels. The SIS unit attached to 21st Army Group Headquarters also entered the city. The following day, Belgian troops and other Allied forces swarmed into the capital. By the end of that day, the 11th British Armoured Division had also entered Antwerp.

The liberation of Brussels meant that the network's operations around Liège, where fighting was still ongoing, had been temporarily cut off from headquarters. The leaders in Liège wished to re-establish contact with Brussels. Françoise Boseret, granddaughter of Gustave Snoech (the latter a veteran of the White Lady), cycled between Brussels HQ and Liège and became the only line of communication between them for six days, until the liberation of Liège on 8 September 1944.[3] While German forces were still fighting in Liège, Boseret courageously crossed the Val-Benoît bridge and took valuable intelligence back to the Americans. Later she undertook several undisclosed, perilous intelligence missions for the American forces.

The advance by these liberating forces had been made easier by the wider work of the Belgian resistance in sabotage and guerrilla warfare. Clarence Service agents from occupied regions of Belgium crossed into liberated parts of the country to brief Allied commanders on troop positions behind the German lines. Two Clarence Service agents were killed in the process of one of these dangerous missions.[4]

During this period immediately after liberation, radio operators Tinsel and Brulage, who had parachuted into the country a few months earlier, prepared to penetrate the German lines and broadcast to London from the last remaining occupied regions. A first attempt failed, but the subsequent speed of the Allied advance made a part of their mission redundant and it was aborted.

On 8 September 1944, as US forces advanced near the Fort de la Chartreuse, information from agent Jacques Jansen enabled American tanks to liberate one side of the Meuse and chase German light armoured vehicles as they tried to escape.[5] Jansen had spent the previous six months monitoring the Chartreuse barracks from an observation post and reported all that he saw, including the movement of German soldiers, to one of the Clarence Service sectors. Aged just sixteen, he hoisted a Belgian flag at the top of the bell tower, but 400 SS troops were still in the area, surrounded by Belgian resistance fighters. Jansen held the flag until he was hit by a German bullet and seriously wounded. He died two days later.

By the time of the liberation, the entire country was covered by intelligence networks, with more than forty clandestine radio transmissions being used, or in reserve solely, for Belgian intelligence purposes. Tens of thousands of documents were produced via these networks for British intelligence; 25,000 were said to have been 'of incontestable, often even of highest, importance'.[6] The Clarence Service was the largest of these networks.

Agents into Germany

On 11 September 1944, Jempson ('Page') landed at Arromanches in Normandy, accompanied by Fernand Lepage, the chief of the Belgian security service, the Sûreté de l'État.[7] Two days later Jempson arrived at the Hotel Metropole in Brussels with Ruth Stowell, and they began the important work of routing out Belgians who had collaborated with the Nazis, to ensure that they did not serve in public posts or in the police force. Stowell and Jempson also sent new agents deep into Germany. The secret V-2 sites had to be tracked down and intelligence on them sent to London, including details of the V-2 tests being carried out at Venlo in eastern Holland.[8]

On 13 September, Ostend was liberated and the MI6 double agent codenamed '0500' handed over the names of eleven German radio operators, leading to their arrests.[9] The Clarence Service received its final message from MI6 the following day, in which the organisation expressed deep gratitude from His Majesty's Government for the network's achievements.[10] However, operations were far from over. The following day, Jempson reported back to London that he was sending a man into Germany for the Clarence Service to prepare a reception committee to receive six agents, to be dropped by parachute during the next full moon.[11] Observation cells were established.

On 18 October, SIS headquarters in London informed the head of the SIS unit attached to 21st Army Group Headquarters that he should speed up the delivery of information and prioritise operational intelligence, including from well behind the lines.[12] Before the unit continued its advance into Holland, intelligence officers were hived off to form the nucleus of an SIS station, initially to liaise with the Sûreté de l'État, which was in the process of re-establishing itself in Brussels.

Few files of the Clarence Service have been declassified for this period, with only a handful surviving in the National Museum of the Resistance in Brussels. These offer a glimpse into some of the activity at this time. Henri Chauvin, a veteran of the White Lady and a founding member and leader of the Clarence Service, was overseeing radio transmissions in the region of Liège.[13] He was asked to urgently find radio telegraphic specialists who could speak German: they were to be sent on a secret mission into Germany.[14] A report commented that among the leaders of the Clarence Service were those who would 'possess both the culture and guts required to serve in the new concept of cell organisation in enemy territory'.[15]

Parts of Liège were still being bombed by the Germans – two devices an hour, day and night, killing eighteen people and seriously injuring 202 people.[16] The American hospital was hit and patients were injured by shards of glass. Six children were killed in a nursery, and in the market square four were killed and thirty injured. Alice Weimerskirch and her parents were some of those hurt in the attack. The Weimerskirch family, who had been involved in both the White Lady and the Clarence Service, survived.

As 1944 drew to a close, on New Year's Eve, Chauvin wrote to Demarque:

> I present you warmest wishes for the year which is about to begin and hope that it will bring the crowning of your work that we have undertaken under our late leader Mr Clement [Dewé] and yours. I send my best wishes to Colonel Page in London, as well as officers around him with whom we collaborate in such a friendly manner.[17]

He informed Demarque that he was setting up secret groups in Germany to establish contact with resistance groups there, and that he had already made contact with 'Edelweiss', a resistance group in the Aachen region.[18] In the same correspondence Chauvin told Demarque that his own wife and son had been compromised at the time of the liberation and he had arranged for their evacuation to his brother-in-law in Hastière-Lavaux. Chauvin reported that the agent Monsieur Maxime had made a perilous expedition through a region criss-crossed by German tanks and he was able to relay messages to Clarence sector chiefs.[19] Chauvin reinforced his commitment to the Allied cause by offering to continue his services for Page and Demarque, in the event that the German forces did not fully withdraw.

Counter-Offensive in the Ardennes

In the late winter of 1944, the Germans mounted their last counter-offensive in the Ardennes region, known as the Battle of the Bulge, led by Field Marshal Gerd von Rundstedt. Henri Chauvin had created a mobile Directorate of Radio Broadcasts company to cover the Liège–Luxembourg region. This mobile unit acted as observers during the von Rundstedt offensive.[20] Clarence Service agents played a critical role in the battle that has been hitherto unrecognised. Although only a few files are available, we do know which agents were active in the Ardennes. Chauvin's agents were involved and were dispatched deep behind the German line from Liège. Chauvin planned a final operation to penetrate the region of Waismies, Saint-Vith and the river Lienne – a mission that was completed on 19 January 1945.[21]

Another Clarence Service agent who took part in the network's clandestine operations and spied on von Rundstedt's forces was thirty-six-year-old Pierre Michiels, who lived in Hasselt and had been recruited with agent number 7500. He undertook a special mission in the Ardennes in autumn 1944, the nature of which has not been disclosed but was almost certainly to gain information on German troops.[22] Georges

Withofs, who was recruited as late as 7 September 1944, undertook missions in the Luxembourg region to gather military information.[23]

The female agents were as important in the final stages of the war as at any point since 1940. Among them was Frédérique (Baroness Germaine de Menten), who, having already run a sub-sector of agents that secured intelligence on V-weapons, now carried out a dangerous liaison mission that involved travelling forty-four miles among German troops.[24] During the Ardennes campaign of winter 1944, she carried out a successful attack behind the German lines in the province of Luxembourg. No further details of her mission have been disclosed in the files. Another aristocrat, Countess Marthe de Meeus, gave over the Château de Tharoul in the province of Liège to the Red Cross in September 1944; from there she and two nurses observed German military activity during the whole of the Ardennes offensive.[25] She had been recruited in May 1940 and had hidden a British parachutist, William Castley, as well as Walthère Dewé's son, Jacques (who had been operating as a courier), until the liberation of Belgium. Frédérique saved many Clarence Service agents from being sent into forced labour in Germany and participated in the liberation of the region.

During September 1944, Jeanne Delwaide – who had served in the White Lady, had spent a year in Siegburg prison in Germany in the last war and was on the board of the Clarence Service from 1940 – saved the bridge over the Nèthe at Walem. The Germans had rigged explosives in a nearby house that would knock out the bridge.[26] Following a shoot-out between a German officer and the head of a sector of the Clarence Service, Delwaide entered the house and defused the two batteries. She left the house safely and, thanks to her heroism, just a few hours later, British tanks were able to cross the bridge.

Stay-Behind Agents

Towards the end of November 1944, Chauvin wrote again to Demarque, informing him that he and 'Daniel' had had a conversation about the final missions into Germany. Chauvin wrote, 'There needs to be a support point (stay behind) mission in enemy countries. This is the most perilous part of the final mission. A mission has been carried out in central Germany. This serves as a valuable support point.'[27] He was referring to the need for 'stay-behind' units in the event of further conflict. These were 'sleeper' agents who remained in the field when all other operatives had been withdrawn. They could be reactivated at any time.

Thus far only one 'stay-behind' agent of the Clarence Service can be named from a study of the network's declassified files, and it was a woman.[28] Ghislaine Marie de Moreau, born in Namur in 1908, had been recruited to the Clarence Service by Thérèse de Radiguès on 10 May 1940. Moreau operated from her home at Château d'Andoy in Naninne, and under the false identity of Pauline Cornil, in the rank of warrant officer. She was listed as having no profession. She had created a group of men and women who constituted the first nucleus of agents in the sector of Namur. She was the chief of a sub-section of the sector until the liberation of the region and gained military, economic and political intelligence for MI6. She ran couriers, oversaw the dead letter boxes and set up observation posts. Her brother headed the whole section around Namur until his arrest in August 1944. After his arrest, she continued the work and demonstrated great initiative in organising her agents to gain intelligence in readiness for combat along the Namur–Meuse front. She remained deep undercover for the Allies during the last German offensive in the Ardennes.

By mid-January 1945, the war on Belgian soil was drawing to a close, with the final German troops being driven out in early February. On 27 January, Soviet forces liberated Auschwitz. Images of the concentration camp shocked the world, but there was more horror to be revealed as the other death camps were liberated by Allied forces in the coming months. Buchenwald concentration camp was liberated on 11 April and Bergen-Belsen on the 15th.

The fate of some of the Clarence Service agents who had been held in the other camps was still unknown. On 30 April, the vanguard of the

Soviet army arrived at Ravensbrück concentration camp. Only thirteen days earlier, on 17 April, Walthère Dewé's daughter Madeleine had died in the camp, comforted by her sister Marie, who did survive. The first liberated Belgian prisoners, including the agents of the Clarence Service, began to return home to Belgium. They had endured terrible conditions and unimaginable torture, been medically experimented on by the Nazis, and had survived death marches. Walthère Dewé junior returned to Liège from captivity in May 1945.

Thérèse de Radiguès and her family paid a great personal price for their work for the Allies. Her son Jean arrived home during the night of 28–29 June 1945 after three years in German captivity and a few weeks in a Russian prison. His joy at being freed was shattered by the news that his eldest son Charles had been arrested at Château Ostin for his part in the Belgian Secret Army. Charles was deported to Mauthausen concentration camp, where he died on 22 October 1944. He was just twenty-one years old.

Of the 300 agents parachuted into Belgium in clandestine missions across the war, around 100 did not survive their mission and were captured, not usually during their landing but while operating within the country.[29] Fifty-two members of the Clarence Service lost their lives in the fight for freedom; some had been shot in Liège, Ghent, Brussels and Utrecht.[30] They are named on a special memorial in Liège. Among them are the names of the women who died in Ravensbrück concentration camp.[31]

Mill

Adrien Marquet ('Mill'), who had led the Mill network for SIS, formally ended his services on 7 August 1945.[32] However, he remained in touch with SIS, and after learning that the German ambassador, who was imprisoned in St Gilles prison, was prepared to hand over details and plans of the V-2 in return for concessions by the Allies, he sent a telegram to London to inform SIS.[33] From his time as leader of Mill,

Marquet would have appreciated how important this information would be. Jempson, now stationed in Brussels, was asked by SIS to find out whether it was true, and to arrange for a Belgian officer and one of his British colleagues to interrogate the German ambassador in prison. Nothing further is revealed about this case in the files.

Marquet was asked to hand over all files and documents relating to the Mill network to the Belgian State Security Service, and they remained classified for over eighty years.[34] He was awarded an OBE, on the recommendation of Page (Jempson).[35] The farmer who had hidden and looked after Marquet and René Clippe on their parachute landing was tracked down by British intelligence and given a reward. Marquet was rarely seen at post-war commemorations or parades, and wrote and said very little about his war. For a man who had delivered so much, he remained quietly in the background and requested a quiet funeral, no fuss. That is exactly what happened after his death in 1972.

Marquet is an example of how these agents and leaders continued their civilian lives, rarely speaking of the war outside their own family circle. In addition, the files relating to their work remained classified for decades afterwards.

Recognition

With the war over, the process began of cataloguing the agents' files and documents, all of which formed a comprehensive archive and were kept classified by the Belgian Security Service. In 1954 Hector Demarque was asked to return all radio equipment used by the network.[36] The official figure given for the number who operated in the Clarence Service is 1,547.[37] Today, with the benefit of the declassified files, it is possible to see that there was a greater number of women and men who aided the network, even though they were not recognised as agents.

On 30 March 1946, Field Marshal Montgomery, commander of the 21st Army Group, expressed his appreciation and admiration to the agents. A certificate has survived in the Tandel archives, personally signed by Montgomery, which states, 'By this Certificate of Service I record my appreciation of the aid rendered by Mademoiselle Laure Tandel and Louise Tandel as a volunteer in the service of the United Nations for the great cause of Freedom.'[38]

For their bravery, members of the Clarence Service were given various awards by their own country as well as Britain and America. The agents were given the status of 'Agent in the Intelligence and Action Services' (IAA agent) with retroactive effect. The leaders Walthère Dewé (posthumously) and Hector Demarque were appointed Colonel IAA and Lieutenant Colonel IAA respectively. The five women on the board of directors, Thérèse de Radiguès, Henriette Dupuich, Rose Houyoux, Violette Verhoogen and Germaine de Menten, were appointed Captain IAA.[39] All received the King's Medal for Courage in the Cause of Freedom, except Germaine de Menten, who received an OBE. Thérèse de Radiguès lived to the great age of ninety-eight and died in Brussels on 16 June 1963.[40]

Hector Demarque was awarded the DSO and died on 7 March 1975. Henri Chauvin received the King's Medal for Courage in the Cause of Freedom. Dewé was posthumously awarded the King's Commendation for Brave Conduct (military). On 19 October 1945 a memorial service was held in Liège Cathedral to commemorate his life.[41]

Frederick Jempson and Ruth Stowell, the two SIS officers who ran the Clarence Service from MI6's Belgian desk in London, were honoured by the Grand Duchy of Luxembourg.[42] Jempson was made a Commander of the Order of the Oaken Crown, and Stowell was made a Chevalier of the Order of the Oaken Crown. Her citation reads: 'In recognition of valuable service rendered during the war, in the organisation and maintenance of effective intelligence services between this country [Britain] and occupied Luxembourg, and in the training of Luxembourg Intelligence Agents parachuted into enemy occupied territory.'[43]

During 1945, Stowell returned to the UK from Belgium and married her second husband, Leslie Scarman (later Baron), who himself had a distinguished war and went on to have an eminent career as a High

Court judge and barrister. Jempson moved to Aachen in Germany, where he remarried and later died. In the official MI6 history there is no mention of Stowell's central role in the Belgian and Luxembourg missions; only Jempson is cited in it. Given that she had been responsible for the missions of parachutists and agents into the Grand Duchy of Luxembourg, as well as being an agent handler alongside Jempson for the Belgian missions, mention could, indeed should, have been made of her. It is quite possible her absence was due to the closed files surrounding MI6, but it has meant that the part she played in the success of agent missions has thus far been invisible – until now. Telling her story in this book has been part of restoring the contribution of women to our narratives – women who have been absent for far too long in the history of intelligence.[44]

On 21 September 1952, a private Catholic chapel was inaugurated on a hilltop in Liège and it was here that Walthère Dewé was finally laid to rest. It is called Chapelle Saint-Maurice. On its exterior wall stands a colossal white statue of a robed woman, carved by the sculptor Jules Brouns, with her finger to her lips in a 'hush' gesture. As leader of both networks across two world wars, Dewé left an enormous legacy.

EPILOGUE

A HUSH WAR

The stories of the White Lady, Clarence Service and Mill are astonishing tales of selfless heroism from behind the German lines in Belgium in two world wars. Some of these stories have been told here for the very first time. A study of the declassified files has revealed just how significant Belgium was to intelligence operations in these wars, and, importantly, how the networks sprang from the initiative and courage of ordinary Belgians. The vast intelligence-gathering operation by the Belgian agents across Belgium, northern France and the Grand Duchy of Luxembourg was simple but effective. They developed techniques in espionage and contributed to methods of intelligence-gathering at a time when the nascent British Secret Service itself was developing new forms of spycraft. They proved to be so effective in World War One with the White Lady network that they did it all over again in the next war under the Clarence Service and Mill. By World War Two, the former leaders and agents of the White Lady were in their sixties and seventies, yet they were prepared to revive the network and develop the spy techniques that they had used before. They were uniquely placed to help MI6 because they had the expertise on and knowledge of how to successfully run an intelligence organisation behind German lines. Clarence and Mill succeeded precisely because they were the direct successors of the White Lady.

The Belgian networks provided a comprehensive picture for the British Secret Service of the enemy's fighting capability and operations within German-occupied Belgium, and even beyond its own borders into Germany itself. They amassed an extraordinary quantity of detailed and reliable information that ranged from technical military details about infrastructure and airfields, to the location of troops and supplies, defences, the top-secret V-weapon programme, the results of Allied bombing raids, enemy communications and so much more.[1]

It is pertinent to ask – without the intelligence coming out of Belgium, could the Allies have won these two wars? Intelligence had the power to influence and change the fighting on the ground, and in World War Two in the air, too. Intelligence from the White Lady gave the Allies the advantage: the British Secret Service could pass strategic information to its military commanders on areas of the front line and where Germany was reinforcing with new troops. On several occasions during World War One, the White Lady gave a real indication of where the next major German offensive would take place. In the end, these networks saved lives and shortened the war. From the intelligence files for the Clarence Service in World War Two, it is possible to understand the sheer scale of the detailed information being provided to MI6 from behind German lines. This network acted as an important early-warning sign for the rest of Western Europe, prior to German forces sweeping across the Low Countries and France. No wonder Claude Dansey, not a man prone to flattery, concluded that the Clarence Service was the most crucial network providing military information in all of occupied Europe.[2]

The Belgian networks are a reminder of how women were quite literally the invisible spies of both wars. Their part in this work was not incidental but essential, and they readily volunteered. They operated as leaders of intelligence sectors, ran agents, dead letter boxes and courier lines, and became couriers themselves. They coded messages into their knitting and provided safehouses for compromised leaders, agents and parachutists. Crucially, they undertook the same roles and risks as the men, on an equal basis, and were given military status like the men. The White Lady became the first known network of agents with military rank to be attached to the British army in combatant roles, albeit without uniform.

As we have seen, this work was not without its risks, as agents and operatives lost their lives in this fight for freedom while helping the Allies. The Belgian networks paid a heavy personal price for their devotion to the cause of freedom. Many agents were shot by the Germans for espionage, or sent to their death in concentration camps (in the case of the 1939–45 war). They understood the personal risks, yet knew that their covert work could help the Allies turn the tide of the war.

Over a hundred years after the end of World War One and over eighty years since the end of World War Two, an examination of a wealth of files in Belgium and London has yielded a rich, exciting history that has too often been forgotten or overlooked. This comprehensive history of the White Lady, Clarence Service and Mill enables a fuller understanding of these highly effective networks, and firmly places them within intelligence history and the wider mainstream history of two world wars.

Today, the archives in Brussels and London attest to an extraordinary web of agents that was operational right across Belgium, and these files deserve much more study by historians outside Belgium. Thousands of brave Belgian women and men operated behind the German lines and risked their lives to ensure that MI6 had the intelligence it needed. They understood just how important their clandestine operations were for the Allies and the impact their intelligence-gathering could have on the outcome of the war. Their story provides a window onto an organisation – MI6 – that continues to be, quite rightly, highly secretive and remains reluctant to speak about its operations and intelligence successes.

Through their devotion and courage, the Belgian agents played an enormous part in the defeat of the occupying German forces and the restoration of democracy in Europe during the twentieth century. It is time for Belgium to receive due recognition and step into the historical limelight for delivering what numbered among the greatest intelligence networks of the two world wars for the British Secret Service. It is a history of heroism and selfless sacrifice of which Belgium can be so very proud.

PLATES

1. Statue of the White Lady, Chapelle Saint-Maurice, Liège. Author's collection.
2. View of Liège. Author's collection.
3. Dieudonné Lambrecht. Courtesy of the State Archives of Belgium.
4. Walthère Dewé with his wife Dieudonnée. Courtesy of the State Archives of Belgium.
5. Original map of the White Lady's operations in Belgium. Author's collection.
6. Code used by Post 49. Author's collection.
7. Information sheet concerning military information, issued to agents of the White Lady. Author's collection.
8. Original tiny messages written by hand. Author's collection.
9. Thérèse de Radiguès. Courtesy of François de Radiguès.
10. Conneux Castle near Ciney. Courtesy of François de Radiguès.
11. White Lady oath of allegiance. Author's collection.
12. The Boompjes, Rotterdam. Penta Springs Limited / Alamy.
13. German intelligence headquarters, Rotterdam. Author's collection.
14. Fort de la Chartreuse, Liège. Author's collection.
15. Remnants of the high-voltage electric fence along the Belgian–Dutch border. Author's collection.

16. Villa des Hirondelles, Wandre. Author's collection.
17. Louis and Antony Collard. Courtesy of the State Archives of Belgium.
18. Jeanne Goeseels. Courtesy of the State Archives of Belgium.
19. Madame Tutiaux. Author's collection.
20. Farm cottage of Monsieur and Madame Tutiaux. Author's collection.
21. Safehouse used by the White Lady. Author's collection.
22. Stewart Menzies, photograph by Walter Stoneman, 1953. © National Portrait Gallery, London.
23. Hector Demarque. Courtesy of the Belgian State Security Archive.
24. Seal of the Clarence Service. Courtesy of the Belgian State Security Archive.
25. Ruth Clement Stowell. Courtesy of John Scarman.
26. Clarence Service certificate for Alice Matthys. Courtesy of the Belgian State Security Archive.
27. Walthère Dewé at Château Ostin. Courtesy of the family de Radiguès.
28. Clarence Service intelligence report for October 1941. Courtesy of the Belgian State Security Archive.
29. Clarence Service report for Page, 1941. Courtesy of the Belgian State Security Archive.
30. Personal record for agent Francine Blondin. Courtesy of the Belgian State Security Archive.
31. Identity card for Louise Tandel. Courtesy of SGRS, Belgian Military Archives.
32. Thérèse de Radiguès. Courtesy of François de Radiguès.
33. Rue de la Brasserie, Brussels. Author's collection.
34. Memorial plaque to Walthère Dewé. Author's collection.

NOTES

Prologue

1. The children were Louis (b. 2.2.1887), born of Henri de Radiguès's first marriage, Carlos (30.10.1889), Marguerite (10.9.1891), Jean (21.2.1893), Xavier (15.8.1895), Marie-Antoinette (31.5.1898), Gérard (6.5.1901) and Agnès (6.3.1903).
2. Unpublished memoirs of Agnès de Radiguès, youngest child of Thérèse and Henri de Radiguès. Copy given to the author by François de Radiguès.
3. Unpublished memoirs of Agnès de Radiguès.
4. Unpublished memoirs of Agnès de Radiguès.
5. David Stevenson, *1914–1918: The History of the First World War*, Penguin, 2012, p. 93; and Henri Bernard, *Un géant de la resistance: Walthère Dewé*, La Renaissance du Livre, 1971, p. 17.
6. Verified by the consular stamps on Marguerite's passport, de Radiguès family archive.
7. During Marguerite's second visit to England in April 1915, Edmond died of appendicitis and peritonitis.
8. Agnès wrote about their time in England in her unpublished memoirs, entry for 9 February 1915.
9. Unpublished memoirs of Agnès de Radiguès, entry for 15 February 1915.
10. Memoirs of Gabrielle de Monge, copy given to the author, pp. 177–9.
11. Thérèse de Radiguès (née Minette) was born on 27 June 1865.
12. Henri de Radiguès was the father of Louis from his first marriage to Marguerite, sister of Thérèse.
13. Names listed for awards in the *London Gazette*, 1919. The list is reproduced in Decock, *La Dame Blanche: Un réseau de renseignements de la Grande Guerre*, Histoire Contemporaine ULB, 2010 edition, pp. 263–8.

Introduction

1. Particularly helpful for a solid historical background to World War One are Jim Beach, *Haig's Intelligence: GHQ and the German Army*, Cambridge University

Press, 2013; Hew Strachan, *The First World War*, Simon & Schuster, 2014; and Stevenson, *1914–1918*.

2. Arthur Weiner to his wife in Germany, letter dated 18 December 1914, quoted by kind permission of his grandson Arthur Weiss.

3. The women of the White Lady network have been analysed in a chapter in Tammy Proctor, *Female Intelligence: Women and Espionage in the First World War*, New York University Press, 2003, pp. 75–98. The network also featured in Christopher Andrew, *Secret Service: The Making of the British Intelligence Community*, Book Club Associates, 1985; and Michael Occleshaw, *Armour Against Fate: British Military Intelligence in the First World War*, Columbus Books, 1989.

4. A brief history of the White Lady appears in Keith Jeffery, *MI6: The History of the Secret Intelligence Service 1909–1949*, Bloomsbury, 2010, pp. 78–87; and the Clarence Service: Jeffery, *MI6*, pp. 388–9 and 521–3.

5. Jeffery, *MI6*, p. 81.

6. Jeffery, *MI6*, p. 521.

7. *David Jason's Secret Service*, produced by October Films for Channel 4, 2017.

8. A number of historians, including myself, were interviewed for the series, alongside relatives of former agents.

9. The history is told in Janet Morgan, *The Secrets of Rue St Roch: Intelligence Operations Behind Enemy Lines in the First World War*, Allen Lane, 2004. Lise was the wife of Dr Camille Rischard, a doctor to the railway workers in Luxembourg. He was in an excellent position to recruit railway workers to give information on the movement of trains across the rail network.

On the subject of Luxembourg, there can be some misunderstanding as there is a region of Belgium known as Luxembourg: this is distinct from the country of Luxembourg (the Grand Duchy). The White Lady operated in Belgian Luxembourg, which covers the southernmost province of Wallonia in Belgium and borders the Walloon provinces of Liège and Namur (the latter less than twenty miles from Conneux Castle), as well as into the Grand Duchy of Luxembourg.

10. It was run from Paris by Captain Bruce, and not from Rotterdam by Captain Tinsley.

11. Morgan, *The Secrets of Rue St Roch*, p. 366.

12. For more on Gabrielle Petit, see Sophie de Schaepdrijver's biography, *Gabrielle Petit: The Death and Life of a Female Spy in the First World War*, Bloomsbury, 2015; also Proctor, *Female Intelligence*, pp. 115–18; and Helen Fry, *Women in Intelligence: The Hidden History of Two World Wars*, Yale University Press, 2023, pp. 28–30.

13. For over twelve months, Petit and her agents sent out fifty intelligence reports for British intelligence on enemy troop movements and positions, uniforms, units and weapons. Report entitled 'The Journeys of Gabrielle Petit at Tournai', dated 2 July 1920, ref: Folder Petit, File 173, Services Patriotiques, State Archives, Belgium. See also Kathryn Atwood, *Women Heroes of World War I: 16 Remarkable Resisters*, Chicago Review Press, 2014, p. 60.

14. 'The Journeys of Gabrielle Petit at Tournai', dated 2 July 1920, signed by Henri Philippart and witnessed by L. Tandel, ref: Folder Petit, File 173, Services Patriotiques, State Archives, Belgium. The three agents in her network alongside her were Laure Butin, Adèle Collet and Hélène Petit. See also Folder Petit, File 40 in the same archive.

15. A 420-page inventory compiled by Anne Lannoye in collaboration with Debruyne, Tallier, Bailly and Funck, 'Inventaire des archives de la Commission des Archives des Services patriotiques établis en Territoire occupé au Front de l'Ouest (1914–1930)', I 581, State Archives, Belgium, copy given to the author.

16. These are catalogued under La Dame Blanche, ref: Documents.17076. At the end of 1918 and into 1919, the agents were asked by the leadership to write up their personal account of their activities for the White Lady.

17. La Dame Blanche, ref: LDB [CAP 10] BE-A0510/1 581. Also, the personal papers and archive of Walthère Dewé, ref: BE-A0547/FICINV_1699.

18. SGRS, Belgian Military Archives, Brussels.

19. Thanks to the help and generosity of François de Radiguès, grandson of Thérèse de Radiguès.

20. Clarence Service papers in the IWM, ref: Documents.17074; and AA1311, individual files of intelligence and action agents, Belgian State Security Archives, Cegesoma.

21. Used by kind permission of the archivist Samuel Pauwels.

22. AA1333, individual files of intelligence and action agents, Belgian State Security Archives, Cegesoma.

23. It is a huge privilege to have been granted early access to these files by the Belgian State Security. I am extremely grateful to Robin Libert.

24. Personal notes and files in AA1333, the individual files of intelligence and action agents, Belgian State Security Archives, Cegesoma. For example, Octave Delvaux (a courier and a reception point for agents) was recruited in June 1942 as agent number 9006. Armand Philippot (agent) was recruited on 1 October 1942 as agent number 9051.

25. Most notably the extensive research and publications by Professor Emmanuel Debruyne, Henri Bernard and Dr Pierre Decock, as referenced in the bibliography of this book.

26. This has been reprinted by Biteback as *The Spy Net: The Greatest Intelligence Operations of the First World War*, 2015, with an introduction by Michael Smith.

27. Jeffery, *MI6*, p. 244. In *Spreading the Spy Net: The Story of a British Spy Director*, Jarrolds, 1938, Landau drew on his earlier books and included new interviews with former agents and extra material about the German counter-espionage operations against the network.

28. In defending his actions, Landau maintained that the damage had been done after the names of 3,000 Belgian agents were published in the *London Gazette* in 1919 when they were awarded various medals. Even so, his memoirs did risk the lives of Belgian agents in the next war.

29. See Jeffery, *MI6*, pp. 243–4.

30. Landau was arrested in Rotterdam in 1917 and questioned about 'immoral sexual behaviour' towards at least one errand boy. He was released as there was no independent third witness to the acts. See Edwin Ruis, *Spynest: British and German Espionage from Neutral Holland 1914–1918*, History Press, 2012, p. 200.

31. Jeffery, *MI6*, p. 77. Sigismund Payne Best, who served alongside Landau in Rotterdam from 1917, also praised Landau. See his unpublished memoirs, chapter entitled 'Active Service', p. 6, ref: 09/51/5, IWM. Tinsley and other officers gave Best a hard time; they themselves engaged in their own shady, illegal activities.

32. An example of this is Cumming's recruitment of Landau for the job in Rotterdam in 1916. Jeffery, *MI6*, p. 77.

33. This is a view with which historian Alan Judd concurs. See Alan Judd, *The Quest for C: Mansfield Cumming and the Founding of the Secret Service*, HarperCollins, 1999, p. 361.

34. Jeffery, *MI6*, p. 77. For the file buttressing Landau's version, see WO 339/12456, which provides a helpful, accurate timeline of the recruitment by Cumming and reasons for the one-month delay in Landau's arrival in Rotterdam.

35. Judd, *The Quest for C*, p. 362.

36. For Cameron's recruitment to Cumming's organisation, see Jeffery, *MI6*, p. 35 and p. 71.

37. Jeffery, *MI6*, p. 71; Michael Smith, *Six: A History of Britain's Secret Intelligence Service*, Dialogue, 2010, p. 47; and Sigismund P. Best, unpublished memoirs, chapter entitled 'London Office', p. 10.

38. The latter are unnamed in the official MI6 history: Jeffery, *MI6*, p. 35.

39. Smith, *Six*, p. 44. See also Beach, *Haig's Intelligence*, pp. 117–19.

40. Smith, *Six*, p. 44. See also Beach, *Haig's Intelligence*, pp. 117–19.

41. From October 1914 GHQ moved to the French town of Saint-Omer, then in March 1916 to Montreuil. Beach, *Haig's Intelligence*, p. 32.

42. Jeffery, *MI6*, pp. 68–9.

43. Jeffery, *MI6*, p. 69.

44. Beach, *Haig's Intelligence*, p. 118. By March 1915, Long's contract with Cumming's organisation was not renewed, as Long had been a failure. See Jeffery, *MI6*, p. 72.

45. Jeffery, *MI6*, p. 69; and Beach, *Haig's Intelligence*, p. 119.

46. Jeffery, *MI6*, pp. 69–70; and Smith, *Six*, p. 39.

47. Smith, *Six*, p. 44.

48. Jeffery, *MI6*, p. 72.

49. Jeffery, *MI6*, p. 70.

50. Ruis, *Spynest*, p. 201.

51. Alastair Smith Cumming's personal army record, WO 339/7419. For an account of the accident, see also Judd, *The Quest for C*, pp. 283–5 and Jeffery, *MI6*, pp. 71–2.

52. Jeffery, *MI6*, pp. 71–2.

53. Captain Bruce (later Lord Balfour) was a descendant of Robert the Bruce (King of Scots).

54. Told in full by Janet Morgan in *The Secrets of Rue St Roch*. From September 1917 Bruce's office in Paris was finally separated from Folkestone and operated independently.

55. 'History of Intelligence, British Expeditionary Force, France from January 1917 to April 1919: The Secret Service', in WO 106/45, TNA (The Secret Service, in History of Intelligence and Secret Service Organisations, 1 January 1917–30 April 1919). See also Jeffery, *MI6*, p. 71.

56. Sigismund Payne Best, unpublished memoirs, chapter entitled 'Le Cateau', p. 4, personal papers, 09/51/5, folder 22, IWM.

57. 'History of Intelligence (B), British Expeditionary Force, France from January 1917 to April 1919', in WO 106/45, TNA (The Secret Service, in History of Intelligence and Secret Service Organisations, 1 January 1917–30 April 1919).

58. Smith, *Six*, pp. 55–60; and Jeffery, *MI6*, p. 46.

59. Smith, *Six*, p. 50.
60. 'History of the British Secret Service in Holland, World War I', 1917, WO 106/6189, TNA.
61. Jeffery, *MI6*, p. 76. Ernest Wallinger was not permitted to expand his organisation.
62. Jeffery, *MI6*, p. 73.

1. A Pioneer of the Resistance

1. Decock, *La Dame Blanche*, p. 12.
2. Smith, *Six*, p. 48; and Landau, *Spreading the Spy Net*, p. 53.
3. Dewé, 'Historique du service Lambrecht', P/24, State Archives, Belgium.
4. Bernard, *Un géant*; and Decock, *La Dame Blanche*, pp. 12–15.
5. 'Copies des billets de prisons dactylographiés du Révérend Père Des Onays, de Philippe Montfort et de Delhaise, 1919–1921', BE-AO510_002182_002443, 1043, State Archives, Belgium. See Dewé's report, 'Historique du Service Lambrecht', P/24, State Archives, Belgium; and also Decock, *La Dame Blanche*, p. 13 and Bernard, *Un géant*, p. 27.
6. The structure is explained in more detail in Decock, *La Dame Blanche*, pp. 84–91.
7. For Dewé's background and life in the White Lady and the Clarence Service, see Emmanuel Debruyne, 'La maison de verre: Agents et réseaux de renseignements en Belgique occupée, 1940–1944', Université Catholique de Louvain, 2005–6; Bernard, *Un géant*; and E. Roche, *Walthère Dewé: Commandant en chef de la Dame Blanche (1914–1918) et du Service Clarence (1940–1944)*, Liège, 1956.
8. La Régie des Téléphones et des Télégraphes. Bernard, *Un géant*, p. 11.
9. Their children were Marie Dewé (b. 1907), Walthère (b. 1911), Madeleine (b. 1914) and Jacques (b. 1920).
10. Henry Landau, *Secrets of the White Lady*, G.P. Putnam's Sons, 1935, p. 15.
11. Landau, *Secrets of the White Lady*, p. 15.
12. Decock, *La Dame Blanche*, p. 122, citing report by Father Des Onays, 30 December 1918, LDB archive, Brussels.
13. See Landau, *Secrets of the White Lady*, p. 15. Sigismund Payne Best also writes about the network's early spycraft in his unpublished memoirs, ref: 09/51/5, IWM.
14. Sigismund Payne Best, unpublished memoirs, chapter entitled 'Active Service', p. 6, ref: 09/51/5, IWM.
15. Best, unpublished memoirs, p. 7. In 2023, I was given private information that an original knitted item does exist with coded information embedded in it. In a similar SIS network run by Madame Lise Rischard in Luxembourg, information was coded into knitting patterns. See Michael Smith, *Foley: The Spy Who Saved 10,000 Jews*, Politico's, 2004, p. 13.
16. Best, unpublished memoirs, p. 5.
17. Best, unpublished memoirs, p. 5.
18. Letter dated 18 December 1914, copy given to the author and quoted thanks to his grandson Arthur Weiss.
19. Letter dated 6 October 1915.
20. Letter dated 16 January 1915.

21. The letters are now in possession of his grandson, Arthur Weiss, in the UK. Weiner was awarded an Iron Cross for his country in World War One; but he was subject to Germany's racial actions against Jews in Germany after Adolf Hitler came to power in January 1933. Less than three months later, Weiner was murdered by the Nazis in April 1933.

22. Service de Monge, [CAP 437], 2964-2972, State Archives, Belgium.

23. 'Service de Passage: Vicomtesse Gabrielle de Monge de Franeau', Box 1, LDB archive, IWM. Unpublished version of the memoirs of Gabrielle de Monge, copy given to the author, pp. 177–9. See also Service de Monge, [CAP 437], 2964-2972, State Archives, Belgium.

24. 'Service de Passage', pp. 177–9.

25. 'Service de Passage', pp. 24–8.

26. 'Service de Passage', pp. 24–8.

27. 'Service de Passage', p. 26. Translated from the original French.

28. 'Service de Passage', p. 33.

29. Reports on Léon Parent's sector of the White Lady, Folder 6, Box 1, LDB archive, IWM. It contains a report on Parent's own activities, including for Gabrielle de Monge. See Service Parent, [CAP 432], 2940-2942, State Archives, Belgium; and also Landau, *Secrets of the White Lady*, pp. 243–51.

30. Report on Léon Parent's activities, Folder 6 (entitled Léon Parent), Box 1, LDB archive, IWM.

31. 'Notice Historique sur le Service Léon Parent', pp. 1–2, Folder 6, Box 1, LDB archive, IWM, and Service Parent, [CAP 432], 2940-2942, State Archives, Belgium.

32. 'Notice Historique sur le Service Léon Parent', pp. 1–2; and Gabrielle de Monge, 'Service de Passage', p. 177.

33. 'Service de Passage', p. 177.

34. 'Service de Passage', p. 177.

35. Bernard, *Un géant*, pp. 19–21. Remnants of the original electrified fence and guard post can still be seen today at Zondereigen, in the province of Antwerp, bordering the Dutch province of North Brabant.

36. Bernard, *Un géant*, pp. 20–1.

37. Sigismund P. Best, 'Origins of the Intelligence Corps BEF, 1914', ref: 09/51/5, folder 22, IWM.

38. Tammy Proctor, *Female Intelligence*, p. 111.

39. Peter Verstraeten, 'The Secrecy of Awards to Belgian Secret Service Agents', *Journal of the Orders and Medals Society of America*, vol. 70, no. 2, 2019.

40. Marie-Antoinette de Radiguès, *Carnets de Guerre 1915–1919*, copy given to the author by the family.

41. 'Services de renseignements créés par des aviateurs: C'est-à-dire des agents deposes par avion en territoire occupé', [CAP 401 – 410], 2886-2903, State Archives, Belgium.

42. For Paul Jacquemin's sector, see report entitled 'Notice Historique sur le Service Paul Jacquemin', Box 1, LDB archive, IWM. See also Service Paulin Jacquemin, [CAP 401], 2886-2889, State Archives, Belgium.

43. 'Notice Historique sur le Service Léon Parent', p. 6, Box 1, LDB archive, IWM.

44. 'Notice Historique sur le Service Léon Parent', p. 5.

45. 'Source des Renseignements', report from Conneux dated 1 July 1920, Box 1, LDB archive, IWM. Other women working for the Paulin Jacquemin platoon were Madame Tutiaux, Hélène Jacquemin, Marthe Baijot, Madame Bottes (a guide), Madame Leleuch, Madame Remacle and Madame Jacquemin.
46. Report of espionage (rapport d'espionnage) by Hélène Levy, n/d, Box 1, LDB archive, IWM.
47. Copy of the citation for Louise Josserand (Sister Marie Angèle), among the reports for Paul Jacquemin, Box 1, LDB archive, IWM.
48. Landau, *Secrets of the White Lady*, pp. 250–1.
49. 'Pièce concernant agent fusillé Léon Parent', [CAP 432], 2942, State Archives, Belgium; and 'Notice Historique sur le Service Léon Parent', p. 6, Box 1, LDB archive, IWM. Recounted in Landau, *Secrets of the White Lady*, pp. 250–1.
50. Judd, *The Quest for C*, p. 336.
51. 'History of the British Secret Service in Holland, World War I', 1917, WO 106/6189, TNA. For background, see also Untitled report, p. 2, 5 May 1919, WO 106/45, TNA (The Secret Service, in History of Intelligence and Secret Service Organisations, 1 January 1917–30 April 1919).
52. Lambrecht's network was not the only British intelligence network in Belgium. The Service Frankignoul had more than forty observation posts by 1915 that were watching the trains, and over 200 agents. Service Frankignoul was compromised and did not recover. See Smith, *Six*, p. 53; and also Beach, *Haig's Intelligence*, p. 115, which cites 4,350 agents in 130 British networks on the Western Front.
53. Untitled report, p. 2, 5 May 1919, WO 106/45, TNA.
54. Untitled report, p. 2, 5 May 1919, WO 106/45, TNA.
55. To further understand the relationship between GHQ and Cumming's organisation and their respective intelligence operations, see Jim Beach, *Haig's Intelligence*, pp. 125–31 and Jeffery, *MI6*, p. 76.
56. Judd, *The Quest for C*, p. 363.
57. Untitled report, p. 2, 5 May 1919, WO 106/45, TNA.

2. Betrayal

1. On 20 October 1915, spymistress Louise de Bettignies was arrested near Tournai in Belgium. She died in prison before the end of the war. Operating under the pseudonym 'Alice Dubois', she had founded a British intelligence network called the Alice Service. It covered the region around Lille in France for Major Cameron who was based in Folkestone.
    Atwood, *Women Heroes of World War I*, pp. 70–8; Proctor, *Female Intelligence*, pp. 117–20; and Fry, *Women in Intelligence*, pp. 18–20.
2. 'Notice Historique sur le Capitaine Evrard', report p. 1, written from Conneux, 27 October 1920, Box 2, LDB archive, IWM; and Service Evrard, [CAP 402], 2891-2892, State Archives, Belgium.
3. 'Notice Historique sur le Capitaine Evrard', p. 2. Schwenck gave the Germans his real name and they decided to send him back to France, where the authorities shot him as a deserter on 4 March 1916 at Fort des Ayvelles.
4. 'Notice Historique sur le Capitaine Evrard', p. 3.
5. Some of Evrard's agents remained in the Ardennes to conduct espionage. They were Désiré Lambert and Mrs Lambert and their son; Colonel Denau of Givet;

Louis Martin, his wife and children (in Fumay); and Mr and Mrs Joseph Defoin (Fumay). In Givet were Mr Goetz, Georges Kugler, Clothilde Gilet, Constant and Rose Houpillart, Charles Furcy, Jules and Irma Yon, Chauvier de Hargnies, Mrs and Mrs Charles Collin, Alfred Delditte, Albert Pirot, Xavier Collin and Arnolds Honnay. Listed in file 'La Mission du Capitaine Evrard', Box 2, LDB archive, IWM.

6. Official booklet 'Un pionnier de la Résistance Dieudonné Lambrecht', pp. 5–6, Box 2, LDB archive, IWM. See also Verstraeten, 'The Secrecy of Awards to Belgian Secret Service Agents'.
7. See Stevenson, *1914–1918*, pp. 159–60; and Strachan, *The First World War*, pp. 175–6.
8. Marie-Antoinette de Radiguès, diary entry for 1 September to 1 October 1915. By this time, she had decided to write in her diary only once a month.
9. 'Notice Historique sur le Capitaine Evrard', p. 10.
10. Evrard's personal file in a folder on Evrard's mission, Box 2, LDB archive, IWM. This shows he came under the sector of Charleville. The reports were signed off at Conneux, 27 October 1920 (Thérèse de Radiguès).
11. 'Notice Historique sur le Capitaine Evrard', p. 12.
12. Unpublished memoirs of Gabrielle de Monge, p. 297, copy given to the author.
13. 'Un pionnier de la Résistance Dieudonné Lambrecht', p. 7.
14. Letter to Lambrecht, 26 January 1916 from Mr Afchain, quoted in Landau, *Secrets of the White Lady*, p. 16.
15. 'Un pionnier de la Résistance Dieudonné Lambrecht', pp. 5–6.
16. Decock, *La Dame Blanche*, p. 21.
17. Landau, *Secrets of the White Lady*, pp. 101–10.
18. Landau, *Secrets of the White Lady*, p. 103.
19. Landau, *Secrets of the White Lady*, p. 30.
20. For an overview on this period, see Judd, *The Quest for C*, pp. 359–70.
21. Information in ref: Folder Keurvers, File 90, Services Patriotiques, State Archives, Belgium.
22. Landau, *The Spy Net*, p. 63.
23. Folder Keurvers, File 90, Services Patriotiques, State Archives, Belgium.
24. Letter from Afchain to Lambrecht, dated 24 February 1916, Landau, *Secrets of the White Lady*, p. 19.
25. The episode is recounted in detail in Landau, *Secrets of the White Lady*, pp. 18–21.
26. Landau, *The Spy Net*, p. 66.
27. 'Lettre de Dieudonné Lambrecht à Jeanne après avoir appris sa condamnation à mort, citadelle de La Chartreuse', 17 avril 1916, [CAP 540], 3420, State Archives, Belgium. The letter is reproduced in full in Landau, *Secrets of the White Lady*, pp. 22–3.
28. 'Un pionnier de la Résistance Dieudonné Lambrecht', p. 10.

3. The Michelin Service

1. Landau, *Secrets of the White Lady*, p. 24.
2. Judd, *The Quest for C*, p. 363.
3. Bernard, *Un géant*, pp. 23–5; and Landau, *Secrets of the White Lady*, pp. 26–8.
4. Bernard, *Un géant*, pp. 18–25; and Emmanuel Debruyne and Jehanne Paternostre, *La Résistance au quotidien 1914–1918: Témoignages inédits*, Racine, 2009, p. 140.

5. Landau, *Secrets of the White Lady*, pp. 27–8.

6. According to Cumming's diary, he met Landau on 8 June 1916. See Jeffery, *MI6*, p. 77. Landau's version suggests the previous month. Reading between the lines of Landau's account in *Secrets of the White Lady*, his declassified personal army record and the MI6 archives, Landau may have had two meetings with Cumming and conflated them into a single account.

7. Details in his personal army record, WO 339/2456. Landau was born at Farm Rotterdam, Bethal District, Transvaal, South Africa to Charles and Chrislina Landau. See also Jeffery, *MI6*, pp. 76–7.

8. Landau says he was recovering from German measles; see *The Spy Net*, p. vii. His personal army record records his precise medical condition and says that he was receiving treatment for a urinary infection, and was admitted to Millbank hospital (London) in early April 1916, WO 339/2456.

9. Landau, *The Spy Net*, p. vii.

10. Landau, *Spreading the Spy Net*, p. 29. For background on Colonel Freddie Browning, see Jeffery, *MI6*, pp. 56–7.

11. It was renamed the Secret Intelligence Service (SIS) in 1919; Jeffery, *MI6*, p. 162.

12. Judd, *The Quest for C*, p. 362.

13. Landau, *The Spy Net*, p. 27. Repeated in Judd, *The Quest for C*, pp. 360–1.

14. Judd, *The Quest for C*, pp. 360–1.

15. Landau, *Spreading the Spy Net*, p. 30.

16. Cumming to MI1, 19 June 1916, WO 339/2456.

17. Note in Landau's personal army file, WO 339/12456.

18. Jeffery, *MI6*, p. 77.

19. See Landau's personal army file, WO 339/12456.

20. Note dated 10 July 1916 in WO 339/12456. This now provides an accurate date for Landau's arrival in Rotterdam in July 1916, rather than May 1916 as stated by Landau, *The Spy Net*, p. 41.

21. Cumming to MI1(d), 29 July 1916, WO 339/12456.

22. Landau, *The Spy Net*, p. 29.

23. Judd, *The Quest for C*, p. 363.

24. 'Notice sur le Corps D'Observation Allie, attaché à L'armee Anglaise', papers of La Dame Blanche (Brussels).

25. 'Notice sur le Corps D'Observation Allie, attaché à L'armee Anglaise'.

26. Ruis, *Spynest*, p. 198.

27. Affaire Michelin, [CAP 10], 1065-1070, State Archives, Belgium.

28. 'Copie d'extraits de lettres adressées au S.A et à Saint-Lambert par B.149, Michelin', [CAP 10], 1069, State Archives, Belgium.

29. Landau, *Secrets of the White Lady*, p. 34.

30. For the episode with Snoeck and Liévin, see Landau, *Secrets of the White Lady*, pp. 37–43.

31. Ruis, *Spynest*, p. 159.

32. Ruis, *Spynest*, p. 159.

33. Letter dated 7 July 1917 from Dewé to Rotterdam, in Archives famille Dewé, FICINV_1699, State Archives, Belgium.

34. Letters between Dewé and Rotterdam about the financing of the network survive in FICINV_1699, State Archives, Belgium. See also Landau, *Secrets of the White Lady*, p. 53.

35. Written correspondence confirming this military status is found in papers, ref: FCI-MNRA, National Museum of the Resistance, Brussels.
36. The following in the State Archives, Belgium: 'Copies de notes concernant l'arrestation du Père Des Onays et les dirigeants de l'organisation', 1920, BE-AO510_002182_002443, 1044; report entitled 'L'Affaire Desonay' in Archives famille Dewé, FICINV_1699; and 3rd peloton d'observation à Charleroi, [CAP 115].
37. For more on this betrayal, see Landau, *Secrets of the White Lady*, pp. 40–5.
38. Copie de la note de Walthère Dewé concernant le role de l'agent Saint Georges, [CAP 10], 1076, State Archives, Belgium.
39. Smith, *Six*, p. 77.

4. The White Lady

1. 'Notice sur le Corps D'Observation Allie, attaché à L'armee Anglaise'.
2. Letter, 7 July 1917, from the White Lady to Landau in Rotterdam confirming that the network agreed to the terms of military status, ref: FCI-MNRA, National Museum of the Resistance, Brussels. There are a number of letters on this subject in this archive, especially during September and October 1917.
3. Letter, 7 July 1917, from the White Lady to Landau in Rotterdam, ref: FCI-MNRA, National Museum of the Resistance, Brussels.
4. Written confirmation is in letter dated 7 July 1917, from the White Lady to Landau in Rotterdam, ref: FCI-MNRA, National Museum of the Resistance, Brussels.
5. Eva Muys, 'Vrouwen in de inlichtingendiensten: De zussen Laure en Louise Tandel', copy given to the author. Letters between Dewé and Rotterdam in the Dewé archive, FICINV_1699, State Archives, Belgium.
6. 'Notice sur le Corps D'Observation Allie, attaché L'armée Anglaise'.
7. Landau, *The Spy Net*, p. 73.
8. In Squad 1 were Juliette Durieu, Lucie Neujean and Camille Hemon. Squad 2: Marie Delcourt, Jenny Jacques and Jeanne Foettinger. Squad 3: Marie Thérèse Collard and Irène Bastin. Squad 4: Marguerite de Radiguès, Françoise de Villermont, Anne de Villermont, Clémie de l'Epine and Marie-Antoinette de Radiguès. 'Conseil Supreme du Corps' in Commission des Archives des Services Patriotiques, Secretariat de Liège.
9. Landau, *The Spy Net*, p. 245.
10. It has not been possible to independently verify this claim. Debruyne, 'La maison de verre', p. 619; Proctor, *Female Intelligence*, pp. 79–81. See also Fry, *Women in Intelligence*, pp. 30–6.
11. Judd, *The Quest for C*, pp. 364–5. See also Decock, *La Dame Blanche*, p. 7.
12. Muys, 'Vrouwen in de inlichtingendiensten'.
13. On the couriers, see Lettres, télégrammes, copies et transcription de ceux-ci, [CAP 10], 974-977, State Archives, Belgium.
14. Ruis, *Spy Net*, p. 88.
15. Other women known to have been working for La Dame Blanche were Lieutenant Henriette Dupuich; sisters Sergeant Jeanne Henne and Lieutenant sécretaire Yvonne Henne; Julienne Cambier and her three sisters Sergeant Jeanne Cambier, Corporal Valentine Cambier and Corporal Marguerite Cambier; Marcelle Dutilleux; and Mrs Walthère Dewé.

16. Bernard, *Un géant*, p. 30.
17. Proctor, *Female Intelligence*, p. 76.
18. Working also in the Service of the Guard (Security) were Anna Barée, Rosa Collin, Eliza Renward, Joseph Bory, Christine Molitor, Angelina Timmermans, Marie Crahay, Desirée Crahay, Emilie Jamme, Dieudonnée Salmon and Henri Ville.
19. See her citation for an OBE: BA_OBE_Props_Ldb_EM-12, State Archives, Belgium. Her sister Alice received an MBE.
20. Jeffery, *MI6*, p. 80.
21. For Jeanne Delwaide's story, see Proctor, *Female Intelligence*, pp. 75, 94–5; and Landau, *Secrets of the White Lady*, pp. 122–31.
22. Landau, *Secrets of the White Lady*, p. 126.
23. Landau, *Secrets of the White Lady*, p. 125.
24. Landau, *Secrets of the White Lady*, p. 126. Also Jeanne Delwaide report, 10 janvier 1919, folder 7, [CAP 222], State Archives, Belgium.
25. Landau, *Secrets of the White Lady*, p. 126.
26. Mariette was responsible for the arrest of members of the Hemptinne Service, an espionage organisation attached to the Belgian Secret Service.
27. Bernard, *Un géant*, p. 6.
28. Landau, *Secrets of the White Lady*, pp. 252–6; and reports of LDB at IWM.
29. Landau, *Secrets of the White Lady*, p. 256.
30. See note 8.
31. Letter dated 21 March 1919, British Military Intelligence Commission, Tandel archive.
32. BA_OBE_Props_Ldb_EM-19, State Archives, Belgium. After the war, both Laure and Louise Tandel were awarded an OBE by the British. Laure's citation: BA_OBE_Props_Ldb_EM-7; Louise's citation: BA_OBE_Props_Ldb_EM-8, State Archives, Belgium.
33. Dossier No. 134605, 7 October 1929, Archive of Laure and Louise Tandel, SGRS, Belgian Military Archives.
34. Archive of Laure and Louise Tandel, SGRS, Belgian Military Archives, Brussels.
35. Muys, 'Vrouwen in de inlichtingendiensten'.
36. Jeanne Menage and Josephine Detrooz aided Louise Tandel with administration.
37. OBE citation: BA_OBE_Props_Ldb_EM-7, State Archives, Belgium. See also Jeffery, *MI6*, p. 80.
38. Records of the Service Patriotique (1914–18), Corps d'Observation Anglais, P-224, State Archives, Belgium. See also P-222 for reports on the battalion's organisation.
39. Proctor, *Female Intelligence*, p. 82.
40. BA_OBE_Props_Ldb_EM-19, [CAP 10], 158, 1149-1174, State Archives, Belgium.
41. Landau, *Secrets of the White Lady*, p. 176.
42. Landau, *Secrets of the White Lady*, p. 80.
43. Landau, *Secrets of the White Lady*, pp. 81–2.
44. This method is explained by Landau, *Secrets of the White Lady*, p. 88.
45. Landau, *Secrets of the White Lady*, p. 89. For other codes see numerous examples, ref: FCI-MNRA, National Museum of the Resistance, Brussels.

5. The Hirson Platoon

1. Rapports d'organisation et copies de rapports d'organisation concernant le Peloton d'élite d'Hirson, [CAP 10], 997-998, State Archives, Belgium. Landau, *Secrets of the White Lady*, pp. 65–79.
2. Jeffery, *MI6*, pp. 80–1.
3. Landau, *Secrets of the White Lady*, pp. 66–7.
4. Landau, *Secrets of the White Lady*, p. 74. Examples of military intelligence coded as ordinary items on lists can be found in Box 1, LDB archive, IWM.
5. Landau, *Secrets of the White Lady*, p. 75.
6. Landau, *Secrets of the White Lady*, p. 75; and Landau, *Spreading the Spy Net*, p. 76.
7. Landau, *Secrets of the White Lady*, p. 75.
8. Landau, *Secrets of the White Lady*, pp. 114–16.
9. Landau, *The Spy Net*, p. 88.
10. BA_OBE_Props_Ldb_EM-3, [CAP 10], 158, 1149-1174, State Archives, Belgium. See also Landau, *Secrets of the White Lady*, p. 75.
11. Landau, *Secrets of the White Lady*, p. 76.
12. For the Chimay Company, see 1st peloton à Chimay, [CAP 10], 1113-1114, and 1294-1296, State Archives, Belgium.
13. Service Aubijoux-Valtier, [CAP 403], 2893-2895, State Archives, Belgium.
14. Landau, *Secrets of the White Lady*, pp. 111–13.
15. Landau, *Secrets of the White Lady*, p. 119.
16. Landau, *Secrets of the White Lady*, p. 75 and p. 117.

6. Villa des Hirondelles

1. The primary sources for this chapter are eyewitness reports of agents in a folder entitled 'Archives des familles de Radiguès et de Moffarts, Folder 4: L'Affaire de la Villa des Hirondelles', in Box 1, LDB archive, IWM. See also Laurent Lombard, *Le drame de la Villa des Hirondelles*, Editions Vox Patriae, Stavelot, 1939; and Landau, *Secrets of the White Lady*, pp. 141–51.
2. Report by Henri Chauvin about the activities of Louis and Antony Collard, entitled 'L'Affaire de la Villa des Hirondelles', Box 1, LDB archive, IWM. See also Felstead, *Under the German Heel*, pp. 207–11.
3. Report of Irene Bastin, 9 September 1920, Box 1, LDB archive, IWM.
4. Report of Irene Bastin, 9 September 1920.
5. Report of Irene Bastin, 9 September 1920.
6. Franchimont's report, 10 January 1919, Box 1, LDB archive, IWM. See also Bernard, *Un géant*, pp. 61–6.
7. See Franchimont's report, 10 January 1919, Box 1, LDB archive, IWM. Box 1 of this archive at the IWM contains numerous eyewitness accounts from the agents who were there during the Villa des Hirondelles affair.
8. After the war Goeseels received an MBE for her role in the White Lady.
9. Letter from LDB to Mr Reymen, no date, in LDB archive, IWM.
10. Franchimont's report, 10 January 1919, LDB archive, IWM.
11. Copie de la correspondence de prison des agents Emile Fauquenot, Marie Birkel et Franz Creusen, [CAP 10], 978, State Archives, Belgium.

12. Landau, *Secrets of the White Lady*, p. 146.
13. Report for LDB by Joseph Bastin, 25 December 1918, LDB archive, IWM.
14. Report for LDB by Joseph Bastin, 25 December 1918, LDB archive, IWM.
15. Dossier concernant les projets d'évasion de la prison de St. Léonard des agents Fauquenot, Creusen et Birckel, [CAP 603], 509, State Archives, Belgium.
16. Report for LDB by Joseph Bastin, 25 December 1918.
17. Landau, *Secrets of the White Lady*, p. 159.
18. Landau, *Secrets of the White Lady*, p. 163.
19. Franchimont's report, 10 January 1919, LDB archive, IWM.
20. Landau, *Secrets of the White Lady*, p. 148.
21. Marie-Thérèse Collard eyewitness account, 'L'Affaire de la Villa des Hirondelles', in Box 1, LDB archive, IWM.
22. Report by Irene Bastin that includes the Villa des Hirondelles affair and her own experiences as an agent of the White Lady, LDB archive, IWM.
23. Landau, *Secrets of the White Lady*, p. 150.
24. Landau, *Secrets of the White Lady*, p. 151.
25. They received an OBE from the British, and Knights of the Cross of the Order of Leopold by the Belgian government.
26. Report by Jeanne Goeseels, 13 December 1918 for LDB archive, IWM.
27. 'L'Affaire de la Villa des Hirondelles', in Box 1, LDB archive, IWM.

7. Post 49

1. Decock, *La Dame Blanche*, p. 123, quoting directive from the British Secret Service dated 30 January 1918.
2. Unpublished memoirs of Agnès de Radiguès. For reports and this post, see Peloton de chevauchement de Conneux et les postes 49 et 520, [CAP 10], 930, and Peloton de chevauchement de Conneux, Direction Générale, [CAP 10], 936, State Archives, Belgium.
3. Report dated 27 January 1919 by Marie-Antoinette de Radiguès, Box 1, LDB archive, IWM. Others working for Post 49 included Arthur Tonet, Mrs Dubois-Lefevre, Lucien Woltèche, Maurice Evrard and Henri Balfroid, as well as Sister Valentine of the Carmelites.
4. For personal files of frontier guides who operated for the sector of Conneux Castle, see Folder 10, Box 2, LDB archive, IWM.
5. François de Radiguès, correspondence with the author, 2023. See also Report on Establishment of Post 49, LDB archive, IWM.
6. BA_OBE_Props_Ldb_EM-21, VSSE archives. Other Belgian female agents listed for awards by the British were Marie Louise Donnay de Casteau and Emma van Hamme de Corte, who each were awarded the British Medal. See WO 372/23/1008. Reports in LDB archive, IWM.
7. Report on Post 49, dated 27 January 1919, LDB archive, IWM.
8. For the history of the Conneux Flying Squad, see Dossiers concernant l'expédition de Charleville, [CAP 10], 1006-1007, State Archives, Belgium.
9. Report on Post 49, 27 January 1919, LDB archive, IWM.
10. Report on Post 49, 27 January 1919, LDB archive, IWM.
11. Reports on Post 49, Box 2, LDB archive, IWM.
12. Reports on Post 49, Box 2, LDB archive, IWM.

13. Reports on Post 49, Box 2, LDB archive, IWM.

14. Report by Clémie L'Epine, 27 October 1918, LDB archive, IWM.

15. Members known to have been part of the small Conneux Flying Squad were Henri Domelier, Mrs Grafetiaux, Abbé Emile Gérard, Jean-Baptiste Martin, Lucien Voltèche and Louis Crépel.

16. Proctor, *Female Intelligence*, p. 92.

17. Landau, *Secrets of the White Lady*, p. 166.

18. Dossier concernant l'affaire Van Houdenhuyse, [CAP 10], 1015, State Archives, Belgium; and Bernard, *Un géant*, p. 71.

19. Landau, *Secrets of the White Lady*, p. 172.

20. Report from Post 49, 9 January 1918, LDB archive, IWM.

21. Report from Post 49, 8 July 1918, LDB archive, IWM.

22. Report from Post 49, 10 September 1918, LDB archive, IWM.

23. Report from Post 49, 11 August 1918, LDB archive, IWM.

24. Report from Post 49, 15 August 1918, LDB archive, IWM.

25. Report from Post 49, 14 August 1918, LDB archive, IWM.

26. Report from Post 49, 28 October 1918, LDB archive, IWM.

27. Report from Post 49, 28 October 1918, LDB archive, IWM.

28. Report from Post 49, 10 September 1918, LDB archive, IWM.

29. Landau, *Secrets of the White Lady*, p. 176.

30. Barnard, *Un géant*, p. 74. See also Muys, 'Vrouwen in de inlichtingendiensten'.

31. Julienne and Anne Demarteau: BA_OBE_Props_Ldb_EM-10 and BA_OBE_Props_Ldb_EM-11, [CAP 10], 158, 1149-1174, State Archives, Belgium.

32. Report dated 21 October 1918, LDB archive, IWM.

33. Instructions to La Dame Blanche, dated 2 November 1918, LDB archive, IWM.

34. Instructions to La Dame Blanche, dated 2 November 1918, LDB archive, IWM.

35. Walthère Dewé, 'Notice Historique sur le Corps d'Observation allié attaché à l'armée anglaise'; AB 2261, Cegesoma.

8. We Have Done Our Duty

1. Report, 16 October 1918, Box 1, LDB archive, IWM.

2. Report by Sigismund Payne Best on his interrogation of Jeanne Cleve on 24 July 1918, KV 2/844.

3. Report, 21 October 1918, Box 1, LDB archive, IWM.

4. Letter from Ernest Wallinger to General Sir Walter Kirke, dated 2 November 1925, written from Knowle, Cuckfield, in Sussex, in Box 1, LDB archive, IWM.

5. According to Ernest Wallinger, it was approximately 200 agents. See letter from Ernest Wallinger to General Sir Walter Kirke, dated 2 November 1925, written from Knowle, Cuckfield, in Sussex, Box 1, LDB archive, IWM. Intelligence historian Alan Judd writes that forty-five agents were arrested, five condemned to death, two shot and one killed on duty. See Judd, *The Quest for C*, p. 365.

6. Newspaper report from *Moniteur*, 31 January 1919, folder 13, Box 2, LDB archive, IWM.

7. Report, 21 November 1918, Box 1, LDB archive, IWM.

8. History of Post 49, dated 27 January 1919, Box 1, LDB archive, IWM.

9. Marie-Antoinette de Radiguès, *Carnets de Guerre 1915–1919*, p. 12.

10. De Radiguès, *Carnets de Guerre*, p. 12.

11. Letter, 1 January 1919, Archive of Laure and Louise Tandel, SGRS, Belgian Military Archives.

12. Landau, *Secrets of the White Lady*, p. 173.

13. Letter from Henry Landau to Captain Vigors of MI1(c), 24 February 1919, in Folder 12a/b, Box 2, LDB archive, IWM.

14. Landau, *Secrets of the White Lady*, p. 252.

15. De Radiguès, *Carnets de Guerre*, p. 16.

16. Muys, 'Vrouwen in de inlichtingendiensten', p. 9.

17. Other members of the committee were Baron Adolphe de Moffarts, Mr Parent (from Charleroi), Edmond Hallfue (judge at the court in Liège), Mr de Potter from Ghent, Gustave Snoeck, Paul Philippart and Madame Merry. Their names are recorded in the minutes of the meeting.

18. Bernard, *Un géant*, p. 91.

19. Jeffery, *MI6*, p. 195; and Smith, *Foley*, p. 15.

20. Sigismund P. Best, unpublished memoirs, chapter called 'Kirkpatrick Joins the Staff', p. 6, ref: 09/51/5, IWM.

21. This conclusion is endorsed by Debruyne in his online article, 'Resistance (Belgium and France)' for *1914–1918 Online*.

22. Henry Landau's attestation on 16 March 1919 to the British Military Intelligence Commission, in 'Notice sur le Corps d'Observation Allie, attaché à L'armée Anglaise', papers of La Dame Blanche, [CAP 10] BE-A0510/1 581, State Archives, Belgium; and see also Judd, *The Quest for C*, p. 365.

23. Keith Jeffery, *MI6*, p. 85; Occleshaw, *Armour Against Fate*, p. 192. Cumming's figure of over 70 per cent is quoted by Landau – see the note above. A copy of Landau's attestation can be found in Historical Notes, P-212, Services Patriotiques, State Archives, Belgium.

9. The Clarence Service

1. Thérèse de Radiguès, personal file, AA1333, the individual files of intelligence and action agents, Belgian State Security Archives, Cegesoma.

2. Thérèse de Radiguès's two daughters had married: Marguerite to Georges Clérinx and Marie-Antoinette to Henri de Moffarts.

3. Interview with the author in 2022.

4. See AA1333, the individual files of intelligence and action agents, Belgian State Security Archives, Cegesoma. The committee (age of members in brackets) consisted of Alexandre Neujean (71), Arsène Scheurette (66), Herman (Henri) Chauvin (64), Jeanne Goeseels (64), Jeanne Delwaide (59), Franz Creusen (47), Robert Boseret (55), the two sisters Laure and Louise Tandel (65/61), the two sisters Emma and Alice Weimerskirch (61/57), the three sisters Jeanne, Valentine and Marguerite Cambier (53/49/46) and Henriette Dupuich (59).

5. The five female members of the board were Thérèse de Radiguès, Henriette Dupuich (1881–1971), Rose Houyoux (b. 1895), Violette Verhoogen (1898–2001) and Germaine de Menten (1903–1998). See Bernard, *Un géant*, p. 175.

6. Bernard, *Un géant*, p. 130.

7. Bernard, *Un géant*, p. 197.
8. Bernard, *Un géant*, p. 105.
9. Bernard, *Un géant*, p. 106.
10. Bernard, *Un géant*, p. 106.
11. Detailed examples and explanations of these codes are in ref: FCI-MNRA, National Museum of the Resistance, Brussels. See also Bernard, *Un géant*, p. 104.
12. Bernard, *Un géant*, p. 106.
13. This book does not seek to provide a detailed analysis of such complex questions. Consideration would have to be taken into account of Belgium's international position, the scale of Belgian mobilisation and the diplomatic friction with Allied forces over Belgium issuing any pre-emptive action. For a good discussion of this, see Jonathan A. Epstein, *Belgium's Dilemma: The Formation of Belgian Defense Policy, 1932–1940*, Brill, 2014.
14. Bernard, *Un géant*, pp. 106–7.
15. Bernard, *Un géant*, p. 107.
16. Marguerite Clérinx, 'Notes et souvenirs du 10 mai au 22 juillet 1940', p. 1, copy given to the author by the family.
17. Clérinx, 'Notes et souvenirs'.
18. Colonel Blake's escape from occupied Belgium is told in Helen Fry, *MI9: A History of the Secret Service for Escape and Evasion in World War Two*, Yale University Press, 2020, pp. 30–1.
19. Bernard, *Un géant*, p. 112.
20. Bernard, *Un géant*, p. 114.
21. The Orders of the Day for 30 May 1940 issued by General Jules Derousseaux. See Bernard, *Un géant*, p. 114.
22. Walthère Dewé, personal file, AA1333, the individual files of intelligence and action agents, Belgian State Security Archives, Cegesoma.
23. Jean Demarque, personal file, AA1333, the individual files of intelligence and action agents, Belgian State Security Archives, Cegesoma.
24. After the war Jean Demarque ('Saturne') was awarded the King's Medal for Courage in the Cause of Freedom.
25. Hector Demarque and his father lived at 127 rue Emile Banning. Their personal files are in AA1333 (folder 166), the individual files of intelligence and action agents, Belgian State Security Archives, Cegesoma.
26. Correspondence with the author.
27. Rose Houyoux, personal file, AA1333, the individual files of intelligence and action agents, Belgian State Security Archives, Cegesoma.
28. Violette Verhoogen, personal file, AA1333, the individual files of intelligence and action agents, Belgian State Security Archives, Cegesoma.
29. These agents' personal files are also in AA1333/166/2.
30. Baroness Germaine de Menten lived at 496 chaussée de Waterloo.
31. Bernard, *Un géant*, pp. 175–6; see also her personal file in Cegesoma.
32. Debruyne, 'La maison de verre', p. 119.
33. Creusen had received an OBE for his part in the White Lady.
34. Laure Tandel and Louise Tandel, personal file, AA1333, the individual files of intelligence and action agents, Belgian State Security Archives, Cegesoma.
35. Among those whom the sisters sheltered were Paul Jacquemin, Gérard Waucquez, Jules Stercq and François De Kinder.

36. Paul Janssens was assisted by Fernand Guillemyn, who had been an agent for the White Lady in World War One. Janssens and Guillemyn collected information about the movements of enemy troops in the region of Mons, Kortrijk and Mouscron and tracked down data about the airfields of Chièvres and Wevelgem.

37. Citation signed by Chief of the Clarence Service, Brussels, 7 February 1946, in their personal files at Cegesoma.

38. See AA1333, the individual files of intelligence and action agents, Belgian State Security Archives, Cegesoma.

39. Correspondence headed 'Room 900 (War Office)' from Major Page survives in AA1333 (folders 161 and 162), the individual files of intelligence and action agents, Belgian State Security Archives, Cegesoma. For further historical background to Room 900, see several references in Fry, *MI9*.

40. Jeffery, *MI6*, p. 520.

41. Frederick John Jempson, warrant number 103893. Joined on 25 May 1914 and last posted to Special Branch, Division as Inspector (CID – 1st Class). He left on 7 September 1939 to join MI6.

42. MEPO 4/350/152 for his service record with Special Branch.

43. The 1939 Register lists him as living at 2 Forest Road, Guildford, occupation civil assistant, War Office (MI6).

44. Other personnel connected to SIS's work in Belgium were Commander Kenneth Cohen, RN and Captain A.T. Caplin.

45. Chevalier of the Order of the Oaken Crown, WO 373/107/179.

46. Obituary for Jean Nicodème, *Le Soir*, 26 September 1972.

47. Interview with the author, January 2025.

48. Interview with the author, January 2025.

49. As with so many relationships between different intelligence organisations, the reality was more complicated than this, but this book cannot go into more detail here.

50. All this is evident in correspondence from Room 900 (War Office) and Nicodème which survives in AA1333, the individual files of intelligence and action agents, Belgian State Security Archives, Cegesoma.

51. Correspondence from Room 900 (War Office) survives in AA1333, the individual files of intelligence and action agents, Belgian State Security Archives, Cegesoma. For Room 900's historical work, see numerous references in Airey Neave, *Saturday at MI9: The Classic Account of the WWII Allied Escape Organisation*, Pen & Sword, 2010; and for Room 900 as part of MI6, see Fry, *MI9*, pp. 72–7.

52. See Vigurs, *Mission Europe*; and Fry, *Women in Intelligence*.

53. 'Mission Richard: Captain Ducq', Clarence Service files, ref: FCI-MNRA, National Museum of the Resistance, Brussels. See also Bernard, *Un géant*, p. 140.

54. Bernard, *Un géant*, pp. 140–1.

55. Mission Aristide, report dated 12 December 1940, Clarence Service files, ref: FCI-MNRA, National Museum of the Resistance, Brussels.

56. Jules Delruelle, personal file, AA1333 (folder 166), the individual files of intelligence and action agents, Belgian State Security Archives, Cegesoma.

57. Jules Delruelle, personal file, AA1333 (folder 166), the individual files of intelligence and action agents, Belgian State Security Archives, Cegesoma.

58. The following month, January 1941, SIS organised a parachute drop of radio transmitters into Belgium for the Clarence Service.

59. Bernard, *Un géant*, p. 146.
60. Maurice van Gijsel, personal file, AA1333 (folder 166), the individual files of intelligence and action agents, Belgian State Security Archives, Cegesoma.
61. This material, in French, survives in eight boxes in the Imperial War Museum, London. The files for the Clarence Service in its entirety do not appear to be complete: there are no Clarence Service reports for the period September 1939 to January 1941, nor from September 1944 to the end of the war in Europe in May 1945. These may still be classified or might not have survived.
62. For a history of agents leaving for occupied Europe, including into Belgium, from RAF Tempsford, see Freddie Clark, *Agents by Moonlight: The Secret History of RAF Tempsford during World War II*, Tempus, 1999.

10. The Parachutists

1. Jean Lamy, personal file, AA1333 (folder 160), the individual files of intelligence and action agents, Belgian State Security Archives, Cegesoma. Jean Lamy was born in Vauchavanne, Belgium, on 4 February 1906.
2. The other agents dropped between 1941 and 1944 were Captain Paul Jacquemin ('Marble'), Paul Godenne ('Student'), Adrien Marquet ('Parent'), Joseph Leblique ('Frantz'), Jules Stercq ('Player'), Elie Nubourg ('Tweed'), Jean Bonsang ('Brulage II') and Gaetan Vervoort ('Tinsel'). Their missions and personal files are in AA1333 (folder 163).
3. Bernard, *Un géant*, p. 145.
4. Jeffery, *MI6*, pp. 388–9.
5. Bernard, *Un géant*, p. 144.
6. Paul Jacquemin, AA1333 (folder 160), the individual files of intelligence and action agents, Belgian State Security Archives, Cegesoma.
7. Report of Paul Jacquemin's mission by his cousin Rachel Machorot-Valat, dated 20 February 1944, AA1333/163, Cegesoma.
8. Bernard, *Un géant*, pp. 146–7.
9. Paul Jacquemin, AA1333/160, Cegesoma.
10. Letter dated 5 February 1943 in Jacquemin's mission file, AA1333 (folder 163), the individual files of intelligence and action agents, Belgian State Security Archives, Cegesoma.
11. According to his prisoner file in the Bundesarchiv, Jacquemin was executed in Essen on 28 May 1943. This is repeated in Bernard, *Un géant*, p. 147 and p. 245. His personal Clarence Service file notes that he was shot in Bochum, Germany in February 1943. See Jacquemin's mission file, AA1333 (folder 163), the individual files of intelligence and action agents, Belgian State Security Archives, Cegesoma. This difference in date may be due to the Clarence Service being informed it was February 1943, when in fact German files released later confirm today that he was shot in May 1943.
12. Report by Rachel Machorot-Valat.
13. Bernard, *Un géant*, p. 147.
14. Report by Rachel Machorot-Valat.
15. Paul Godenne was born in Namur in 1903, and was a garage owner by occupation. Paul Godenne, AA1333, the individual files of intelligence and action agents, Belgian State Security Archives, Cegesoma.

16. Cable from Student to MI6 on 31 January 1942, AA1333 (folder 160), the individual files of intelligence and action agents, Belgian State Security Archives, Cegesoma.

17. Cable sent to MI6 on 24 February 1942, AA1333 (folder 160), the individual files of intelligence and action agents, Belgian State Security Archives, Cegesoma.

18. Letter from Page in Room 055 to Nicodème, 27 February 1942, Box 1, Clarence Service archive, IWM.

19. Among those radio operators were 'Bravery', who was to link up with agent 'Brave', and another sent to 'Baldric'. 'Bouquet' and 'Sand' were sent in during March 1942 to found their own service.

20. Bernard, *Un géant*, p. 151.

21. Jeffery, *MI6*, pp. 388–9.

22. Jeffery, *MI6*, pp. 388–9.

23. Agent Frantz was arrested on 16 July 1942; AA1333/160, Cegesoma.

24. The reports for 1941 survive in Box 1, Clarence Service archive, IWM.

25. Report dated 27 March 1941, Box 1, Clarence Service archive, IWM.

26. Report 1, dated 20 February 1941, Box 1, Clarence Service archive, IWM.

27. Report 2, dated 6 March 1941, Box 1, Clarence Service archive, IWM.

28. Report 2, dated 6 March 1941, Box 1, Clarence Service archive, IWM.

29. Report 4, dated 19 March 1941, p. 5, Box 1, Clarence Service archive, IWM.

30. Report 6, dated 3 April 1941, Box 1, Clarence Service archive, IWM.

31. Report 6, dated 3 April 1941, p. 3, Box 1, Clarence Service archive, IWM.

32. Report 6, dated 3 April 1941, p. 3, Box 1, Clarence Service archive, IWM.

33. Report 6, dated 3 April 1941, p. 4, Box 1, Clarence Service archive, IWM.

34. Report dated 29 August 1941, Box 1, Clarence Service archive, IWM.

35. This might be Clotilde Coppens, although her personal file states that she joined Clarence on 1 July 1942. It is possible that she was working for the network earlier; or maybe it is a different Clotilde.

36. One of the planes bore the designation B72798 9662 Pat40-A72815 H.

37. Report dated 29 August 1941, Box 1, Clarence Service archive, IWM.

38. Report dated 20 September 1941, Box 1, Clarence Service archive, IWM.

39. Report dated 28 September 1941, Box 1, Clarence Service archive, IWM.

40. Report dated 7 October 1941, Box 1, Clarence Service archive, IWM.

41. Report dated 7 October 1941, Box 1, Clarence Service archive, IWM.

42. Report dated 11 October 1941, Box 1, Clarence Service archive, IWM.

43. Personal correspondence from Robin Libert (Chairman RUSRA-KUIAD, Royal Union of Intelligence and Action Services) to the author, 1 July 2025.

11. Mill

1. Information in René Clippe, personal file, AA1333, the individual files of intelligence and action agents, Belgian State Security Archives, Cegesoma.

2. Mill agent files are in AA1333 (folder 213), the individual files of intelligence and action agents, Belgian State Security Archives, Cegesoma.

3. Mill had a strong hub of agents in Brussels, Charleroi, Tirlement, Liège, Erquelinnes and the Chimay districts.

4. Separate intelligence reports for Mill cannot be located. They may be among those for the Clarence Service, or not declassified yet, or missing.

5. A manual, dated 1939, provided instructions on what information to collect. Copy in the National Museum of the Resistance, Brussels (FCI-MNRA).

6. History sheet for Marquet in his personal file, AA1333, the individual files of intelligence and action agents, Belgian State Security Archives, Cegesoma.

7. Gobeaux was awarded the OBE at the end of World War One for his part in the White Lady.

8. Message dated 7 September 1941, Clarence Service and Mill correspondence in files, ref: FCI-MNRA, National Museum of the Resistance, Brussels.

9. The courier service was headed by Hervé Close (codename 'M.23'), who worked for Mill from 28 September 1941 until 1 November 1944.

10. Adrien Marquet, personal file in AA1333 (folder 163), the individual files of intelligence and action agents, Belgian State Security Archives, Cegesoma.

11. Report from Paul Marquet quoted on his personal agent proposition sheet, personal file in AA1333, the individual files of intelligence and action agents, Belgian State Security Archives, Cegesoma.

12. Obituary, 3 January 1972, copy in his personal agent file, AA1333 (folder 163), the individual files of intelligence and action agents, Belgian State Security Archives, Cegesoma.

13. Jean Denis, personal file, AA1333 (folder 213), the individual files of intelligence and action agents, Belgian State Security Archives, Cegesoma.

14. Yvonne Collet, personal file, AA1333, the individual files of intelligence and action agents, Belgian State Security Archives, Cegesoma. Another courier for Mill was Marthe Balleux. Fernande Hazette in Sirault ran the Mill letter box to Mons. Alphonse Declère was a courier to Brussels. Louis Wallez of Leuze ran a letter box for the sector.

15. Germaine Crabbe, personal file, AA1333, the individual files of intelligence and action agents, Belgian State Security Archives, Cegesoma.

16. Numa Bouté, personal file, AA1333 (folder 213), the individual files of intelligence and action agents, Belgian State Security Archives, Cegesoma.

17. Observations along the line of Mouscron–Lille–Douai–Valenciennes–Mons–Lens–Renaix–Courtrai.

18. Wallez began in auxiliary rank in Mill, then ended in 1944 in the rank of captain.

19. Marius Salveniac, personal file, AA1333 (folder 213), the individual files of intelligence and action agents, Belgian State Security Archives, Cegesoma.

20. Robert Mathieu, personal file, AA1333 (folder 213), the individual files of intelligence and action agents, Belgian State Security Archives, Cegesoma.

21. Gérard Marchard, personal file, AA1333 (folder 213), the individual files of intelligence and action agents, Belgian State Security Archives, Cegesoma.

22. Andrée Leruth, personal file, AA1333 (folder 213), the individual files of intelligence and action agents, Belgian State Security Archives, Cegesoma.

23. Pierre Kauten, personal file, AA1333 (folder 213), the individual files of intelligence and action agents, Belgian State Security Archives, Cegesoma.

24. Jean Dardenne was born on 15 May 1909 and lived in Lodelinsart.

25. Another report states that he died in Groos-Strélitz on 30 November 1944. Ref: AA1333 (folder 213), the individual files of intelligence and action agents, Belgian State Security Archives, Cegesoma.

26. Letter dated 14 July 1945, ref: AA1333 (folder 213), the individual files of intelligence and action agents, Belgian State Security Archives, Cegesoma.

27. Extract of a letter from Major Page to Mr Lepage, 25 February 1942, in Adrien Marquet, personal file, AA1333 (folder 213), the individual files of intelligence and action agents, Belgian State Security Archives, Cegesoma.
28. Jean Denis, personal file, AA1333 (folder 213), the individual files of intelligence and action agents, Belgian State Security Archives, Cegesoma.
29. Jean Denis, personal file, AA1333 (folder 213), the individual files of intelligence and action agents, Belgian State Security Archives, Cegesoma.
30. Jean Denis, personal file, AA1333 (folder 213), the individual files of intelligence and action agents, Belgian State Security Archives, Cegesoma.
31. One source says he was arrested on 25 May 1944, another 5 June 1944.
32. SIS to the Clarence Service, AA1333 (folder 213), the individual files of intelligence and action agents, Belgian State Security Archives, Cegesoma.
33. Report from Paul Marquet quoted on his personal agent proposition sheet, and in his obituary 3 January 1972, both in his personal file in AA1333, the individual files of intelligence and action agents, Belgian State Security Archives, Cegesoma. See also AA1333 (folder 213), the individual files of intelligence and action agents, Belgian State Security Archives, Cegesoma.
34. Email of 1 July 2025 to the author from Robin Libert (Chairman RUSRA-KUIAD, Royal Union of Intelligence and Action Services).
35. History sheet for Marquet, Adrien Marquet, personal file, AA1333 (folder 213), the individual files of intelligence and action agents, Belgian State Security Archives, Cegesoma.

12. A Vast Web

1. Report, 4 January 1942, Box 1, Clarence Service, IWM.
2. Report, 4 January 1942, Box 1, Clarence Service, IWM.
3. Jeffery, *MI6*, p. 521. The report was dated 17 February 1942, Box 1, Clarence Service, IWM.
4. Report dated 28 March 1942, Box 1, Clarence Service, IWM.
5. The sending of agents into Germany is attested by personal agent files in AA1333 (folder 162), the individual files of intelligence and action agents, Belgian State Security Archives, Cegesoma.
6. Report, 4 January 1942, Box 2, Clarence Service archive, IWM.
7. Report No. 75, dated 13 December 1942, Box 3, Clarence Service archive, IWM.
8. They were Jacques Basyn, Herman Vos, Walter Ganshof, Van der Meersch and Edgard De Bruyne; and Aristide of the Clarence Service.
9. Bernard, *Un géant*, pp. 157–8.
10. Transmissions were also sometimes sent to the Gilles Group via a resistance network, Zéro.
11. Bernard, *Un géant*, p. 157. The armed resistance movement was founded by Antoine Delfosse, along with Pierre Clerdent, Joseph Fafchamps, René Wéra and Jules Malherbe.
12. Obituary for Jean Nicodème, *Le Soir*, 26 September 1972.
13. Jeffery, *MI6*, p. 522.
14. This section draws on the unpublished memoirs of Jean de Radiguès and material from the family.

15. The children of Jean and Jacqueline de Radiguès were Françoise (1921), Charles (1922), Yves (1924), Eliane (1926), Guillain (1929) and Olivier (1932).
16. Unpublished memoirs of Jean de Radiguès, copy given to the author by the de Radiguès family.
17. Among those he helped were Léon van de Werve de Vorsselaer; Pierre, Antoine and Emmanuel Jooris; Baron Charles Moncheur; Étienne de Wasseige; and Albert Regout.
18. The papers of Georges Theunis survive in the United States Holocaust Memorial Museum, having been given by the National Archives of Belgium in January 2011 as part of an international Holocaust archives project.
19. Cited in the unpublished memoirs of Jean de Radiguès, p. 2.
20. Unpublished memoirs of Jean de Radiguès, p. 3.
21. Cited in the unpublished memoirs of Jean de Radiguès, p. 3.
22. Among them were Queen Elisabeth, Princess Ruspoli, Alexandre Galopin (governor of the Société Générale de Belgique), Albert Janssen (president of the Société Belge de Banque) and various diplomats (Baron Pierre van Zuylen, Bernard de l'Escaille and Viscount Joe Berryer).
23. Jeffery, *MI6*, p. 522. It must have been an internal complaint, because nothing currently exists in the Clarence Service archives in London or Brussels to suggest that a delay was causing problems.
24. Bernard, *Un géant*, p. 174.
25. Letter dated 20 May 1943, AA1333 (folder 161), the individual files of intelligence and action agents, Belgian State Security Archives, Cegesoma.
26. 'Historique Clarence', report in AA1333 (folder 160), the individual files of intelligence and action agents, Belgian State Security Archives, Cegesoma.
27. It is not possible here to go into the technical details of the specialist equipment used by the network. For more information see Clarence Service files, ref: FCI-MNRA, National Museum of the Resistance, Brussels.
28. Bernard, *Un géant*, p. 176.
29. For details of Verhamme's mission see 'Historique Clarence', report in AA1333 (folder 160), the individual files of intelligence and action agents, Belgian State Security Archives, Cegesoma; and his personal file in AA1333 (folder 166). Verhamme was agent number 11 and recruited in September 1941.
30. Details of Verhamme's mission in AA1333 (folder 160) and his personal file, the individual files of intelligence and action agents, Belgian State Security Archives, Cegesoma; and Hector Demarque, personal file, AA1333. See also Bernard, *Un géant*, pp. 170–2.
31. Bernard, *Un géant*, p. 171.
32. Clotilde Coppens joined the Clarence Service on 1 July 1942. After the war she was awarded the King's Commendation for Brave Conduct (civilian).
33. Laure Tandel and Louise Tandel, personal files, AA1333, the individual files of intelligence and action agents, Belgian State Security Archives, Cegesoma. See also Eva Muys, 'Vrouwen in de inlichtingendiensten: De zussen Laure en Louise Tandel', p. 15.
34. Laure Tandel and Louise Tandel, personal files, AA1333, the individual files of intelligence and action agents, Belgian State Security Archives, Cegesoma. See also Eva Muys, 'Vrouwen in de inlichtingendiensten: De zussen Laure en Louise Tandel', p. 15.

35. Laure Tandel, personal file, AA1333, the individual files of intelligence and action agents, Belgian State Security Archives, Cegesoma.
36. Sohngen was arrested by the French resistance movement 'Les Forces Françaises de l'Intérieur'. Eva Muys, 'Vrouwen in de inlichtingendiensten: De zussen Laure en Louise Tandel', p. 15.
37. After the war, Laure and Louise Tandel and Albert Sohngen were in contact. In September 1947, Sohngen wrote to them and thanked them for the help they had provided to his family while he was imprisoned in England. He asked them to use their contacts to obtain Belgian nationality for him. He was finally granted Belgian citizenship on 3 February 1955.
38. They included Wolf, De Beer, Lenaerts, Ernest Feys (deputy leader of a sector in Ostend), Léon Lambert, Father Paul Désirant, and Fathers Hugues and Etienne from Val-Dieu Abbey.
39. Letter from Page of Room 900 to Captain Nicodème, 16 September 1943, AA1333 (folder 160), the individual files of intelligence and action agents, Belgian State Security Archives, Cegesoma. Serge's parachute mission included three containers for the clandestine Zéro network, which provided information of a political, financial and social nature to the British and Belgian intelligence services.
40. See list dated 14 March 1943 with items in a container dropped to Student, AA1333 (folder 161), the individual files of intelligence and action agents, Belgian State Security Archives, Cegesoma. The same file has a complete list of items dropped in containers at other times during 1943. The estate was owned by the family of Léon Pirlot-Orban.
41. Keith Jeffery, *MI6*, pp. 521–2.
42. Report 106, Box 4, Clarence Service archive, IWM.

13. Women of Clarence

1. Fry, *Women in Intelligence*, pp. 329–37.
2. Marie Thérèse Dewé, personal file, AA1333 (folder 166), the individual files of intelligence and action agents, Belgian State Security Archives, Cegesoma. She joined the Clarence Service on 1 September 1940. She was recruited for the Comet Line too, by Miss Poswick in July 1942.
3. Marie Thérèse Dewé, personal file, AA1333, the individual files of intelligence and action agents, Belgian State Security Archives, Cegesoma. See also Neave, *Saturday at MI9*, pp. 247–50.
4. Thérèse de Radiguès's agents are listed in her personal file in AA1333, the individual files of intelligence and action agents, Belgian State Security Archives, Cegesoma.
5. Thérèse de Radiguès recruited Marie-Joseph Poswick on 11 August 1943; Viscountess Coraly-Alexienne van Eyll, who served from 1 February 1942 until 1 April 1943; and Viscountess Marie-Antoinette de Parc of Herzele, who operated from 1 November 1939 to 15 September 1944. De Radiguès also enlisted Thérèse Plissàrt on 10 May 1940 and her sister Elisabeth on 20 June 1940, and Louisa de Marotte de Montigny on 15 August 1940.
6. Thérèse Plissàrt enlisted on 10 May 1940, was arrested on 6 June 1942, then was deported to Germany on 22 August 1942. Her sister Elisabeth died in Ravensbrück in January 1945. Louisa de Marotte de Montigny was arrested on 14 February

1943, and finally deported to Germany on 28 November 1943, where she later died. Their personal files are in AA1333, the individual files of intelligence and action agents, Belgian State Security Archives, Cegesoma.

7. Marie-Antoinette de Radiguès, personal file, AA1333 (folder 166), the individual files of intelligence and action agents, Belgian State Security Archives, Cegesoma.

8. Marie-Antoinette de Radiguès, personal file, AA1333 (folder 166), the individual files of intelligence and action agents, Belgian State Security Archives, Cegesoma.

9. Henri de Moffarts was recruited on 1 September 1941 and served until 31 January 1945.

10. Marguerite de Radiguès, personal file, AA1333 (folder 166), the individual files of intelligence and action agents, Belgian State Security Archives, Cegesoma.

11. Marguerite de Radiguès, 'Journal d'Ostin', copy given to the author by the family.

12. Notes at the beginning of Marguerite's 'Journal d'Ostin'.

13. Marguerite de Radiguès, 'Journal d'Ostin', entry notes for July 1944.

14. Others arrested that day at the castle included Lieutenant Jacques Robin, André Schepdryver (radio operator), Edmond Servais, vicar of Vedrin, and Gaston and Georges Sevais. They are listed in the notes to the journal.

15. 'Journal d'Ostin', entry for 17 August 1944.

16. 'Journal d'Ostin', entries from 19 August to 23 August 1944.

17. 'Journal d'Ostin', entry for 22 August 1944.

18. Georges Clérinx, personal file, AA1333 (folder 166), the individual files of intelligence and action agents, Belgian State Security Archives, Cegesoma.

19. Olga Leclair was born in March 1907 and given agent number 3712. Her husband Richard Hoornaert was given agent number 3612. Their personal files are in AA1333 (folder 166), the individual files of intelligence and action agents, Belgian State Security Archives, Cegesoma.

20. Olga Leclair, personal file, AA1333, the individual files of intelligence and action agents, Belgian State Security Archives, Cegesoma.

21. Clotilde Lucie Coppens entered the Clarence Service on 1 July 1942. She was born in March 1890 and lived at 59 avenue du Parc in Brussels.

22. For her part in the White Lady, Henriette Dupuich had been awarded an OBE: personal file, AA1333, the individual files of intelligence and action agents, Belgian State Security Archives, Cegesoma.

23. Clarence Service report dated 17 December 1945, in Henriette Dupuich, personal file, AA1333, the individual files of intelligence and action agents, Belgian State Security Archives, Cegesoma.

24. Thérèse Liénart, personal file, AA1333 (folder 166), the individual files of intelligence and action agents, Belgian State Security Archives, Cegesoma.

25. Report dated 16 February 1944 by evader Jean de Haubert, and report dated 23 May 1944 by evader Georges Benekens in Anspach, personal file AA1333, the individual files of intelligence and action agents, Belgian State Security Archives, Cegesoma.

26. Letter dated 15 September 1949 from Clarence Service to chief of SGARA, Brussels, Simone Anspach, personal file, AA1333, the individual files of intelligence and action agents, Belgian State Security Archives, Cegesoma.

27. Mariette Baldauf, personal file, AA1333, the individual files of intelligence and action agents, Belgian State Security Archives, Cegesoma.

28. Report in her personal file, HS 9/460/3, TNA.

29. Letter from Page (Jempson), 5 April 1945, HS 9/460/3, TNA.

30. Report by Clarence Service, 28 April 1944, HS 9/460/3, TNA.

31. Frédérique Dupuich was dropped in the Loire region at around 3 a.m. on 6 August 1944. For this operation she came under the Belgian section of SOE, headed by Hardy Amies, although he always maintained that she was an SIS agent, not SOE: Letter to Aronstein, dated 3 November 1944, HS 9/460/3. She returned to England and enlisted in the First Aid Nursing Yeomanry (FANY) in 1945. She went on to serve as a welfare officer in East Asia in uniform. See HS 9/460/3 and HO 334/339/12445, TNA. Her name appears on the SOE memorial in Tempsford.

32. Jean Orban-Englebert, personal file, AA1333, the individual files of intelligence and action agents, Belgian State Security Archives, Cegesoma.

33. Antonina Grégoire, personal file, AA1333, the individual files of intelligence and action agents, Belgian State Security Archives, Cegesoma.

34. Alice Cheramy, personal file, AA1333, the individual files of intelligence and action agents, Belgian State Security Archives, Cegesoma.

35. Countess Marie Thérèse de Meeus, personal file, AA1333 (folder 166), the individual files of intelligence and action agents, Belgian State Security Archives, Cegesoma.

36. Alice Marlier, personal file, AA1333 (folder 166), the individual files of intelligence and action agents, Belgian State Security Archives, Cegesoma.

14. 1944

1. Countess Marthe de Meeus, personal file, AA1333 (folder 166), the individual files of intelligence and action agents, Belgian State Security Archives, Cegesoma.

2. Countess Marie Thérèse de Meeus, personal file, AA1333 (folder 166), the individual files of intelligence and action agents, Belgian State Security Archives, Cegesoma.

3. Bernard, *Un géant*, p. 244.

4. Personal file of Marie Dewé in AA1333 (folder 166), the individual files of intelligence and action agents, Belgian State Security Archives, Cegesoma. According to her personal testimony in her file, she was liberated on 22 April 1945. Mauthausen was officially liberated on 5 May 1945.

5. For Dewé and Demarque operating as co-leaders of the Clarence Service, see 'Reseau Clarence', AA1333 (folder 161), the individual files of intelligence and action agents, Belgian State Security Archives, Cegesoma.

6. Jean de Radiguès, unpublished memoir, p. 6.

7. Bernard, *Un géant*, pp. 203–9. Jean de Radiguès also wrote about it in his unpublished memoir, p. 6, copy given to the author by the family.

8. Jean de Radiguès, unpublished memoir, p. 6.

9. Her own account of what happened is quoted in Bernard, *Un géant*, p. 204. See also Jean de Radiguès's unpublished memoir, p. 6 (which has some variants on the account). This momentous event in Thérèse de Radigues's life has been passed down as an oral story in the family because she talked about it. It has been recounted to the author during a visit to them in Belgium.

10. Correspondence from François de Radiguès with the author. See also Bernard, *Un géant*, p. 207.

11. Bernard, *Un géant*, p. 211.
12. Jean de Radiguès, unpublished memoir, pp. 6–7.
13. Jean de Radiguès, unpublished memoir, p. 7.
14. They were Léon Calmeau from Luxembourg on 7 February 1944 and Jean de Moreau d'Andoy from Namur on 1 August 1944. They were replaced by two new chiefs, Aimé Lahaut and Louis Delvigne, both engineers.
15. Report by Clarence Service, 5 February 1946, AA1333 (folder 160), the individual files of intelligence and action agents, Belgian State Security Archives, Cegesoma.
16. Maud Mary de Cort, née Leadbeater, was born on 15 May 1886 in Hackney, London. Maud Mary de Cort, personal file, AA1333, the individual files of intelligence and action agents, Belgian State Security Archives, Cegesoma.
17. 'Historique Clarence', report in AA1333 (folder 160), the individual files of intelligence and action agents, Belgian State Security Archives, Cegesoma.
18. Maud Mary de Cort, citation in her personal file, AA1333, the individual files of intelligence and action agents, Belgian State Security Archives, Cegesoma.
19. Citation medal in Maud Mary de Cort, personal file, AA1333, the individual files of intelligence and action agents, Belgian State Security Archives, Cegesoma.
20. Elie Nubourg died in Flossenbürg concentration camp on 5 April 1945, and Pierre Walkiers on 15 April 1945.
21. At the end of the war, Godenne was awarded the King's Commendation for Brave Conduct (military).
22. Bernard, *Un géant*, p. 219.
23. From mid-August 1944, the Liège sector that Chauvin headed sent its messages direct to SIS. Bernard, *Un géant*, p. 219. Herman Chauvin, personal file, AA1333, the individual files of intelligence and action agents, Belgian State Security Archives, Cegesoma.
24. Jeffery, *MI6*, p. 543.
25. Reports in Box 6, Clarence Service files, IWM.
26. Message sent 1 June 1944; Bernard, *Un géant*, p. 215.
27. Report No. 140, Annex 4, November 1943, Box 5, Clarence Service archive, IWM.
28. Fernand Pironet, personal file, AA1333/166/3, the individual files of intelligence and action agents, Belgian State Security Archives, Cegesoma.
29. Message of 21 February 1944, AA1333 (folder 161), the individual files of intelligence and action agents, Belgian State Security Archives, Cegesoma.
30. Message of 31 March 1944, AA1333 (folder 161), the individual files of intelligence and action agents, Belgian State Security Archives, Cegesoma.
31. Message of 31 March 1944, AA1333 (folder 161), the individual files of intelligence and action agents, Belgian State Security Archives, Cegesoma.
32. Report 151, Box 6, Clarence Service archive, IWM.
33. Message of 26 May 1944, AA1333 (folder 161), the individual files of intelligence and action agents, Belgian State Security Archives, Cegesoma.
34. Gaston Lebrun, personal file, AA1333, the individual files of intelligence and action agents, Belgian State Security Archives, Cegesoma.
35. Marcel Hermans, personal file, AA1333 (folder 166), the individual files of intelligence and action agents, Belgian State Security Archives, Cegesoma.

36. Joseph de Wilde, personal file, AA1333, the individual files of intelligence and action agents, Belgian State Security Archives, Cegesoma. Joseph de Wilde was recruited in Zeebrugge in May 1941.
37. Report 151, Box 6, Clarence Service archive, IWM. See also Jeffery, *MI6*, p. 542.
38. Jeffery, *MI6*, p. 542.
39. Message of 25 August 1944, AA1333 (folder 161), the individual files of intelligence and action agents, Belgian State Security Archives, Cegesoma. See also Jeffery, *MI6*, p. 542.
40. Report 160, Box 7, Clarence Service archive, IWM.
41. Report 160, Box 7, Clarence Service archive, IWM.
42. Clarence Service to London, report for 25–31 August 1944, Box 6, Clarence Service archive, IWM.
43. Message of 25 August 1944, AA1333 (folder 161), the individual files of intelligence and action agents, Belgian State Security Archives, Cegesoma.
44. This report covered the week immediately after 25 August 1944.
45. Robert Dupuis, personal file, AA1333 (folder 166), the individual files of intelligence and action agents, Belgian State Security Archives, Cegesoma.
46. Jean-Pierre Bobsang had already founded the Delbo-Phénix network in France.
47. Brief paragraph headed 'Annex VIII: Mission BOBSANG Jean Pierre (alias BRULAGE II)', the individual files of intelligence and action agents, Belgian State Security Archives, Cegesoma.
48. Jeffery, *MI6*, p. 543.
49. Gaetan Vervoort, personal file, AA1333, the individual files of intelligence and action agents, Belgian State Security Archives, Cegesoma.

15. V-Weapon Intelligence

1. Other MI6 agents operating in Germany and France were sources of V-weapon intelligence: see Jeffery, *MI6*, pp. 533–5.
2. Jeffery, *MI6*, pp. 533–4.
3. Transcript of bugged conversation of General Walter Dornberger, GRGG 341, 11 August 1945, WO 208/4178, TNA. For background to this, see Helen Fry, *The Walls Have Ears: The Greatest Intelligence Operation of World War II*, Yale University Press, 2019, pp. 263–6; and Michael Neufeld, *The Rocket and the Reich: Peenemünde and the Coming of the Ballistic Missile Era*, Smithsonian, 2013, pp. 41–72.
4. Fry, *The Walls Have Ears*, pp. 6–23.
5. R.V. Jones, *Most Secret War*, Coronet, 1978, p. 424.
6. Copies of the photographs from these missions exist in the archives of the RAF Medmenham Collection.
7. Chiefs of Staff memorandum, COS(43) 592 (O), entitled 'German Long Range Rockets', section 3: 'First Report of the Long Range Rockets', 29 September 1943, CAB 80/75.
8. Fry, *The Walls Have Ears*, pp. 150–71.
9. The source is General Dornberger, who was in conversation with Major General Bassenge. See 'Report on Information Obtained from Senior Officer PW on 2–7 Aug 45', GRGG 341, CSDIC Camp 11, WO 208/4178, TNA. There are other transcripts of bugged conversations about the V-weapons between the generals in this file. See new research in Fry, *The Walls Have Ears*, pp. 150–71. Professor R.V. Jones gives a figure of 720 people killed; see Jones, *Most Secret War*, p. 441.

10. New research from declassified intelligence files now shows that the V-1 was closer to being operational than previously thought by scholars. It was nearly operational by July 1943. See transcript of bugged conversations, SRN 1986 and SRX 1848 in WO 208/3437, TNA, and 'Rockets and Invasion', 26 July 1943, WO 208/3437, TNA. See also Helen Fry, *Spymaster: The Man Who Saved MI6*, Yale University Press, 2021, pp. 236–7.

11. Jones, *Most Secret War*, p. 441. See also Fry, *The Walls Have Ears*, pp. 150–71.

12. Details in his father's Clarence Service file: Henri Roth, personal file, AA1333, the individual files of intelligence and action agents, Belgian State Security Archives, Cegesoma. See also Jones, *Most Secret War*, p. 431.

13. Henri Roth was born in Luxembourg in 1893. Henri Roth, personal file, AA1333, the individual files of intelligence and action agents, Belgian State Security Archives, Cegesoma.

14. Adolphe Godart, personal file, AA1333 (folder 166), the individual files of intelligence and action agents, Belgian State Security Archives, Cegesoma.

15. Jeffery, *MI6*, p. 533.

16. Jeffery, *MI6*, p. 533.

17. Information on what the agents discovered on the V-1 and V-2 is contained in their personal files, AA1333, the individual files of intelligence and action agents, Belgian State Security Archives, Cegesoma.

18. Joseph Moutchen, personal file, AA1333/166/8. Joseph Moutchen, born 1905, was recruited in May 1942. In another mission into Germany in April 1944 he conducted surveillance around Heppenbach, and between June and July 1944, he documented defences along the Siegfried Line.

19. Jeffery, *MI6*, p. 522.

20. Report 160, dated 30 July 1944, Box 7, Clarence Service archive, IWM. See also Bernard, *Un géant*, p. 216.

21. Pierre Vanderveken, personal file, AA1333 (folder 166), the individual files of intelligence and action agents, Belgian State Security Archives, Cegesoma. Pierre Vanderveken was born in 1910 and enlisted on 1 October 1940. He operated under a number of pseudonyms: Lindt, Speth, Verhaegen and Van Ashoeck.

22. Details in Pierre Vanderveken, personal file, AA1333 (folder 166), the individual files of intelligence and action agents, Belgian State Security Archives, Cegesoma.

23. Camille van Welput, personal file, AA1333 (folder 166), the individual files of intelligence and action agents, Belgian State Security Archives, Cegesoma.

24. Bernard, *Un géant*, pp. 216–17.

25. Daniel Lefebvre, personal file, AA1333, the individual files of intelligence and action agents, Belgian State Security Archives, Cegesoma. Daniel Lefebvre was born in 1911 and lived in Bruges.

26. Marie Levez was born in 1905, joined the Clarence Service on 1 June 1942 and was given agent number 3619.

27. Marie Levez, personal file, AA1333 (folder 166), the individual files of intelligence and action agents, Belgian State Security Archives, Cegesoma.

28. Jean Balteaux, personal file, AA1333 (folder 166), the individual files of intelligence and action agents, Belgian State Security Archives, Cegesoma.

29. Baroness Germaine de Menten, personal file, AA1333 (folder 166), the individual files of intelligence and action agents, Belgian State Security Archives, Cegesoma.

NOTES TO PP. 223–229

30. André de Callatay, personal file, AA1333 (folder 166), the individual files of intelligence and action agents, Belgian State Security Archives, Cegesoma. Recruited 1 March 1943 by Baroness Germaine de Menten.
31. Thomas Vinaimont, personal file, AA1333 (folder 166), the individual files of intelligence and action agents, Belgian State Security Archives, Cegesoma. Details of the transport of V-1s recorded by him on 15 April 1944.
32. Jean Lefeure, personal file, AA1333 (folder 166), the individual files of intelligence and action agents, Belgian State Security Archives, Cegesoma.
33. Léon Destenay, personal file, AA1333 (folder 166), the individual files of intelligence and action agents, Belgian State Security Archives, Cegesoma.
34. Report 160, Clarence Service archive, Box 7, IWM.
35. Jones, *Most Secret War*, pp. 527–8.
36. Jones, *Most Secret War*, pp. 527–8.
37. Francine Blondin, personal file, AA1333 (folder 166), the individual files of intelligence and action agents, Belgian State Security Archives, Cegesoma. Francine Blondin was born in Belgium in June 1919, of Belgian nationality, and lived at 100 rue de la Gare, Halanzy. She worked for Clarence from 17 December 1943 until 15 October 1944.
38. Albert Onghena, personal file, AA1333 (folder 166), the individual files of intelligence and action agents, Belgian State Security Archives, Cegesoma. Albert Onghena was born in 1894, lived in Ixelles and was recruited to the Clarence Service in July 1943 by R. de Keyser (agent number 100).
39. Report 160, Box 7, Clarence Service archive, IWM.
40. Stéphane Felix Noël (agent number 8760) operated for Clarence from 1 November 1943 to 15 October 1944. His personal file is in AA1333 (folder 166), the individual files of intelligence and action agents, Belgian State Security Archives, Cegesoma.
41. Bernard, *Un géant*, p. 216.
42. Report 160, dated 30 July 1944, Box 7, Clarence Service archive, IWM.
43. Report 160, dated 30 July 1944, Box 7, Clarence Service archive, IWM.
44. Report 160, Box 7, Clarence Service archive, IWM.
45. Report 160, dated 30 July 1944, Box 7, Clarence Service archive, IWM.
46. This transport took place on 21 July 1944.
47. Report 160, dated 30 July 1944, Box 7, Clarence Service archive, IWM.
48. Messages from the Clarence Service to London, for the period 25 to 31 August 1944. Information confirmed in report dated 25 July 1944, Box 7, Clarence Service archive, IWM. Details also contained in AA1333/166/2.
49. Included in radio messages from the Clarence Service to London (SIS), 25 to 31 August 1944.
50. Report dated 25 July 1944, Box 7, Clarence Service archive, IWM.
51. Report 160, dated 30 July 1944, Box 7, Clarence Service archive, IWM.
52. Report 160, dated 30 July 1944, Box 7, Clarence Service archive, IWM.
53. Messages from the Clarence Service to London for the period 25 to 31 August 1944, Box 7, Clarence Service archive, IWM.
54. Messages from the Clarence Service to London for the period 25 to 31 August 1944, Box 7, Clarence Service archive, IWM.
55. Report 161, Box 7, Clarence Service archive, IWM.

56. Report 162, Box 7, Clarence Service archive, IWM.
57. Report 162, Box 7, Clarence Service archive, IWM.
58. Report 163, Box 7, Clarence Service archive, IWM.
59. Report 163, Box 7, Clarence Service archive, IWM.
60. Report 163, Box 7, Clarence Service archive, IWM.
61. Report 163, Box 7, Clarence Service archive, IWM.

16. Liberation

1. Bernard, *Un géant*, p. 220.
2. Bernard, *Un géant*, p. 216.
3. Bernard, *Un géant*, p. 221. The American VII Corps entered Liège on 9 September 1944, commanded by J. Lawton Collins.
4. They were Auguste Thys, killed in Antwerp on 6 September, and Jean van Ooteghem, near Berendrecht the following day.
5. Bernard, *Un géant*, pp. 223–4. Jacques Jansen enlisted in the Clarence Service in February 1944.
6. Obituary for Jean Nicodème, *Le Soir*, 26 September 1972.
7. Jeffery, *MI6*, p. 544.
8. Jeffery, *MI6*, p. 544.
9. Bernard, *Un géant*, p. 218.
10. Bernard, *Un géant*, p. 244.
11. Jeffery, *MI6*, pp. 544–5.
12. Jeffery, *MI6*, p. 544.
13. Herman (Henri) Chauvin, personal file, AA1333, the individual files of intelligence and action agents, Belgian State Security Archives, Cegesoma.
14. Report for the period 18–25 November 1944, Clarence Service files, ref: FCI-MNRA, National Museum of the Resistance, Brussels.
15. Report for the period 18–25 November 1944, Clarence Service files, ref: FCI-MNRA, National Museum of the Resistance.
16. Report, 26 November 1944, Clarence Service files, ref: FCI-MNRA, National Museum of the Resistance, Brussels.
17. Letter in Henri Chauvin file, Clarence Service files, ref: FCI-MNRA, National Museum of the Resistance, Brussels.
18. Letter in Henri Chauvin file, Clarence Service files, ref: FCI-MNRA, National Museum of the Resistance, Brussels.
19. Letter in Henri Chauvin file, Clarence Service files, ref: FCI-MNRA, National Museum of the Resistance, Brussels.
20. Henri Chauvin, personal file, AA1333, the individual files of intelligence and action agents, Belgian State Security Archives, Cegesoma.
21. Henri Chauvin file, Clarence Service files, ref: FCI-MNRA, National Museum of the Resistance, Brussels.
22. Pierre Michiels, personal file, AA1333 (folder 166), the individual files of intelligence and action agents, Belgian State Security Archives, Cegesoma.
23. Georges Withofs, personal file, AA1333 (folder 166), the individual files of intelligence and action agents, Belgian State Security Archives, Cegesoma.
24. Germaine de Menten, personal file, AA1333 (folder 166), the individual files of intelligence and action agents, Belgian State Security Archives, Cegesoma.

25. Marthe de Meeus, personal file, AA1333 (folder 166), the individual files of intelligence and action agents, Belgian State Security Archives, Cegesoma.
26. Bernard, *Un géant*, p. 223.
27. Letter from Chauvin to Demarque, 25 November 1944, Clarence Service files, ref: FCI-MNRA, National Museum of the Resistance, Brussels.
28. Revealed for the first time in Fry, *Women in Intelligence*, p. 336.
29. Bernard, *Un géant*, p. 136.
30. A full list is in Bernard, *Un géant*, p. 244.
31. The female members who lost their lives are listed in Appendix 5 of Bernard, *Un géant*. Madame Dewé (née Dieudonnée Salmon) died in service on 14 January 1943. The following women died in Ravensbrück concentration camp: Madeleine Dewé (17 January 1945); Elisabeth Plissàrt (January 1945); Nelly Durieu (29 January 1945), Juliette Durieu (March 1945); and Bertha Morimont (née Lambrecht, died in March 1945).
32. Letter, n.d., from Bihin (administrator of the Sûreté de l'État) to Marquet, in Marquet's personal file.
33. Letter from Page (Jempson at SIS) to Bihin, 18 September 1944, in Marquet's personal file.
34. Letter, n.d., from Bihin to Marquet, in Marquet's personal file, AA1333, the individual files of intelligence and action agents, Belgian State Security Archives, Cegesoma.
35. Letter dated 25 August 1947, confirming the award of an OBE, and a letter from Page, dated 7 May 1946, written from Brussels. Both letters are in Marquet's personal file, the individual files of intelligence and action agents, Belgian State Security Archives, Cegesoma.
36. Letter from A. Hauzeur to Hector Demarque, 28 October 1954 which gives a list of all the radio equipment returned, in a folder marked 'Radio equipment, 1939', Clarence Service files, ref: FCI-MNRA, National Museum of the Resistance, Brussels.
37. Bernard, *Un géant*, p. 226.
38. In the Tandel papers, Belgian Military Archives, Brussels. After the war, Laure and Louise were both members of the Association of Former Political Prisoners of Siegburg and regularly met with other members in Brussels.
39. Laure and Louise Tandel were appointed Adjutant IAA. They both received the Cross of Knight in the Order of the Crown with palm, the War Cross 1940 with palm, the Medal of Resistance and the Remembrance Medal 1940–1945.
40. Her daughter Marguerite Clérinx (de Radiguès) died in 1976.
41. Invitation to Dewé's memorial service, copy in the Archive of Laure and Louise Tandel, SGRS, Belgian Military Archives.
42. Awards for Jempson and Stowell in WO 373/107/178 and WO 373/107/179, TNA, respectively.
43. Ruth Stowell, citation in WO 373/107/179, TNA.
44. For a panoramic history of women's intelligence roles across two world wars, see Fry, *Women in Intelligence*.

Epilogue

1. Jeffery, *MI6*, pp. 521–2.
2. Jeffery, *MI6*, p. 521.

BIBLIOGRAPHY

Papers and Archives

State Archives of Belgium, Brussels

Inventaire des archives de la Commission des Archives des Services patriotique établis en Territoire occupé au Front de l'Ouest (1914–1930): I 581.

Corps d'observation anglais au front de l'Ouest (C.O.A.), alias Dame Blanche: I 581 [CAP 10].

Papers and archive of Walthère Dewé: FICINV_1699.

Records of the Service Patriotique (1914–1918), Corps d'Observation Anglais, P-207 to P-224.

Cegesoma Studies and Documentation Institute, Brussels

Clarence Service papers: AA1333/160-166.

Mill Service: AA1333/213.

Archives partielles de et relatives au service de renseignements Mill (1941–1944): AA1136, inventory code: FCINV_0990.

Individual files of intelligence and action agents, Belgian State Security Archives: AA1333.

SGRS, Belgian Military Archives

Archive of Laure and Louise Tandel.

National Museum of the Resistance, Brussels

Papers of the Clarence Service, ref: FCI-MNRA.

Imperial War Museum, London

Papers of La Dame Blanche, ref: Documents.17076.

Papers of the Clarence Service, ref: Documents.17074.
Papers of Sigismund Payne Best, ref: Documents.09/51/5.
Diaries and papers of General Sir Walter Kirke, IWM 82/28/1.

National Archives, Kew

MEPO 4/350/152, Register of leavers from the Metropolitan Police, Frederick John Jempson.
WO 106/45, The Secret Service, in History of Intelligence and Secret Service Organisations.
WO 106/6189, History of the British Secret Service in Holland, World War I.
WO 208/4178, 301–365, Combined Services Detailed Interrogation Centre.
WO 339/7419, Lieutenant Alastair Mansfield Smith Cumming.
WO 339/12456, Captain Henry Landau, Royal Field Artillery.
WO 373/107/178, Recommendation for award for Jempson, Frederick John.
WO 373/107/179, Recommendation for award for Stowell, Ruth Clement.

Selected Published Works

Andrew, Christopher. *The Defence of the Realm: The Authorized History of MI5*, Allen Lane, 2009.
Andrew, Christopher. *Secret Service: The Making of the British Intelligence Community*, Book Club Associates, 1985.
Beach, Jim. *Haig's Intelligence: GHQ and the German Army, 1916–1918*, Cambridge University Press, 2013.
Bernard, Henri. *Un géant de la résistance: Walthère Dewé*, La Renaissance du Livre, 1971.
Bijl, Nick van der. *Sharing the Secret: The History of the Intelligence Corps, 1940–2010*, Pen & Sword, 2020.
Brown, Anthony Cave. *C: The Secret Life of Sir Stewart Graham Menzies*, Macmillan, 1987.
Clark, Freddie. *Agents by Moonlight: The Secret History of RAF Tempsford during World War II*, Tempus, 1999.
Clayton, Anthony. *Forearmed: A History of the Intelligence Corps*, Brassey's, 1993.
Debruyne, Emmanuel. 'La maison de verre: Agents et réseaux de renseignements en Belgique occupée, 1940–1944', Université Catholique de Louvain, 2005–6.
Debruyne, Emmanuel, and Jehanne Paternostre. *La Résistance au quotidien 1914–1918: Témoignages inédits*, Racine, 2009.
Decock, Pierre. *La Dame Blanche: Un réseau de renseignements de la Grande Guerre*, Histoire Contemporaine ULB, 2010 edition.
Epstein, Jonathan. *Belgium's Dilemma: The Formation of the Belgian Defense Policy, 1932–1940*, Brill, 2014.
Felstead, S. Theodore. *Under the German Heel: Revelations of Life in Belgium under the German Occupation 1914–1918*, George Newnes Ltd, 1940.
Foot, M.R.D., and Jimmy Langley. *MI9: Escape and Evasion 1939–1945*, BCA, 1979.
Fry, Helen. *MI9: A History of the Secret Service for Escape and Evasion in World War Two*, Yale University Press, 2020.
Fry, Helen. *Spymaster: The Man Who Saved MI6*, Yale University Press, 2021.

Fry, Helen. *The Walls Have Ears: The Greatest Intelligence Operation of World War II*, Yale University Press, 2019.

Fry, Helen. *Women in Intelligence: The Hidden History of Two World Wars*, Yale University Press, 2023.

Jeffery, Keith. *MI6: The History of the Secret Intelligence Service 1909–1949*, Bloomsbury, 2010.

Jones, R.V. *Most Secret War*, Coronet, 1978.

Judd, Alan. *The Quest for C: Mansfield Cumming and the Founding of the Secret Service*, HarperCollins, 1999.

Landau, Henry. *Secrets of the White Lady*, G.P. Putnam's Sons, 1935.

Landau, Henry. *Spreading the Spy Net: The Story of a British Spy Director*, Jarrolds, 1938.

Landau, Henry. *The Spy Net: The Greatest Intelligence Operations of the First World War*, Biteback, 2015 edition.

Lombard, Laurent. *Le Drame de la Villa des Hirondelles*, Editions Vox Patriae, Stavelot, 1939.

Macintyre, Ben. *Double Cross: The True Story of the D-Day Spies*, Crown, 2012.

Masterman, John. *The Double-Cross System*, Yale University Press, 1950.

Morgan, Janet. *The Secrets of Rue St Roch: Intelligence Operations behind Enemy Lines in the First World War*, Allen Lane, 2004.

Muys, Eva. 'Vrouwen in de inlichtingendiensten: De zussen Laure en Louise Tandel', in Marc Cools et al. (eds), *1915–2015: Het verhaal van de Belgische Militaire Inlichtingen- en Veiligheidsdienst: L'histoire du service de renseignement militaire et de sécurité belge*, Maklu, 2016, pp. 225–50 (copy translated from the original Dutch given to the author).

Neave, Airey. *Saturday at MI9: The Classic Account of the WWII Allied Escape Organisation*, Pen & Sword, 2010.

Neufeld, Michael. *The Rocket and the Reich: Peenemünde and the Coming of the Ballistic Missile Era*, Smithsonian, 2013.

Occleshaw, Michael. *Armour Against Fate: British Military Intelligence in the First World War*, Columbus Books, 1989.

Parritt, Brian. *The Intelligencers: British Military Intelligence from the Middle Ages to 1929*, Pen & Sword, 2011.

Proctor, Tammy. *Female Intelligence: Women and Espionage in the First World War*, New York University Press, 2003.

Read, Anthony, and David Fisher. *Colonel Z: The Life and Times of a Master of Spies*, Hodder & Stoughton, 1984.

Roche, E. *Walthère Dewé: Commandant en chef de la Dame Blanche (1914–1918) et du Service Clarence (1940–1944)*, Liège, 1956.

Ruis, Edwin. *Spynest: British and German Espionage from Neutral Holland 1914–1918*, History Press, 2012.

Schaepdrijver, Sophie de. *Gabrielle Petit: The Death and Life of a Female Spy in the First World War*, Bloomsbury, 2015.

Smith, Michael. *Foley: The Spy Who Saved 10,000 Jews*, Politico's, 2004.

Smith, Michael. *Six: A History of Britain's Secret Intelligence Service*, Dialogue, 2010.

Stevenson, David. *1914–1918: The History of the First World War*, Penguin, 2012.

Strachan, Hew. *The First World War*, Simon & Schuster, 2014.

van Ypersele, Laurence, and Emmanuel Debruyne. *De la guerre de l'ombre aux ombres de la guerre: L'espionnage en Belgique durant la guerre de 1914–1918, histoire et mémoire*, Editions Labor, 2004.

Verstraeten, Peter. 'The Secrecy of Awards to Belgian Secret Service Agents', *Journal of the Orders and Medals Society of America*, vol. 70, no. 2, 2019, pp. 3–14.

Vigurs, Kate. *Mission Europe: The Secret History of the Women of SOE*, Yale University Press, 2025.

Unpublished Works

Judge, A.F. 'The Intelligence Corps 1914 to 1929', unpublished history, copy in the Military Intelligence Museum.

Monge, Gabrielle de. *Memoirs of Gabrielle de Monge, WWI*, unpublished, written in French, 1928, copy given to the author [published as *Les Heures tragiques de ma vie*, Asbl Syndicat d'Initiative et de Tourisme d'Ohey, 2014].

Radiguès, Agnès de. *Memoirs of WW1*, unpublished memoir, written in French. Copy given to the author by François de Radiguès.

Radiguès, Marguerite de (Clérinx). *Journal d'Ostin*, unpublished memoir, written in French. Copy given to the author by the family.

Radiguès, Marguerite de. 'Notes et souvenirs du 10 mai au 22 juillet 1940'. Copy given to the author by the family.

Radiguès, Marie-Antoinette de. *Carnet de Guerre: 1915–1919*, unpublished memoir, written in French. Copy given to the author by the family.

Documentary Programmes

David Jason's Secret Service, three-part series, Channel 4, 2017.

INDEX